DATE DUE

MAR 0 2 1993	MAR 2 2 2001
MAR 1 0 1993	NOV - 1 2001
APR 1 3 1993	SEP 1 1 2002
FEB 1 4 1994	
MAR 0 3 1994	
APR 1 3 1994	
NOV 2 4 1994	
FEB - 7 1995	
FEB 1 4 1995	
MAR 2 0 1995	
MAR 1 0 1996	
APR - 2 1996	
APR	
FEB 2 4 1998	
MAY - 8 1998	
MAY 2 2 1998	

MODERN POLITICAL THEORY
AND
CONTEMPORARY FEMINISM

SUNY Series in Feminist Political Theory
Marion Smiley, editor

MODERN POLITICAL THEORY
AND
CONTEMPORARY FEMINISM

A Dialectical Analysis

BY
JENNIFER RING

State University of New York Press

Published by
State University of New York Press, Albany

© 1991 State University of New York

For information, address State University of New York
Press, State University Plaza, Albany, N.Y. 12246

Production by Marilyn P. Semerad
Marketing by Dana E. Yanulavich

Library of Congress Cataloging-in-Publication Data

Ring, Jennifer, Date
    Modern political theory and contemporary feminism : a dialectical
analysis / Jennifer Ring.
        p. cm. — (SUNY series in feminist political theory)
    Includes bibliographical references and index.
    ISBN 0–7914-0753–5 — ISBN 0–7914-0754–3 (pbk.)
    1. Feminist theory. 2. Knowledge, Theory of. I. Title.
II. Series.
HQ1190.R56 1991
305.42—dc20
                                                                90–46118
                                                                CIP

10 9 8 7 6 5 4 3 2 1

For Johanna and Lillian

CONTENTS

ACKNOWLEDGMENTS

It is with delight that I take advantage of the opportunity to acknowledge the people who have inspired, encouraged, and witnessed the writing of this book. I have been blessed with teachers who have personified scholarly and pedagogical excellence and provided constancy and guidance from my earliest efforts with political theory. I was drawn to the academic life in Eugene Victor Wolfenstein's undergraduate seminars at UCLA, and his energy continues to inspire me. Hanna Pitkin heard the first ideas that evolved into this book almost a decade ago in Berkeley, and helped shape my thoughts with her willingness to read and reread the many drafts her exacting criticism compelled me to write. In the beginning, certainly, this book was a dialogue with her, and her importance to me as teacher and friend cannot be adequately expressed here. Arlene W. Saxonhouse and Elisabeth Young-Bruehl have been extraordinary friends and colleagues, and I am profoundly grateful for their rare gifts of intellectual independence and professional generosity. Without them this book might still be looking for a way into print. Nannerl Keohane read an early draft, and her detailed and encouraging critique emboldened me to continue; John H. Schaar by his example showed me the importance of sticking to the work.

My husband, Norman Jacobson, whose love and confidence have sustained me, has been untiring in his willingness to read, edit, and offer his knowledge and experience, as well as to live with my doubts. Hilda Kessler has given me the gifts of her wisdom and friendship and taught me to trust the future. My daughters, Johanna and Lillian, whose births marked the beginning and completion of the writing, have filled my life with love and laughter and taught me to forget about finishing things on time. I dedicate this book to them.

CHAPTER 1

INTRODUCTION

I. THE PROBLEM OF SUBJECTS AND OBJECTS IN MODERN THEORY

An issue lurks beneath the surface of contemporary feminist theory. It possesses different guises and traverses boundaries, from feminism's most conservative to its most radical thought. Although it concerns questions of moment, it has been gathering strength for centuries. The issue encompasses the old question of the nature of women and assumes, in its ultracontemporary form, the question of *difference.* Are women really so different from men? Does it matter politically? What might be the basis of the politically significant differences between men and women? How do we know?

The question about how we know marks the point of departure of this book. Although it is easy enough to assume that there are significant differences between women and men, it is difficult to know what they are, beyond the obvious physical and biological appearances. Yet much of contemporary feminist theory regards the differences between men and women, and their social consequences, as settled. The prevailing feminist contention, which assumes a variety of political shapes, is that women are somehow more at peace with nature than are men, experience less metaphysical angst, less tension between "inside" and "outside." The meaning of inside and outside, which changes depending upon the interest of the theorist, may focus upon the relationship between mind and the world, abstract and concrete, reason and emotion, thought and action, consciousness and history, or theory and praxis. Some argue that men experience the world dichotomously while women travel more easily between different arenas of life. Women live in a world with soft borders; the division between self and the world is easy and permeable. Men, in contrast, live in a harshly divided world, isolated from each other and their environment. It is sometimes even supposed that the notion of divided arenas of life is an entirely male construct.

Problems exist in all of the work I have read on the concept of gender difference. Even assuming that the descriptions of difference are accurate, the theories are all laden with unexplored assumptions about the sources of the difference. Although the concept of feminine "nature" (or "human nature") is somewhat archaic to a twentieth-century theorist, the notion of difference seems to call for discussion of that concept. Are the differences between men and women "natural," or are they the result of environment and history? Is nature itself, perhaps, a part of history? To build a political theory around the concept of difference, one must surely have some ideas about the basis of difference. The contention that men and women experience existence differently involves metaphysical questions about what existence in the world is like, as well as epistemological questions about how one knows anything about the world or oneself. How can one know what another person experiences?

The terms I prefer to use to address these questions are *subjectivity* and *objectivity*. They are sufficiently general to be flexible about the problem of division that contemporary feminists have come to associate with men. They may be used to address a problem that has preoccupied philosophers and metaphysicians for millennia, and that may be described as puzzlement over an apparent gap between the tangible world and our ability to know about it. Hannah Arendt regards this problem as particularly poignant in the modern age, concerning doubt about whether we can trust our own senses. In *The Human Condition* Arendt associates this relatively recent phenomenon, which she calls "world alienation," with modern loss of the stability of the objective world. The loss is characterized by a breakdown of the boundaries that once made the world, in Arendt's view, a more habitable place: private and public spaces, a stable objective world to survive generations of people and to "stand against" nature. Alienation, for Arendt, is associated with the loss of secure divisions between household and political life, the loss of anything in the world that is expected to last beyond the lifetime of a single generation. In her terms, this amounts to relinquishment of the objective world, which carries an enormous psychological price. She believes that being human involves the creation of permanence external to human beings. She reminds us of the etymology of the word *objective*. It means "stand against."

> It is this durability which gives the things of the world their relative independence from men who produced and use them, their "objectivity" which makes them withstand, "stand against" and endure, at least for a time, the voracious needs and wants of their living makers and users. From this viewpoint, the things of the world have the function of stabilizing human life, and their objectivity lies in the fact that—in contradiction to the Heraclitean saying that the same man can never enter the same stream—men, their ever-changing nature notwithstanding, can retrieve their sameness, that is, their identity, by being related to the same chair and the same table. In other words, against the subjectivity of men stands the objectivity of the man-made world rather than the "sublime indifference of an untouched nature."[1]

Along with the loss of boundaries to divide the world, Arendt believes that the particularity of basic human activities has disappeared. Not only have formerly distinct public and private arenas become one ill-defined place (referred to by Arendt as "the social"), but the distinction between *labor, work,* and *action*—activities that always used to characterize human life—has become blurred. Of the three, labor, the least peculiarly human, has come to dominate our lives. Labor is cyclical, duplicating biological rhythms. It may have a beginning point, but it has no defined end. In contrast, work is something that distinguishes people from animals. It has a starting and an ending point, and leaves something that lasts. It is the activity of hands and tools. Action is the most distinctly human of the three, according to Arendt. It leaves deeds that can be remembered and talked about, also regarded by Arendt as things permanent. From

Arendt's perspective, the terms can be distinguished most readily when regarded objectively, rather than subjectively. A loaf of bread is a product of labor: it will quickly decay whether or not it is used (consumed). A pair of shoes is an example of a product of work: it may be expected to last, if used properly or if not used at all. The difference between a day spent baking or making shoes is not as significant as the difference between the products, between what is contributed to the world.

The products of work are introjections into the cyclicality of the natural world, as are the results of action, whereas labor itself is cyclical, and natural. In Arendt's view, human beings define themselves by the permanence they impose upon natural cyclicality. Regrettably, we have become a world of laborers and consumers and have lost the comfort of permanence in life. We have acquiesced in the reduction of everything to cycles of production and consumption, lost the firmness of the division between private and public. We expect everything to dissolve before our eyes, expect shoes to go out of style before they wear out, to be as transient in our lives as bread. Instead of acting, asserting ourselves upon the world, we simply *behave* according to predicted norms. Acting is a uniquely public capacity; behaving according to predictable routines is what people normally do in the privacy of their own household. Animals also behave; only human beings are capable of action. The decline of both private and public, and their replacement with the social means that behavior, not action, is dominant. This confusion between what is public and what is private robs people of the capacity to act. The rise of social science, the study of predictable mass behavior, is an indication of what we have lost.

Loss of the objective world is what defines alienation, according to Arendt. An overemphasis on intangible, fleeting human experience—subjectivity—is another way to describe what she regards as unnerving about modern life. Arendt traces the rise of subjectivism (or the centrality of subjectivity) to Descartes. "I think therefore I am" is not a statement about epistemological certainty, but rather about a last refuge taken from the increasingly unlivable world. It is a statement revealing profound uncertainty, doubt, a modern scepticism about the reliability of the world. It is descriptive of modern alienation. Galileo's discovery by means of a telescope (a product of work) that the earth was not the center of the universe contributed to conditions that permitted the rise of Cartesian doubt. People could no longer trust their senses or their reason; appearances were no longer to be relied upon. What had appeared obvious to the naked eye—that the sun revolves around the earth—was, if Galileo was to be believed, now proven false. The startling discovery that one could no longer trust one's senses overshadowed the dichotomy between reason and the senses that had previously characterized the world.

> The old opposition of sensual and rational truth, of the inferior truth capacity of the senses and the superior capacity of reason, paled beside this challenge, beside the obvious implication that neither truth nor reality is given, that neither of them appears as it is, and that only interference with appearance, doing away with appearances, can hold out a hope for true knowledge.[2]

The response to Galileo's discovery was thus not exultation but doubt, "that 'school of suspicion' as Nietzsche once called it," and an accompanying rise of introspection and loss of common sense.[3] However, introspection is thought thinking about itself, cut off from rather than responding to the reality of the external, objective world. It is a description of an overriding subjectivism. "The poignancy of Descartes' doubt is fully realized only if one understands that the new discoveries dealt an even more disastrous blow to human confidence in the world and in the universe than is indicated by a clear-cut separation of being and appearance."[4]

According to Hannah Arendt, then, we live in a world dominated not by objectivity and dichotomy but by subjectivism and a loss of the very distinctions that modern feminists would call dichotomies. Our feeling of unease in our own world is the result of a lack of clarity, crispness, between our internal, subjective existence and our objective "being-in-the-world." This line of thinking runs counter both to other "male" descriptions of modern alienation and to most contemporary feminist theory as well. For example, Marx's theory of alienation, of which Arendt is explicitly critical in *The Human Condition,* offers a description of alienation that is nearly the inverse of Arendt's. To Marx, alienation is characterized by a forced dichotomy between a human subject and the objects of labor. Alienation results when human energy is infused into the material, objective world, in the form of products of labor, and then, because of specific historical conditions, is withheld from the person whose energy has been captured in them. Alienation is the loss of objectivity, but that loss is material; the worker has lost control over the world she produces. Alienation in capitalist society is characterized by a hostile confrontation between subject and object.

Marx's concept of alienation and his ideas about the relationship between subjects and objects will be discussed in detail further on. They are noted here to emphasize the importance in modern thought of the relationship between subjectivity and objectivity, terms that may be used to describe the modern problem of "alienation." Although alienation has been used to describe a psychological state more often than a political problem, it may also be useful in elucidating aspects of political oppression itself. It is certainly related to feminist concerns. The meaning of and relationship between subjects and objects, subjectivity and objectivity, have been increasingly central to efforts to construct the basis of a feminist theory: a feminist epistemology.

II. CONTEMPORARY FEMINISM: SUBJECTS AND OBJECTS, EQUALITY AND DIFFERENCE

If contemporary feminist theorists are in agreement about anything, it is that dichotomies are anathema to feminism. However, contemporary feminists are less explicit about the nature of these troublesome dichotomies. Sometimes the difficulty seems to lie more with objectivity, sometimes with subjectivity. On other occasions "dichotomous" thinking itself is regarded as incompatible with feminist theory, and a world "divided" into subjects and objects is considered suspect. In the immediately following pages, I shall explore feminist use of the terminology meant to indicate the problem with dichotomous thinking. My purpose is not to defend a divided and alienated world but rather to question whether doing away with conventional categories of analysis is prerequisite to formulating an epistemology for feminism. The fact that both radical and conservative feminists share a mistrust of dichotomies is in itself worthy of inquiry. It assumes that a link exists between epistemology and political content, but a single epistemological tendency is criticized, while the political conclusions drawn from it are quite different. Can dichotomous thinking then be held responsible for inhibiting development of a political theory compatible with feminism? Is an emphasis on objectivity, whatever that may mean, incompatible with feminist substance? What about subjectivity? Indeed, is there any correlation between the epistemological structure and the political substance of a theory?

In this book, the links between structure and substance in theorizing about politics will be explored in detail. In the overview of existing feminist positions that follows, I shall argue that the link between epistemology and politics has been insufficiently explored, permitting unwarranted and unconscious assumptions about what those links might be. I do not intend to engage in technical quibbling about some obscure methodological point. I believe that existing feminist theory, whether radical or conservative, that concerns itself with problems about subjects and objects, dichotomies and unities, assumes that the way things are is the result of male thinking. That is, objectivity is male, or subjectivity is male, or dichotomies themselves are male. Women would not have brought the world to its current deplorable state because women think differently than men.

The two directions that can be taken from this assumed starting point are, in my view, equally undesirable. Either one must conclude that women are fundamentally different from men, which assumes some theory of nature, also usually inadequately addressed by contemporary feminist thought, or one can assume that the way the world is currently conceived, that is, the epistemology before the men who use it, is responsible for political circumstances that have oppressed women (and in a different way, men) and so must be changed. The former offers no real opportunity for change because it tacitly accepts concepts of masculine and feminine nature while overlooking what the basis of that nature might be. At best, it offers a change in leadership: "If women were in charge, things would be better, or at least different." In its most conservative form, the former view may argue that women's domain has been undervalued throughout and history ought to be taken more seriously without, however, suggesting any formal change in the power arrangements to which society has become accustomed. By bringing the matter to public attention, the assumption is that people will come to recognize that the private sphere with its intimacy, nurturance, unity, is valuable on its own. The "male sphere," however, is still characterized by competition, aggression, individuation, warfare, etc., while the female sphere is not.

The alternative to assuming that men are just plain different from women, the assumption that a dichotomizing epistemology itself is conducive to oppressive politics and creates hierarchies, contains its own problems. I am in general agreement up to this point: some epistemologies have created difficulties for women. Instead of focusing on what it is about the relationship between subject and object that creates the difficulties—usually described by feminists in terms of dichotomies or hierarchies—feminist theorists have either sought to include women as subjects without questioning the epistemology itself (de Beauvoir), or have attempted to abandon the categories subjectivity and/or objectivity altogether, leaving an unnerving absence of structure in their wake (deconstructionist feminists). More specifically, Simone de Beauvoir, in *The Second Sex,* identified an epistemological problem that had gone unrecognized since the Enlightenment: the problem with mainstream epistemology and its substantive outcome is "homocentrism," the assumed centrality of the male subject. The modern discovery of the individual, which facilitated or accompanied the rise of liberalism, assumes that the individual is male. The centrality of the male subject in post-Enlightenment thought assumes a dichotomy between subject and object. Women, when thought about at all, are assumed to be objects.[5] In the beginning, if we attribute the origin of contemporary feminist theory to de Beauvoir, was the male subject. While de Beauvoir is critical of this asymmetrical and hierarchical view of the world, she is not particularly critical of the subject-object split per se, but only of the male monopoly of subjectivity. She herself is not really a theorist of difference, but the French deconstructionist feminists who claim to be following and going beyond her theories *are,* and would completely eliminate subjects and objects from philosophical vernacular.

The other side of the "epistemology-as-problem" stance assumes objectivity rather than "the male subject" as the problem. The concept of "male objectivity" involves both the making of women into objects and the assumption that truth resides in the world "out there," calling for the withdrawal of subjective, personal involvement. Catharine MacKinnon is one theorist who has written powerfully against the concept of objectivity, which she regards as a "male construct," and against the usefulness of the categories subjectivity and objectivity altogether. In her provocative two-part article, "Feminism, Marxism, Method and the State,"[6] MacKinnon argues that "The male epistemological stance, which corresponds to the world it creates, is objectivity: the ostensibly uninvolved stance, the view from a distance and from no particular perspective apparently transparent to its reality. It does not comprehend its own perspectivity, does not recognize what it sees as subjective like itself..." (1:24).

She does not, however, adequately distinguish between epistemological objectivity and political objectification. She seems to assume that the former invariably leads to the latter: "Objectivity, as the epistemological stance of which objectification is the social process, creates the reality it apprehends by defining as knowledge the reality it creates through its way of apprehending it" (2:636).[7] If she is critical of objectivity, neither does MacKinnon focus upon the desirability of subjectivity. Although psychological distance, not only from what is studied but from oneself, is the problem created by objectivity, MacKinnon tacitly assumes that where there is objectivity there must also be subjectivity, for the two concepts constitute parts of the same whole. Each one assumes a dichotomist stance. The methodology appropriate for feminism transcends the partiality of both objectivity and subjectivity.

> Having been objectified as sexual beings while stigmatized as ruled by subjective passions, women reject the distinction between subjective and objective postures—as the means to comprehend social life. Disaffected from objectivity, having been its prey but excluded from its world through relegation

to subjective inwardness, women's interest lies in overthrowing the distinction itself. (1:22)

In transcending the partiality of both subjectivity and objectivity, MacKinnon also paradoxically envisions the possibility of overcoming the impulse to universalize. The specifically feminist method she seeks will stand outside all traditional categories of epistemology.

> Feminism does not see its view as subjective, partial, or undetermined but as a critique of the purported generality, disinterestedness, and universality of prior accounts. These have not been half right, but have involved the wrong whole. Feminism not only challenges masculine particularity, but questions the universality imperative itself. Aperspectivity is revealed as a strategy of male hegemony. (1:23)

Although MacKinnon does not define the terms *subjectivity, objectivity, objectification,* or *universality* with particular precision, on the whole she seems to be arguing that women, or at least feminists, would not divide the world into subjects and objects but rather would (naturally?) utilize a more unified epistemological stance. In her view, subjectivity seems to be associated with passivity and internality. Objects are associated with activity, externality, and also with tangibility, for in this work she argues that Marx's materialism is as objectivist as liberal empiricism. But objectivity as MacKinnon uses the term is also associated with "the universality imperative." That is, objectivity has to do both with tangible materiality and with aperspectivity; psychological distance, which encourages thinking in terms of universals, gives one the false confidence that it is possible to stand upon an Archimedean point and lift the entire world.

The problems MacKinnon discusses in this work and others[8] are recognizable and have certainly caused difficulties for women. Whether feminists would necessarily think any differently is another matter, for she does not suggest *why* the world divided into subjects and objects is invariably male. The point to be noted in this context, however, is that the difficulties are associated with both objectivity and dichotomous thinking.

Of the two feminist critiques of subjectivity and objectivity discussed so far, de Beauvoir is considered a "moderate" because she accepts the dualist categories subjectivity and objectivity, desiring only to include women as subjects. This stance anticipates the androgyny argument of liberal feminism: women should simply be included in all aspects of public life, regardless of the injustices, inequalities, and economic and racial hierarchies upon which liberal capitalism rests. By refusing to acknowledge that there may be politically significant differences between men and women, it tacitly advocates the "superwoman syndrome." A privileged class of women expect themselves to "do everything": succeed at a professional career, marriage, childbearing and child rearing, on a model of a male life pattern (or "career curve") without public support in the form of federal- or state-funded maternity leaves, childcare, etc. The liberal feminist stance has most recently been referred to in feminist discourse as the argument for "equality." In contrast, the argument for difference assumes that politically significant differences exist between men and women. This stance has become more acceptable to feminists recently and enlists both more radical and more conservative spokeswomen. The difference between radical and conservative is often blurred, although it is related to the sort of solution advocated, and probably also to the amount of anger displayed in writing. MacKinnon is an example of a radical, although she declines to modify feminism with any adjectives at all.

On the conservative side of the difference question is, for example, Carol Gilligan. Her book *In a Different Voice* received a lot of attention when it was first published, arguing as it does that girls and boys have very different perceptions of their relationship to the world. Gilligan, a psychologist, studied the process of moral decision making, taking as her point of departure a well-known scale of moral reasoning developed by Harvard psychologist Lawrence Kohlberg. She argues that the methods used by Kohlberg and his associates, specifically the ranked hierarchy of levels of moral reasoning, assume standards of thinking that are specifically male. Excellence, or a high rating on the moral reasoning scale, involves characteristics that, for whatever reason, are male. Male moral reasoning involves the capacity to "individuate," to create distance between the self and the prob lem, and the capacity to think abstractly, in terms of impersonal rights. The alternative, which Gilligan argues is more character-istic of girls and women, is to become involved, reasoning in terms of personal responsibility to another person.

Although Gilligan doesn't specifically use the vocabulary of subjectivity and objectivity, it is evident that her thinking is com-patible with that vocabulary, and that the difference between men and women has something to do with the relationship between self and other, inside and outside, subjectivity and objectivity. She suggests that women perceive the world as more connected to themselves than do men. The distinction between the male and female voices she hears has to do with "two modes of describing the relationship between other and self."[9] Because women are less inclined to see a clear-cut separation between self and other, they are more reluctant to make decisions based upon abstract moral standards. In a psychological experiment designed to test the process of moral decision making, this tendency may appear as an inability or an unwillingness to distance oneself from a situa-tion—that is, to reason in conventionally abstract (male) terms.[10]

The ability to reason abstractly, to differentiate oneself from others, is in our society defined as adulthood itself. Gilligan argues that such a conception of adulthood is gendered, and specifically male: "When the focus of individuation and individu-al achievement extends into adulthood and maturity is equated with personal autonomy, concern with relationships appears as a weakness of women rather than as a human strength" (17). With-out elaborating on the possible origins of this difference, Gilligan notes that women approach situations differently than men:

> Sensitivity to the needs of others and the assumption of responsibility for taking care lead women to attend to voices other than their own and to include in their judgement other points of view. Women's moral weakness, manifest in an apparent diffusion and confusion of judgement, is thus inseparable from women's moral strength, an overriding concern with relationships and responsibilities. The reluc-tance to judge may itself be indicative of the care and con-cern for others that infuse the psychology of women's devel-opment and are responsible for what is generally seen as problematic in its nature. (16, 17)

Gilligan describes an alternative to the male model of adulthood. Female maturity involves the ability to think in terms of the needs of others, rather than in terms of individuation and autonomy. It operates in a concrete rather than an abstract mode, judging a particular situation in terms of the individuals involved, rather than in terms of abstract theories about justice or equality. Women make decisions that affect other people by thinking in terms of networks of relationships, rather than hierarchies of values.

The difficulty with Gilligan's work is that she does not elaborate, does not offer a theory about how women came to be the way they are. She claims to be offering a description rather than an analysis. At one point she suggests that she is only highlighting a form of moral reasoning that has been overlooked, and that may not be directly related to gender: "The different voice I describe is characterized not by gender but theme. Its association with women is an empirical observation, and it is primarily through women's voices that I trace its development" (2). There is something unsatisfactory, or at least incomplete, about offering a description of so fundamental a difference between men and women while declining to suggest how the difference might have arisen or even whether it really applies only to women. Gilligan mentions that women have been nurturers and seems to imply, however vaguely, that that womanly experience is the source of the difference. Woman's role is devalued in a male-dominated society that views separation and individuation as key developmental tasks, and autonomy and individual achievement as its major values. Does Gilligan mean to imply that the difference between male and female reasoning is desirable? Indeed, how specifically female is it? Is it possible to change it? Is it biological or sociological in origin?

Gilligan is close to assuming a theory about feminine nature without recognizing what she is doing, or taking responsibility for the implications. The problems involved with tacit assumptions about nature in a theory about "the way women are" will be discussed more fully in chapter 3, on John Stuart Mill's *The Subjection of Women*. What one does with the "simple observation" that women are different from men in a given way has much to do with what one assumes about the origins of the difference. To suggest that a particular trait is just plain *there,* that it makes little difference anymore how it came to be, is an example of the ahistoricity of liberal thought. The empiricist believes that she is merely describing what she sees, but acknowledged differences between men and women have proven particularly destructive to women. When not used as an excuse for exclusion, or a polite description of inferiority, they have been the basis of romanticized notions about feminine characteristics. Difference has provided the basis of hierarchy in the past and should be treated with delicacy and wariness by feminists.

There are other examples of theories about women's greater capacity to experience the world as connected to themselves. Nancy Chodorow in *The Reproduction of Mothering* presents separation and individuation as specifically male developmental problems because girls identify with their mothers and are encouraged to maintain a sense of connection with both the mother and others, who characterize the bonds of infancy and childhood.[11] Sigmund Freud and traditional psychologists viewed the maintenance of childhood bonds as the source of weak ego boundaries. Chodorow and other feminist psychologists view the identification with the mother as a source of strength: the capacity for empathy with others.

Dorothy Dinnerstein in *The Mermaid and the Minotaur* makes a similar point, although she is more explicit about the problems that accompany the inability of girls and women to see themselves as separate and autonomous.[12] She comes closer, I think, to presenting an argument for equality rather than difference between men and women when she suggests that it places an impossible burden on women to be singularly associated with the extraordinary dependency of infancy. Dependency inevitably translates into ambivalence toward women in general, because everybody grows, and growth necessarily entails separation and independence, which is both painful and exhilarating. The person who serves as a background for, or the most involved witness to, growth is bound to be the recipient of both anger and gratitude, hatred and love. The other parent, the one who represents the outside world, apart from infancy, will receive extraordinary admiration and fear. Neither parent should bear the weight of such complicated unconscious associations. Dinnerstein emphasizes the importance of both male and female contact with the infant in order to prevent the perpetuation of unconscious association of infancy wholly with one sex or the other. Women should not have the burden of representing empathy and lack of individuation in a society that doesn't publicly value those traits; nor should men have the burden of representing autonomy and independence in society, with all the associated responsibilities. No woman is as powerful as the infant's conception of her mother; no man is as powerful as the child expects her father to be. Whomever the infant encounters first, however, will be the basis of the more powerful associations because of the strength of that first, primal bond. What is called for is a redistribution of primal associations in order to defuse exaggerated attitudes about both sexes. That is, difference may amount to a skewing or exaggeration of traits associated with masculinity and femininity, which is likely to lead to hierarchy.

I find Dinnerstein's argument promising (in spite of its assumption of the heterosexual nuclear family as a norm in society) precisely for its emphasis on the importance of a more equitable distribution of what society regards as masculine and feminine characteristics. She is fairly clear about the *sources* of the differences that can be observed between male and female behavior: they are rooted in the unconscious, rather than any vaguely alluded to concept of nature, and hence can be changed only by changing an infant's primal, unconscious associations with female and male, mother and father. Too often, the feminist theories that rest upon a conception of difference simply avoid discussion of the sources of difference and its implications.

Consider one more example of a feminist theory of difference whose neglect of the basis of difference leads to precisely the same uncertainty that Gilligan displayed when she acknowledged that she might not even be describing a difference unique to women but rather a "theme," or a tendency, characteristic of some women and some men. Sara Ruddick in her article "Maternal Thinking" argues that mothers possess special qualities that have been overlooked and undervalued by society because they have been wrongly regarded as emotional rather than cognitive. Ruddick's purpose is to demonstrate that one important aspect of mothering is in fact *thinking*. She identifies three qualities associated with motherhood, which call for conscious, intellectual thought. "I speak about a mother's *thought*—the intellectual capacities she develops, the judgements she makes, the metaphysical attitudes she assumes, the values she affirms. A mother engages in a discipline. That is, she asks certain questions rather than others; establishes criteria for the truth, adequacy, and relevance of proposed answers; and cares about the findings she makes and can act upon."[13] The three characteristics of maternal thinking, reasons Ruddick, are interest in the preservation, growth, and acceptability of the child.[14] Her description of mothering is poignant, insightful, and interesting, but it soon becomes unclear whether she is actually describing mothers, or even women only. In a single confusing page (346), she suggests (1) that identifying anything with "womanly" is an invitation to oppressive misuse: "Our current gender dichotomies are rigid and damaging. Praising cultures of oppression comes close to praising oppression itself"; (2) that one needn't be a mother to be capable of "maternal thinking": "Maternal thinking is only one example of 'womanly thinking'.... For me, 'maternal' is a social category: Although maternal thinking arises out of actual child-caring practices, biological parenting is neither necessary nor sufficient. Many women and some men express maternal thinking in various kinds of working and caring with others"; (3) that women are after all different from men: "Maternal thought does, I believe, exist for all women in a radically different way than for men"; and finally, once again, (4) that women are not after all so different from men: "Along with biology, I put aside all accounts of gender difference or maternal nature which would claim an essential and ineradicable difference between female and male parents."

Maternal or not, this is an example of confused thinking! What can Ruddick be talking about? Does she mean to say that women are different from men or not? Is the difference biologically or socially rooted? There are probably no definitive answers to these questions, but that doesn't save a theorist from obligation to be clear about what is being assumed, and what the implications of a given stance may be. If an argument for difference is to be made, a theorist must establish the basis of that difference. If the difference to be focused upon is biological, what are the social implications? Does bearing children account for the difference in a woman's relation to the world? How exactly can the relationship be characterized? Are women more at peace with the world, less aware of tension between self and other? Are women more a "life force," who would not, for example, have thought of making war, or of inventing weapons? What about the wild protectiveness of female animals for their helpless young? Or the willingness of some animals to abandon their young? Perhaps, ironically, motherhood gives rise to a tendency towards aggression? In that case, a feminist theorist ought to consult a biologist, or a geneticist, to find out about sources of aggression or the lack of it in hormones, genes, etc.[15]

Then, too, if Ruddick means to suggest motherhood as the source of the difference between women and men, how do women who are not biological mothers fit in? Is womanhood to be reduced to maternity? If adoptive mothers, for example, behave toward their children in much the same way as biological mothers, shouldn't the possibility also be considered that fathers, biological or adoptive, might be capable of similar or identical relationships with their children? Perhaps the difference is physiological more than biological or genetic. Perhaps living in a male body is so different from living in a female body that behavior is affected. But how do we know? If it cannot be established even probabilistically, does it make any sense to focus on difference?

Obviously, I do not think much is accomplished by focusing upon the differences between women and men. Thinking in those terms, even if carefully done, leads inevitably to a theory of nature, and I do not think it is possible to establish once and for all a theory of immutable human, feminine, or masculine nature. It makes more sense to me to focus on the possible similarities between men and women if the relationship between the sexes is to change significantly from what it has been. If men believed they were more like women, and women believed they were more like men, I can't see how the theories that have served to separate and subordinate women from men would continue to be possible.

On a slightly different tack, there is a school of feminist thought that endeavors to transcend traditional dichotomies and traditional categories of analysis completely. The theory of Luce Irigaray, a contemporary French feminist, exemplifies the postmodern effort to transcend both traditional boundaries and traditional language. Her essays in *Speculum of the Other Woman* stress the harshness and limitations of a dichotomous approach to knowledge, drawing our focus to phallic imagery, which she believes is to be found in all traditional male thought. "Plato's Hystera" discusses the parable of the cave in *The Republic* as an effort to escape the darkness of the womb, through a vaginal passage, into the light of the sun. Plato forces unnecessary choices between darkness and light, female and male, and any number of equally false dichotomies. His perspective reflects a distinctly male, that is, phallocentric view of the world. Referring to the path or passageway he describes between the cave and the sunlight, Irigaray writes:

> Between the "world outside" and the "world inside," between the "world above" and the "world below." Between the light of the sky and the fire of the earth. Between the gaze of the man who has left the cave and that of the prisoner. Between truth and shadow, between truth and fantasy, between "truth" and whatever "veils" the truth. Between reality and dream. Between. . . . Between. . . . Between the intelligible and the sensible. Between good and evil. The one and the many. Between anything you like. All oppositions that assume the *leap* from a worse to a better. An ascent, a displacement (?) upward, a progression along a line. Vertical. Phallic even? But what has been forgotten in all these oppositions, and with good reason, is how to pass through the passage, how to negotiate it—the forgotten transition, the corridor, the narrow pass, the neck.
>
> *Forgotten vagina.* The passage that is missing.[16]

That is, dichotomous thinking is inevitably phallocentric, laden with phallic imagery. Plato imagines only the possibilities inside or outside the cave. Irigaray believes these choices to be false, even vicious. To emphasize their oppressiveness, she draws our attention to the force Plato believes will be necessary, and the pain that will occur as the unenlightened prisoners are wrenched, torn from their places in the cave, turned completely about, and forced to gaze directly into the sunlight. The linear imagery, where there is only forward and backward, is a harshly limited view of the world and is distinctly male. Men, she notes, also are agonized by the dichotomies they see as inevitable. They seek relief in unities, but Irigaray believes they also force the unities before they are ready to emerge more spontaneously, because zealous, aggressive man "only asks [himself] questions that he can already answer, using the supply of instruments he has available to assimilate even the disasters in his history" (137).

Even the choice between unity and dichotomy is dichotomous, one-dimensional, phallic, and encourages the masculine will to violent domination.

> A split tears open the arche of presence.... Being stands on high, off stage... and there it referees the life and death rivalries.... But there is no reduction of the gap, the rift between the bewitching spell of the cave and the logic of reason, between the earth's attraction and the sun's allure. Between the more maternal and the more paternal.... (274, 275)

> When the Other falls out of the starry sky into the chasms of the psyche the 'subject' is obviously obliged to stake out new boundaries for his field of implantation to re-ensure—otherwise, elsewhere—his dominance. Where once he was on the heights, he is now entreated to go down into the depths. (136)

This sort of thinking certainly holds radical epistemological promise. My problem with it is that in shattering all conventions, in arguing that subjectivity and objectivity are inevitably dichotomous and that dichotomies inevitably turn into hierarchies, too much may be relinquished. All hold on anything familiar is sacrificed.

Irigaray's solution is worrisome to me because doing away with the security of known epistemological categories, most specifically subjectivity and objectivity, leaves a nerve-wracking world, free-floating, with no structure, no reliable perspective at all. The price of living in such a world is the abandonment of epistemological conventions that have provided the basis of Western philosophy since the time of Plato and Aristotle. However, it is not simply my personal distaste for the relinquishment of solid historical ground that makes me so wary of postmodernism. The call for an antiauthoritarian stance toward history, toward the old authors, courts the danger of utter irresponsibility for the political consequences of any text. Anything is possible in a deconstructed world, in a world where there is no standard for weighing the responsibility of an author against the responsibility of a reader. While that may provide a handy weapon for undermining entrenched traditional authority, it offers no basis, indeed, it self-consciously denies the very *possibility* of a solidly grounded alternative to the past. It surrenders too much.[17]

Most importantly, it surrenders the possibility of confronting injustices of the past by simply "writing them off." If history can be reduced to text, and if a reader's interpretation of text carries as much authoritative weight as the author's, how can one argue that problems *actually* existed, and *still* persist? The power of the past is undone by an act of literary will. It is too facile a solution. In the next chapter we shall see that some feminist philosophers of science have struggled with the political difficulties of the postmodernist epistemological stance. Sandra Harding, in particular, wants to integrate the radical potential of a poststructuralist epistemology with the confrontational power of a "successor science" that accepts conventional terminology precisely because a dialogue with the past can be maintained.

I have a different solution. I think it may be possible to salvage the concepts, at minimum, of subjectivity and objectivity in a way that is compatible with feminist theory. They do not lead inevitably to a dichotomous world, but rather provide the possibility of some psychological distance, or perspective that might not always be as destructive as its historical overvaluation leads many feminist theorists to believe it must be.

Minimalist dialectics is an effort to salvage some central traditional philosophical concepts for feminist theory, an insistence that feminist theory need not reinvent the wheel, but can make use of significant work that has already been done in an effort to understand the world. Minimalist dialectics calls for a specific perspective on the relationship between subjectivity and objectivity, which in turn sheds new light on the concept of nature. The assumption is that one's relationship with nature and with the past is developmental, rather than predictably linear. Minimalist dialectics assumes that all human beings experience tension between mind and the world: perception and consciousness on the one hand, and material experience on the other. The method focuses on the conflict between the two realms and traces the process of the conflict through time. "Truth" is a moment of reconciliation when the border between subject and object is temporarily dissolved.

Truth—or perhaps "understanding" is a better term—thus *does* involve the dissolution of hard boundaries and an end to tension, but this boundary truce is achieved by acknowledging and tolerating, sometimes seeking and sustaining, conflict. The epistemology involves a certain drama and risk. The moments of resolution are not privileged, nor are they guaranteed, but the experience of tension and conflict feels absolute, frightening, perhaps also exhilarating, sometimes hopeless. There is no assurance that peace, understanding, or a unified perspective is forthcoming on any matter, and the frustration of not knowing whether a resolution to a problem is achievable may be discouraging. Conflict, misunderstanding, frustration are prerequisite to understanding, which is, in turn, never complete or final. Moments of understanding themselves give rise to further conflict in the quest for yet fuller understanding.

Subjectivity, objectivity, and dialectics are discussed in greater detail in the chapters on Hegel and Marx. For now it should be noted that minimalist dialectics differs from Marxian and Hegelian dialectics primarily in terms of its professed agnosticism about origins and ends in history, and in its refusal to accept any truth as "world historical." It defines truth as a process of conflict through time, but does not insist that either consciousness or materiality can have primacy so long as the method is dialectical. Minimalist dialectics is thus neither idealist nor materialist: it involves the interplay of materiality *and* ideas, objectivity *and* subjectivity. To anticipate acceptable ends, whether in the form of a workers' revolution, universal self-consciousness, or anything else, is to import content, to impose a political agenda, to rig political outcome and turn epistemology into ideology. My hope is that minimalist dialectics will indeed prove conducive to nonhierarchical, nonauthoritarian political and intellectual outcomes that encourage progressive politics with human freedom as its agenda. However, to postulate those ends as the inevitable outcome of the method is to deprive the method of its legitimacy—indeed, to impose a daunting political smugness. Hence the riskiness, hence the excitement of the method.

To make this initial sketch more concrete, take for example how one person comes to know another. Consider the beginning of a friendship. There is a moment of initial contact, a meeting. Two people first see each other in a classroom, at a dinner party, in the waiting room of a doctor's office, and become interested: "Something about that woman's face is intriguing. I'd like to know her better." At the initial encounter each is object to the other. Each sees surfaces and thinks, "I like her smile, I like her eyes," or perhaps unconsciously, "That person is dressed in a style that says to me she is honest, straightforward, compatible with my values," or even "My goodness, how can she wear that? . . . but I like her face anyway."

A luncheon date is arranged and while any number of outcomes is possible, consider two: either the promise of friendship is not fulfilled, the two women find very little to talk about and leave each other wondering, "How could I have been interested in her? She's really very shallow," or "She's so intense; I feel exhausted." Alternatively, a wonderful meeting might take place, and each woman finds herself listening to the other's story for minutes at a time. The moment when one is "lost" to the other is the moment when the boundary between subject and object is transcended, when the initial perception of the other as object is reversed. The "other," once the object of attraction, is now subject, while the listener becomes object, unconscious of self, so intriguing is the other's story. The listener is object in the sense that the speaker-subject defines and shapes the listener's world. (Think of object only in the sense of passivity; forego the political prejudice that associates "objectification" with abuse.)

The conversation slows, perhaps a waiter arrives and distracts the two and the speaker suddenly "comes to herself": "But I've been talking too much, tell me about yourself." The spell is broken; the listener who was lost to the speaker now also "returns" to herself, perhaps with some disappointment, because it is pleasant to be under another's spell at least momentarily, even as it is necessary to "find oneself" again. With luck, as the listener now begins to speak, the original speaker will also lose herself, and a friendship will blossom.

Now think about what happens after the lunch. Both have experienced moments of lost and regained conscious subjectivity. Each has returned to herself enriched by the experience of having risked something, having surrendered emotional self-protectiveness and made herself vulnerable. Each has undergone a change from that experience alone, and each one's initial vision of the other has also changed. Recall what you first saw in a friend, and think about how that friend now seems to you. Is she the same person? "When I first saw you, you seemed to me so...." Is that appearance, that object first encountered, really the same as the friend you now know so intimately? Even in the case of a friendship that never develops, sufficient exchange takes place to change each person in the eyes of the other, and to add one misjudgment about a person to each one's own store of experiences. Both are "changed" by the meeting.

The scenario is offered as a demonstration of the interpenetrability of subjectivity and objectivity in a dialectical approach to knowledge. An empirical approach would focus instead on the *inviolability* of the object: "Of course your friend is the same person as she was before you knew her. Your knowledge of her is simply cumulative," argues the empiricist. "You simply know *more* now than you did originally, but you and she are the same persons you always were, defined objectively by the perimeters of your bodies." Dialectical method, however, focuses on the challenges to boundaries that constitute the interaction between subject and object, and which result in "more" knowledge or, more accurately, in a changing perception of reality. It is an oversimplification to describe the knowledge acquired between two friends, as in our example, as merely cumulative. The mutuality of influence of subject and object, and the inevitable interchangeability of the two stances (what is subject becomes object and what is object becomes subject), suggests an end to the hierarchical relationship between knowing subject and known object and ensures that both will change, that neither will be the same person who first opened herself up to the other.

What is "minimalist" about this dialectic is the focus upon interaction in a limited time frame, rather than a grander historical sweep. The difficulty with "Big History" as the framework for a dialectical analysis is that it lends itself too readily to assumptions about origins and ends. Minimalist dialectics focuses upon the *process* of interaction, adhering to an agnosticism about origins and outcomes. In contrast a Marxian dialectic would focus upon the economic class structure contained in all human relationships, even with the objective material world. A table, for example, cannot adequately be understood merely as an object in a room. Rather, it is congealed human labor representing the historical development of the class structure of the society in which it was manufactured. Members of the working class felled the trees, extracted the petroleum from the earth, refined the raw materials, manufactured the chemical composites in unpleasant surroundings, and participated in fashioning and assembling a mountain of tables to be sold to a business or university. Members of the working class loaded the table onto trucks, drove the trucks, delivered the tables, and assembled them in offices or classrooms. Members of another class are thereby privileged to use the tables to further their education, retaining membership in the privileged class. A professor truly sees the table before her in the classroom only when she understands the economics that brought it there. A table has much to teach the professor who places her lecture notes upon it.

As ingenious as this perspective is, it is beyond the scope of minimalist dialectics in that it presupposes one, and only one, perspective on truth. Marxian dialectics assumes that the table's economic history is its true story. Minimalist dialectics *could* embrace that perspective, but it could never settle on it as final or ultimate. It might instead be more to the point in a particular classroom situation, to begin by focusing upon the table as a physical barrier, establishing a psychological hierarchy between teacher and students, thereby shaping the relationship between them. Nor would that understanding be regarded as final. Rather it would be one, but only one, perspective leading towards a fuller but never complete understanding of the process of interaction between teacher and students.

There is an additional aspect of dialectics—both minimalist and Marxian-Hegelian—that must be introduced here: the role of conflict in the process of understanding. In order to see the role conflict plays, return to our budding friendship. It may be more immediately obvious that an encounter involving members of two different economic classes will likely involve a conflict of perspective and experience. A relationship between worker and owner will surely involve an aspect of confrontation and challenge before any understanding may be possible. But what about a relationship between two friends? What role can conflict possibly play there?

In friendship, and indeed even in marriage, knowledge and intimacy proceed as a result of argument as much as agreement. A disagreement over a movie seen together may be handled either by avoiding or by evoking confrontation. Our two friends see a movie that one loves and the other hates. Over coffee after the movie they can "agree to disagree," opt for consensus, say to each other, "Well, we're each entitled to our opinion," even though each may be harboring grave doubts about the aesthetic sensibilities of the other. That is, they can repress the conflict. Or, they can use the conflict as a means of pushing for more knowledge about the other person and run the risk of losing the friendship altogether. If pressed, one friend has actually been thinking: "If she liked that sexist trash, I can't possibly imagine staying her friend. She probably hasn't understood a word I've been saying about politics and feminism." Meanwhile, the other thinks: "She's so serious she can't even lighten up long enough to enjoy a comedy without reading politics into everything. I don't know if we can stay friends; it's too basic an element in her personality. She's heavy." Instead of peacefully letting the matter drop, the two friends can let the argument develop and argue the night through. If they let their fears emerge—that disagreement over a movie reflects disagreement about politics and is fundamental to each one's worldview—it may indeed undermine the friendship. They may leave each other angry, certain that this is the end of the relationship. Each is disappointed and depressed; each may doubt her own judgment about people. Perhaps in the next day or two, one calls the other, and both realize that they have a stake in the continuation of the friendship. How much richer will their friendship be for having risked everything over a trifle such as a movie! How much richer are knowledge and understanding when continually challenged and truly risked, rather than allowed to become entrenched. Minimalist dialectics calls for continual challenge to all assumptions—even political beliefs fiercely clung to. Their validity is won only by question and challenge, and even then can never be assumed to be final.

CHAPTER 2

CONTEMPORARY FEMINIST EPISTEMOLOGY

Some recent feminist theory *does* make use of the term dialectics; some *does* make use of the concept of objectivity. What are the differences between the minimalist dialectics I will describe in this book and the work already done that seems to resemble my efforts to integrate objectivity and subjectivity in an epistemology for feminist theory? Three theorists come close to saving aspects of traditional concepts while forging a theory that is unequivocally feminist: Alison Jagger, Sandra Harding, and Evelyn Fox Keller. Jagger in *Feminist Politics and Human Nature* offers an approach she calls socialist feminism, to be distinguished from traditional Marxism, as well as from liberal and radical feminism.[1] She grounds her effort in the assumed necessity of some concept of nature. Harding and Keller are feminist philosophers of science, both of whom offer a sophisticated integration of the concepts of subjectivity and objectivity, and draw upon the term *dialectics*. Unfortunately, however, all three tend to minimize the role of conflict that is at the essence of dialectical learning. In so doing, they associate feminist theory with too facile a unity. The dialectics of Jagger, Harding, and Keller leap over the necessity and the completeness of conflict between subjectivity and objectivity. In undue haste they seize upon a desire for unity, a harmony between subjectivity and objectivity that, because unearned, lacks true power in their formulations.

I. ALISON JAGGER

Alison Jagger offers a comprehensive review of the contemporary varieties of feminist theory and practice. Her preference is for what she terms "socialist feminism," which harnesses the combined virtues of radical and Marxist feminism. She is critical of liberal feminism because it is plagued by ahistoricity and atomism in its political solutions. It assumes a static concept of nature, external to history. Its methodology is rationalist owing to the absence of any role for history, and empiricist in that it presupposes a world of empirical fragments, detached from the mind of the observer. Liberalism and liberal feminism thus offer a worldview plagued by dualisms and hierarchy. Liberalism is "essentialist," dividing body from mind, overvaluing the role of mind in defining human nature, while denying the impor- tance of bodies. Precisely because it denies any connection between mind and body, liberalism assumes too many similarities between men and women. Women and men are potentially "equal" by virtue of the lack of distinction between male and female minds. "Objective" truth is a result of independence from both subjective perception and subjective material experience.

Marxism, in contrast, avoids the rationalist-essentialist limitation, and in principle avoids the liberal tendency to dichotomize. Like liberalism, however, it also denies that any significant differences between men and women exist. Because Marxists believe that economic history is the sole determinant of consciousness, and that the only significant conflict in the modern world is the one between the capitalist and proletariat classes, gender is an entirely secondary element in Marxist theory. Whether one is a man or a woman matters far less than whether one is a proletarian or a capitalist.

Ironically there are many similarities between the substance of Marxist and liberal feminism. Jagger notes that Marxism on its own, in reducing all human consciousness to class consciousness, actually resembles liberal feminist rationalism in its assumption that no significant gender differences exist between men and women: in the marketplace, according to Marxists, such differences are entirely obscured by more important class differences. As Jagger remarks, "The major thrust, indeed, of Marxist theorizing seems to have been toward the abolition of gender distinctions in the market, and thus toward what liberal feminists have called an androgynous future" (67). At the same time, however, Marxism is characterized by tacit assumptions about inevitable consequences of differences: women are probably "destined" to be caretakers as well as bearers of children. And Marxism, much like liberalism, values public life—at least the life of the marketplace—more highly than private life. "The biologistic conception of procreation leads to the devaluation of procreative labor: women's work may be socially necessary, but it is not fully historical and hence not fully human work . . . the apparent gender-blindness of Marxist categories is in reality a gender bias . . ." (78).

Radical feminism, as described by Jagger, runs to the opposite extreme. It overemphasizes the biologically predicated differences between men and women, denying the significance of material history. In her initial discussion of radical feminism, Jagger claims that radical feminist theory is so various it can't be said to assume any one view of human nature. In later discussion, Jagger implies that for most radical feminists the biological differences between women and men, specifically differences in sexual and reproductive experiences, are crucial in determining outlook and potential. The socialist feminism that Jagger offers as the most adequate basis for feminist theory is an effort to integrate the strengths of both Marxist and radical feminism. Radical feminism focuses on the women's perspective, while the Marxist emphasis on material history ensures that a radical feminist perspective will not be reduced to ahistorical assumptions about women's sexual and reproductive experiences.

Jagger assumes that epistemology and content are related in any theory—an assumption with which I heartily agree. However, because Jagger does not adequately distinguish between epistemology and content, her analysis becomes dominated by content, namely, politics and society. Hers is essentially a substantive rather than a methodological argument. For example, she applauds Marxism's historical materialist method as a welcome advance over the polarized categories of liberal theory. She regards the "rationalism" she finds in Marxist theory as an aberration, a departure from its more promising historical materialism. But the social and political content of the Marxian perspective dominates her comparison of Marxism and liberalism and is the basis of the similarities she discovers in both approaches.

Jagger's methodological analysis falters because she holds to a conventional view of conflict as that which must be overcome as quickly as possible. What she regards as a contradiction between rationalism and materialism in Marxism is really the very basis of dialectical method. Were she less reluctant to embrace conflict she might more readily appreciate the difference between dualism and dialectics. Jagger's inadequate treatment of the complexities of dialectical method leads to an oversimplification of the role nature plays in Marxist thought. This is crucial from the standpoint of her thesis because her book is a comparative theoretical analysis centered on the concept of human nature.

Now, nature is a most complicated construct, even in liberal theory, where it seems to fit more comfortably than in Marxism. Liberal epistemology divides the world into things and ideas, objects and essences. Nature is both an essence and a description of the material world, but the relationship between nature's ideal and material meanings remains unexplored. Dialectical theory has the capacity to begin to overcome the unresolved dualism of the liberal view of nature, but because Jagger is not thinking dialectically, the Marxist view of nature is a puzzle to her. She regards it as another aspect of the aberrant rationalism, incompatible with Marxism's focus on history. In dialectical thought—in Marx's theory, if not in its Marxist interpretations—the conflict between history and nature is precisely what recasts the possibilities for the concept of nature and frees dialectical thought from the confines of more traditional empiricist categories. I shall discuss the Marxian concept of nature in due course. For the present, it is necessary to look more carefully at how Jagger imposes a concept of nature upon the theories at which she looks. For it is not clear why Jagger assumes that the theories she examines must *have* a theory of nature. Indeed, she is not very clear about what purpose the concept of nature might serve for feminist theory. Her assumption that human nature exists signifies to me that she herself is thinking in dichotomist terms, even while discussing Marxist and socialist theory.

"Do I have a nature?" "Do I have a human or a feminine nature?" These questions inevitably lead to a consideration of nature itself. Perhaps nature is a theoretical imposition, an objective construct imposed upon subjective experience. I act in a certain way, experience certain things, but does that mean I *have* a given nature? Is my experience of the world unified enough to be described by, or subsumed under, the solitary concept nature? One person generally craves solitude; another is frightened of being alone: is either characteristic natural? One person does not feel fully alive unless she is continually taking physical risks; another feels most content while relaxing at home with his family; a third is a happy blend, needs adventure, work and family, is capable of both solitude and mutuality. Are any of these ways of being in the world natural for a human being, for a man, for a woman?

Perhaps I am being obstinately liberal and individualist in my approach to what is natural for a human being. Perhaps as socialists argue, nature is historically determined and tells us more about economic conditions than individual experience: one's nature is the product of the current stage of economic development. Jagger describes the socialist feminist concept of human nature as "inseparable from the socialist conception of political economy." She claims that "only socialist feminism makes a serious attempt to explain how human beings continuously transform themselves into men and women" (148, 149). In that case why is a concept of nature necessary to understand that process? Isn't Jagger really referring to history, rather than nature? What does nature help us to understand that history does not? Moreover, what is the relationship between nature and history?

Although he may occasionally fall into a conventional use of nature as "essential" or biologically grounded, Marx provides a way of integrating history and nature. Dialectical method requires that we see materiality and consciousness as interrelated, inseparable by virtue of their differences. Nature involves the convergence of material experience and human consciousness. Jagger impatiently dismisses the conflict between the two as a contradiction, while Marx sees conflict as a prerequisite to unity. She does not understand that in Marxism nature is both a historical product and an active, if historically determined, human essence. It would be superfluous to speak of nature if it were simply a historical product. The tenacity of Jagger's own tendency to dichotomize is evident when she declares that essences are incompatible with history and defines a Marxist concept of nature as entirely historical: "In spite of its promise as a critical tool, 'alienation' is a somewhat problematic concept for Marxists because it may be taken to presuppose a human essence from which people under capitalism are alienated, and the concept of a human essence seems quite at odds with the conception of human nature as a product of history" (57).

In Marxian dialectics *both* history and nature exist. They are not reducible to one another, but they are interrelated. Jagger turns this complicated thought into the one-dimensional observation that "If the human essence consists in anything, therefore, it consists in praxis" (208). Essence to a dialectician doesn't "consist in" praxis; it does not "equal" praxis. Essence and praxis exist in conflict with each other and also in a mutually determining relationship.

Jagger's fourfold categorization of approaches to feminism is itself emblematic of her undialectical epistemology. The categories are imposed from the outside rather than emerging as momentarily appropriate descriptions. Certainly some feminists fit the descriptions offered by Jagger, but the fact remains that the descriptions are abstract—as are any categorical descriptions. She does name names: she is explicit about who she would categorize as a radical, and who a socialist feminist. However, the question about the fundamental usefulness of such categories remains unaddressed, as did the usefulness of the concept of nature. Would a feminist voluntarily identify herself as, for example, a "radical feminist"? Catharine MacKinnon's insistence that feminism is a term that can be "modified" only from the outside, by nonfeminists, strikes home here. The establishment of four distinct types of feminism seems an imposition, or at best a pedagogical convenience, rather than something that arises from the works of activists and theorists themselves.

The point is not to belittle Jagger's contribution. Her book is useful as a review of available "feminisms." Jagger also sets forth her own preferences for an effective feminist theory. The thrust of her book, however, is to offer a feminist political agenda rather than a feminist epistemology. Socialist feminism, as she conceives it, is not grounded in a new or specifically feminist epistemology. Jagger herself is still thinking in terms of static categories: socialist feminism appears to be the best of both Marxist and radical feminism by virtue of adding one to the other. The minimalist dialectical method I offer in this book differs from Jagger's approach, and most contemporary feminist theory, in its conviction that conflict and contradiction can be overcome only by recognizing and acknowledging their inevitability. The travails of conflict are embraced as an inevitable part of life. Minimalist dialectics offers feminist theory the presupposition that conflict is a central and unavoidable part of self-awareness and change, and as such is prerequisite to unity, which itself is never permanent.

II. SANDRA HARDING

Sandra Harding in *The Science Question in Feminism* explores the possibility of an epistemology for a feminist science.[2] She offers an argument against traditional notions of "scientific objectivity," yet maintains serious questions about the validity of an innately "special" women's worldview. She offers "feminist standpoint" epistemologies as a promising basis for a feminist science but does not claim that at their current stage of development "standpoint epistemologies" are devoid of problems.

Harding does not turn her back on all objectivity, and in fact believes there is a place for objectivity in science. However, she also believes that the common conception of empirical truth is woefully inadequate because it does not acknowledge the intervention of social and historical context. While "science-as-usual" is not to be confused with "bad science," the good stuff is nonetheless contaminated with gender bias. Harding does not believe method is independent of social environment, and so methodological questions cannot be isolated. One needn't "disprove" the theories of Newton and Einstein, for example. More pertinent for the purposes of a feminist science are questions about how their sort of thinking became paradigmatic. "I have been suggesting reasons for reevaluating the assumption that physics should be the paradigm of scientific knowledge-seeking. If physics ought not to have this status, then feminists need not 'prove' that Newton's laws of mechanics or Einstein's relativity theory are value-laden in order to make the case that the science we have is suffused with...gender" (47).

One of the problems with science-as-usual is the division assumed to exist between subjectivity and objectivity. That border is a product of male minds. For whatever reasons—and Harding does not really probe the basis of the differences between "male" and "female" minds—it is men who have been concerned with differentiating between male and female, and who have insisted that analogies from the animal world are appropriate models for comparison. Men prefer to prove scientifically that they more closely resemble male monkeys than female human beings. "The point here is that if we ask which gendered humans have historically been concerned—indeed, obsessed —to distinguish themselves from the other gender, the answer is 'men.' Similarly it is men who have been preoccupied with finding the continuities between men and males in other species and between women and females in other species..." (100).

Although Harding considers this preoccupation with epistemological and social divisions emblematic of science-as-usual and not just bad science, she insists that "our recognition of the fact that science has always been a social product" does not "require the exaltation of relativist subjectivity on the part of feminism" (137). Postulating an alternative to traditional epistemological categories runs a risk with which feminist epistemologists have been struggling. If dichotomist thinking characterizes modern science, how can feminists set themselves in opposition to dichotomist thinking, without also dichotomizing? A feminist standpoint epistemology, then, runs the risk of opposing "political correctness" to scientific objectivity. Harding softens the effect of this feminist dichotomization by reminding us that feminist science is still "transitional," and by suggesting that a feminist science (which she calls a "successor science") could be complemented by postmodernist pluralism in order to avoid dichotomies. In other words, the successor science could indeed be "oppositional"—self-consciously distinguished from traditional science—but the postmodernist dimension would undermine the dichotomizing effects of the opposition, providing the possibility of a less dichotomist epistemology.

I have doubts about the possibility of such a compromise. I

have, it is true, presented myself here as an advocate of conflict, not one to regard a contradiction as necessarily negative or destructive. However, suggesting *a priori* the possibility of an epistemology that combines a specific standpoint with an epistemology committed to undermining all standpoints seems problematic, and overly optimistic. Harding understands that a total commitment to such a deconstructed world will not permit development of a feminist epistemology precisely because it offers no political ground upon which to stand. She seeks a self-consciously oppositional stance that *also* avoids a rigidly dichotomized view of the world, but she knows how difficult such a combination will be. "Of course this creates a powerful internal tension: the standpoint epistemologies appear committed to trying to tell the 'one true story' about ourselves and the world around us that the post-modernist epistemologies regard as a dangerous fiction. Can the former be sufficiently disengaged from their modernist ancestors to permit their justification of merely partial but nevertheless 'less false' stories?" (195) Harding is more hopeful than I am about the radical potential of postmodern or poststructuralist epistemologies as an alternative to traditional and conservative concepts of subjectivity and objectivity. The problem with poststructuralist thought is that beyond not promising a *positive* feminist epistemology, it raises questions about the very possibility of any epistemology at all. How then can feminists adopt such a stance with the faith that it will lead to politically desirable science, philosophy, or anything else?

Harding's formulations permit at this point some brief indications of how my own approach differs from hers: Harding advances a combination of poststructuralist pluralism and a self-consciously political successor science. She believes that at the current state of development of feminist theory the "tension" between an oppositional stance toward conventional science and a postmodernist "anti-stance" is "simply one that we should learn to live with" (195). I propose to explore in much greater detail the nature of that and other epistemological tension. The minimalist dialectics that I offer provides a way of understanding tension as something with its own developmental history and future. Such tension is not a static concept that we must learn to live with, but rather something that we participate in making.

The relationship between any theorists and their theory is continually changing as the borders between conventionally understood subjectivity and objectivity clash and dissolve. That is to say, if there is the possibility of combining postmodern and standpoint epistemologies, it will be the result only of acknowledging and playing out the contradictions between the two: not assuming at the start that the two are possible in tandem. Rather, one must make a deliberate effort to imagine that the two stances are antithetical from the very outset, and that they will manage to destroy one another. Then stubbornly investigate whatever points they have in common.

There is another way to understand the differences between Harding's discussion of a feminist science and my ideas about a feminist epistemology. She offers two critical perspectives on the validity of scientific truths. One she calls "internalist," and the other, "externalist." The first seeks to understand limitations on scientific certainty from the perspective of science's own standards: the logical and methodological impossibility of objectivity. The other places the "pure objectivity" that science so values in a social and historical context, casting light on the subjectivity that infuses it. Harding attempts an externalist critique, seeking the historical moment when science divorced itself from political and historical influences. That moment, she suggests, marked a radical and political departure from previous science because it accompanied the decline of feudal class structure and the rise of egalitarian liberalism. In the beginning scientific objectivity was a leveler. Knowledge was no longer the sole domain of the privileged class. Understanding the historical emergence of the very concept of scientific objectivity thus constitutes an externalist understanding on the limitations of objective truth.

The internalist critique is usually provided by the scientists themselves, and Harding is less impressed with its political potential. Thomas Kuhn is an internalist in Harding's terms. Even though his theory proposes the mutual influence of a community of scientists on the truths they establish, thereby debunking the myth of the lonely scholar working with his data in isolation, Kuhn still believes in a self-contained isolated community of the initiated. The truths upon which the scientific community collaborates are regarded by it as pure and objective, immune to the influences of society and politics. The concept of scientific objectivity remains intact in Kuhn's theory.

My effort will be to focus on a radical internalist critique of the methodology of social science, not in order to refute an externalist criticism, but rather to enhance it. Scientific objectivity is impossible in its own terms, not only because it will be "contaminated" by social and political influences but because the borders between internal and external, mind and world, subjectivity and objectivity *cannot* be understood as isolated from one another. This is not to suggest that "women don't think in dichotomist terms, but men do." I do not propose any theory of difference between male and female epistemology because any such theory either must embrace a concept of nature, by definition conservative and probably unknowable to boot, or it must embrace a theory of origins, also unknowable. That men and women behave differently proves nothing about the future of gendered difference between the sexes. The theory I offer assumes that men and women live in the same metaphysical universe and have at least compatible problems understanding the relationship between internal experience and the external world.

Like most feminist theorists, Harding raises the question of whether and how women are different from men but does not answer it. How do we come to associate some things with masculinity and other things with femininity? How did women come to be "feminine" and men "masculine"? The assumption always seems to revolve around the term *connectedness:* women are connected to people and the world in a way that men are not. This glorification of sentimental unity is not promising. Surely life involves for both men and women moments of both engagement and detachment. The point is that the two are mutually necessary. Any feminist epistemology will need to take detachment as seriously as engagement. Any critique of existing epistemology must be *both* internalist and externalist and must explore the relationship between internal and external itself.

III. EVELYN FOX KELLER

Evelyn Fox Keller in *Reflections on Science and Gender* also raises questions about the social context, and more specifically the psychological context that permits scientific objectivity to dominate as the standard for truth in Western thought.[3] Keller is more specific than Harding about what might constitute a feminist redefinition of objectivity, and she pays specific attention to the relationship between subjectivity and objectivity. Keller states at the outset that a particular form of relationship to the objective or natural world has predominated since the time of the ancient Greeks. The stance claims to exclude any emotional and subjective involvement. In reality, such an exclusion is impossible. Where Harding traces the emergence of objectivity through a history of modern science that began with the decline of feudalism, Keller returns the gendered development of mind and nature, subjectivity and objectivity, to the time of Plato.

Her analysis reveals that subjects and objects have had complicated dealings with each other throughout the history of Western philosophy, and that even though male thought has shaped and defined the relationship between subjectivity and objectivity, the terms have not always been regarded dichotomously. Plato used a model of unity, specifically erotic unity, as the basis of knowledge. He made use of a "model of unreciprocal but relatively equitable sexuality, in a culture that acknowledged no model of reciprocal sexuality between equals" (27). The "pederastic" model was the only model of love in Athenian culture that disdained aggression, dominance, and submission, all of which Plato regarded as incompatible with the learning experience. Both homosexual and heterosexual relations were perceived by Plato and the culture in which he lived to involve dominance and submission, and the loss of masculinity of the submissive partner. Hierarchy and divisiveness were antithetical to the unity Plato believed was the central characteristic of knowledge. In order to avoid such worldly tension the philosopher must withdraw from actual women and from the natural, objective world. "Plato . . . has discovered a model of sexual love that allows for mutuality of desire without compromising the masculinity or dignity of the beloved, without evoking a division into dominant and subordinate roles, or the aggression that that entails. But such reciprocity is bought at a price, and the price is final sexual constraint. Growth of the wings of the soul requires that actual consummation be avoided. . . . Disregard for the embodied individual in and of itself pervades Plato's entire philosophic system, as it describes his theory of love" (28, 30). Thus, even though his system of knowledge might appear compatible with a feminist epistemology, characterized as it was by the pursuit of love and unity, Plato managed to exclude both the feminine and the physical. Moreover, his epistemology was plagued by a belief in hierarchy, which of course is not regarded as compatible with feminism. "It is important to note, however, that neither Plato's epistemology, his cosmology, nor his model of love is yet free of hierarchy. Everywhere, the eye, the soul and the mind continue to look upward" (29). In Plato's universe, the spiritual is higher and finer than the physical. There is no mutuality between the two.

Modern thinkers have a different epistemological project, but it is not much more promising for women. A desire for knowledge of the material world has preoccupied scientists and philosophers since the time of Sir Frances Bacon. According to the tenets of modern science reality resides in the physical world, and so that world can no longer be ignored. Reentering the physical world, Keller suggests, has forced modern science to deal with the female, and the way men have traditionally "dealt" with what they don't understand is to attempt to dominate it. "In turning his attention to the physical world per se, the modern scientist must of necessity override Plato's stricture against inclusion of the physical; in doing so, he becomes a party to the aggression that Plato sought to avoid" (30). Both the Platonic image and the Baconian goals are united in their unquestioning association of the physical with the female, and "in neither vision is material nature (female for both Plato and Bacon) invited into a partnership of love: in one she is relegated to another realm, in the other she is seduced and conquered" (31).

Still, according to Keller, this is only the beginning. For it becomes evident that knowledge cannot simply be equated with domination: any knowledge calls for some receptivity. How will the Baconian scientist receive knowledge and from whom? The natural world, regarded as female, must certainly be incapable of the activity necessary to infuse a male scientist with knowledge! Keller suggests that Bacon turned to God (and of course to a masculine image of God) and appropriated a passive, receptive (female) stance for the scientist. Once again, actual women were regarded as superfluous for the attainment of knowledge. "When nature becomes divine, not only does 'she' become 'he' but by implication as we shall see, the scientific mind becomes more nearly female" (37).

If Bacon excluded the physical female by appropriating passivity for the male scientist in his purified relationship with God, modern scientists have excluded God by appropriating the capacity to impregnate themselves with knowledge. Male scientists want both the active *and* passive aspects of knowledge for themselves: "The scientist himself has assumed the procreative function that Bacon reserved for God: his mind is now a single entity, both phallus and womb. However, his kinship with Bacon survives in his simultaneous appropriation and denial of the feminine" (42). Keller's analysis thus acknowledges the complexity of the relationship between subjectivity and objectivity. It is a vast oversimplification to associate automatically a male stance with a divided, dichotomous world, and a female stance with unity. For men, too, have been striving after unity since the beginning of time.

What does Keller offer as an epistemological alternative to this male science that excludes the female? In a section of her book entitled "The Inner World of Subjects and Objects," Keller outlines a feminist-compatible epistemology that calls for the integration of subjectivity and objectivity. They are perceived in psychological terms as the merging and differentiation of ego. Still, I believe that Keller, like Harding, associates unity and subjectivity with the feminine, and distance and objectivity with the masculine, without exploring the basis of that association. While aware of the need for psychological distance, Keller leaps over the price that must be paid for an epistemology that truly involves both subjectivity and objectivity. Like many other feminist theorists, she associates objectivity, differentiation, separation, domination, autonomy, and power with male psychology, while subjectivity, "commingling," and a lack of clear boundaries between self and other are bequeathed to the female psyche. Keller's analysis is not so simplistic as to associate "bad" with the former set of qualities and "good" with the latter: her call for "dynamic objectivity" declares that *both* separation and unity are necessary for growth and knowledge.

Still, as Keller describes it, masculine psychology has given us a conception of truth that is one-sided, born in conflict, differentiation, isolation, "To see how the twin goals of science—knowledge and power—are translated into objectification and domination, we need to examine the psychodynamic tools that link these goals together. The key psychological construct is autonomy..." (72). The underlying message is that objectification is not desirable, not compatible with harmony or the permeability of boundaries. The stances that characterize male thought are in fact presented in a thoroughly negative light: "Masculine here connotes, as it so often does, autonomy, separation, and distance. It connotes a radical rejection of any commingling of subject and object, which are, it now appears, quite consistently identified as male and female" (79). In spite of Keller's claim to value both objectivity and subjectivity, objectivity means separation from subjectivity, and subjectivity means the unity of subjectivity and objectivity. This is a confusing, asymmetrical use of the terminology, and one that betrays Keller's fear of objectivity and overeager embrace of subjectivity, again so typical of efforts to construct a feminist epistemology. The etymology and use of subjectivity and objectivity will be explored in detail in chapter 5. In order to begin to appreciate the problems created by associating objectivity solely with male epistemology, consider this paradox: if subjects are male, and objects are female, how did objectivity come to be reserved for men and subjectivity for women?

Keller does acknowledge the necessity for occasional distance, or psychological perspective, but her discussion in general, and specifically her concept of dynamic objectivity, is characterized by an antiadversarial stance, a fear of conflict. She argues that her dynamic conception of autonomy "leaves unchallenged a 'potential space' between self and other..." (99). Conflict and a profound need to differentiate self from other, to distinguish subject from object, are denied in the haste to arrive at a more fully established unity. Keller's message, along with that of a chorus of contemporary feminists, is something like: "real women don't start fights." She does not deny the need for psychological tension, but the strain that she does acknowledge seems guaranteed to be utilized in the service of a greater and sweeter unity. "This ideal [dynamic autonomy]—for most of us only occasionally realized—enables the very real indeterminacy in the distinction between subject and object to function as a resource rather than as a source of confusion and threat. . . . The ideal described here requires an exquisite balancing act. It presupposes that the fears of merging, of loss of boundaries, on the one hand, and the fears of loneliness and disconnection, on the other, *can* be balanced. It also presupposes the compatibility of one's contrasting desires for intimacy and for independence" (99, 100).

The difference between Keller's dynamic objectivity and my "minimalist dialectics" is the role that conflict plays in the quest for an ever fuller but never absolute or complete truth. Keller's epistemological world is more agreeable than mine: conflict is more tolerable because it inevitably leads to unity. The prior expectation of unity will take all the risk from conflict, and it is precisely that risk that I find unavoidable. For the feminist theorists I have been considering, the experience of conflict, alienation, discord is minimized, short-circuited, precisely because the unpleasantness is understood to be for a good end. There is never, in Keller's schema, a moment of letting go, of surrendering to the terror of isolation, alienation, conflict. Without the full experience of those "negative" moments, I will argue, any unity, harmony, intimacy must also be incompletely experienced and understood.

Keller comes as close as any theorist I am familiar with to attempting to utilize negative objective moments in a feminist-compatible epistemology. Yet she does not take seriously the importance of discord and negation fully experienced. Such negative moments are somehow "unfeminist." Consider, for example, how quickly mention of the importance of "independent integrity" turns to the greater desirability of "empathy":

> Dynamic objectivity aims at a form of knowledge that grants to the world around us its independent integrity but does so in a way that remains cognizant of, indeed relies on, our connectivity with that world. In this dynamic objectivity is not unlike empathy. . . . Premised on continuity, it recognizes difference between self and other as an opportunity for a deeper and more articulated kinship. The struggle to disentangle self from other is itself a source of insight—potentially into the nature of both self and other. (117)

Keller is afraid to let go. The "consciousness of self" she applauds does not result from a struggle against a sense of loss of self, which I count essential to the capacity to experience both self and other. This is obvious in her observation that "The capacity for such attention, like the capacity for love and empathy, requires a sense of self secure enough to tolerate both difference and continuity; it presupposes the development of dynamic autonomy" (118). If one "tolerates" difference and continuity, one never loses a sense of oneself. A threat to one's awareness of self may be intolerable, but the experience of discomfort, with no guarantees of blissful unity at the other end, is what grants our most hard-won and precious insights into self and other. While conflict, pain, what is experienced as intolerable tension are not prerequisite to all knowledge, neither can they be avoided or shunned as politically incorrect or undesirable moments in an epistemology.

IV. FEMINIST DIALECTICIANS

Some feminists have been attracted to dialectics as a feminist methodology. How do their efforts to formulate a feminist epistemology differ from minimalist dialectics? Mary O'Brien in *The Politics of Reproduction,* and even more specifically in her essay "Feminist Theory and Dialectical Logic," sees potential in dialectical method, although she has reservations about whether Marx and Hegel made full use of it.[4] She argues that they did not extend the substance far enough to include the concerns of women and that indeed, when it came to the woman question, they simply abandoned dialectical method altogether. "The orchestration of a harmony of Man and Nature was a recurring motif of Classical thought, revived in the modern world by Hegel and Marx. Yet despite the real concern of dialectics to mediate and cancel alienation, Marxism has joined male metatheory in general in perceiving the fundamental opposition of Man and nature as an invitation to cancel Man's alienation from nature in a praxis of domination and control."[5]

O'Brien believes that both Marx and Hegel imposed their own substantive concerns, thereby foreclosing the potential of their method for radical new insights. In Irigaray's terms, they

asked only questions they knew they could answer. This is particularly evident with regard to their ideas about women and reproduction.

> Neither of these thinkers deals with reproduction in a
> dialectical way; rather they retreat ignominiously to the sort
> of crude empiricism that both despise. For Hegel, women
> cannot transcend particularity and thus constitute a hazard
> in the path of Universal Reason: they therefore have their
> ethical being, limited as it is, in the household. For Marx,
> they can only find the transcendence of particularity in
> social labor.[6]

O'Brien, however, is not so much interested in dialectical
method as in how male alienation from the reproductive processes has shaped the course of Western philosophy. In fact, she
becomes rather reductionist, insisting that what Western civilization regards as its greatest moments actually reflect male longing, a form of compensation for male exclusion from and desire
for a more concrete relation to the reproductive process. She
believes that paternity is "in fact an abstract idea" and that men
experience life as dualistic because their relationship with procreation is abstract. They feel excluded and seek unity, universals, grand theories and ultimate truths because they feel impov-
erished by their exclusion. "A whole series of oppositions . . .
haunt the male philosophical imagination: mind and body, subject and object, past and present, spirit and matter, individual
and social, and so forth."[7]

O'Brien argues that dialectics, and specifically the dialectics
of Hegel and Marx, come closer than previous philosophical
methods to acknowledging and transcending dualist thinking.
She is not interested in the potential of dialectical thought
beyond what it can add to our understanding of reproduction
itself, which she regards as the necessary substantive basis of
feminist theory. "Where does feminism start? I answer: Within
the process of human reproduction. Of that process, sexuality is
but a part . . . it is not within sexual relations but within the total
process of human reproduction that the ideology of male
supremacy finds its roots and its rationales."[8] With respect to her

intentions regarding the appropriation of dialectical method, O'Brien states:

> This is a feminist analysis, and the two gentlemen in question were immersed in the tradition of male-stream thought, Hegel in particular being an unrepentant and often bitter misogynist. None the less, the debt to both of these men is acknowledged without reservation, while we proceed quite buoyantly and without embarrassment to ignore, with a calculated naivete, the major propositions of their respective systems, concentrating on the social relations of reproduction which both seriously misunderstood.[9]

I differ from O'Brien in that I do not propose to assume a specific substantive basis, such as reproduction, for feminist theory, but cautiously rather than buoyantly propose to attempt to separate dialectical method from Hegelian and Marxian substance: to use dialectics as a basis for exploring the compatibility of female and male experience.

Other feminist scholars are interested in dialectical theory. For the most part, however, they are more interested in the political substance of Marxism or socialism than in the epistemology of dialectics. Nancy Hartsock in *Money, Sex and Power,* for example, is optimistic about the promise of dialectical theory for feminism, but she focuses on Marx's materialism, specifically the act of producing, as a basis for constructing a feminist theory.[10] She is thus more concerned with political substance than with the method of argument, or "metatheory" (116), although she claims to be using Marx's theory of capitalist production as epistemology. Materialism represents Marx's understanding of the universal importance of the "unities and commonalities of head and hand" in daily life. The activity of labor itself is the basis for a perspective that "stresses the unity of social and natural worlds." Materialism with its substantive focus on production and labor is a welcome basis for feminist theory because "there is ... unification rather than separation of mind and action inherent in the labor process itself" (125). Hartsock assumes the harmonious combination as a universally desirable basis for life in a "rich, concrete and quality-laden world" (124). Her argument is thus ensconced in the specifics of materialism, which she regards as an appropriate substance for feminism, because it permits a unified "nondualist" theory.[11]

In another essay, Hartsock draws the links between materialism and feminism in more explicit epistemological terms. In "The Feminist Standpoint: Developing the Ground for a Specifically Feminist Historical Materialism"[12] she sets forth the theory of the "standpoint epistemology" that so intrigued Harding. Hartsock attempts the delicate task of explicating the potential for unity in an epistemological stance that is self-consciously oppositional. In her provocative essay, she maintains that women's traditional activities provide them with an epistemological standpoint analogous to and yet "deeper" than the perspective Marx associates with the proletariat at a specific moment in history. The sexual division of labor is the basis for this feminist standpoint as the capitalist division of labor is for the proletarian standpoint. As described by Hartsock, a "standpoint" is a self-consciously engaged vision, achieved or mediated with material labor rather than abstractly "obvious" (288). "Each division of labor, whether by gender or class, can be expected to have consequences for knowledge" (286). The knowledge available to women by virtue of the sexual division of labor is "more complete" than the worker's. In a playful paraphrase of Marx, Hartsock offers this unforgettable image:

> If, to paraphrase Marx, we follow the worker home from the factory, we can once again perceive a change in the *dramatis personae*. He who before followed behind as the worker, timid and holding back, with nothing to expect but a hiding, now strides in front while a third person, not specifically present in Marx's account of the transaction between capitalist and worker (both of whom are male) follows timidly behind, carrying groceries, baby and diapers. (291)

Still, Hartsock's argument, although dialectical in its presupposition of the inevitable connection between material experience and idea, is substantive rather than methodological. She presupposes the superiority afforded by woman's engagement with the material world and makes this point explicit at several places in her essay. "The feminist standpoint which emerges through an examination of women's activities is related to the proletarian standpoint, but deeper going" (290). "Reproduction represents a unity with nature which goes beyond the proletarian experience of interchange with nature" (293). Even more telling, Hartsock associates the unity of women with the material world as *life itself.* The male experience is, by contrast, analogous to death. The unity with nature that characterizes feminine experience is once again assumed to result from reproduction and female biology. "Menstruation, coitus, pregnancy, childbirth, lactation—all represent challenges to bodily boundaries" (294). The male stance is by contrast "an abstract ideal to be achieved over the opposition of daily life" (297). The female standpoint *is* the potential for life, and its basis is reproduction. From this privileged perspective, women can save men from the abstractness, indeed, the metaphysical death that results from their experience, and which has resulted in the death and destruction men have visited upon the world. Hartsock describes the isolation and devaluation of women's role as a male response that has the effect of making women's life experiences *seem* like death. It indicates how the male consciousness that has dominated history has inverted reality, turned life into death: "The organization of motherhood as an institution in which a woman is alone with her children, the isolation of women from each other in domestic labor, the female pathology of loss of self in service to others—all mark the transformation of life into death..." (302).

The question still remains: is women's perspective as described by Hartsock superior, as life is to death? Or in fact is the abstractness she associates with the male perspective also necessary and also a part of life? Even from her perspective, where abstraction and death are associated, is Hartsock herself running from an aspect of life, perhaps one she regards as unwomanly? In both material and ideal terms, isn't death a part of life? I dwell upon abstraction and death not to glorify them but rather to point to the hidden assumptions and hierarchies that plague Hartsock's attempt at a feminist materialism. The woman's perspective is now privileged from the start where before the man's had been. Materialism is thus not cast in dialectical terms; it is assumed to provide the "more complete," historically neglected perspective.

V. INTRODUCTION TO MINIMALIST DIALECTICS

I have presented an array of feminist writers who make use of the concept of objectivity and feminist writers who are intrigued with dialectics as a methodological basis for feminist theory. What can I add to their theory? What can minimalist dialectics offer that has not already been covered in the existing literature? In a sense, minimalist dialectics is nothing more than a focus upon that with which feminist theorists seem most uncomfortable: conflict. I seek to retain the vocabulary of subjectivity and objectivity but to avoid the static dichotomies of empiricism; to dismantle the conventional notion of "objective truth" but to avoid deconstructing the very notion of truth; to preserve historical perspective but to avoid a static, authoritarian conception of history. Minimalist dialectics is a method that embraces conflict but avoids static, dichotomous truth. It preserves the importance of history but avoids orthodoxy. It cautions against the romanticization of unity that plagues so much contemporary feminist theory—whether consciously or unconsciously—and is wary of both the chaos of a deconstructed world and the tendency to presuppose substantive historical and political truths that too often characterize Marxist feminism and Marxism in general.

The method is traditional in that it seeks to preserve a world of subjects and objects, but radical in its recasting of the relationship between the two. I have suggested both political and psychological reasons for retaining the epistemological constructs, subjectivity and objectivity. From a political perspective, using conventional categories forestalls the need for a separatist feminism, a feminist theory that excludes itself from traditional history and philosophy. Women have already been excluded; feminist justification of that exclusion is foolhardy. Psychologically, I have indicated that I seek a world with some familiar guideposts, landmarks, some conventional stability. Relinquishing the familiar categories of subjectivity and objectivity places one in a world with no edges, no solidity. Even a strong swimmer cannot survive indefinitely in the wide ocean: she needs a shore, a boat, a dock, an island, *something* solid, unless she is a fish. Solidity is neither antifemale nor antifeminist. The psychological comfort of momentary distance, of perspective, is something feminists should be wary of discarding too quickly. There is nothing antifemale, antifeminist about seeing something from afar. Detachment, disengagement, uninvolvement have their place in a feminist universe.

This is not to say that the world has not suffered from a dangerous *overvaluation* of distance and abstractness on the one hand, concreteness and tangibility on the other. We have suffered from *too much* refusal of engagement, to the point where unthinkable destruction can now be visited upon us by flicking a series of switches. The invention of the gun may well have been the first phallic step down the road toward remote-controlled death and nuclear weaponry: surely evidence of the dangers of disengagement and the overvaluation of emotional distance. It is also likely that scientific studies operating on the assumption that truth results from the ability to withhold involvement from an object of study have created all sorts of irresponsible, uninvolved conclusions about the "other" and her nature. Whites have enslaved blacks, men have debased and degraded women, men have destroyed the ecological balance of the earth because of an overvaluation of objective detachment and the unwillingness or inability to understand that self is implicated in the demise of other. Viewing the world as thus divided, at war with itself, seems to justify the impulse to flee dichotomies, flee objectivity, take refuge in a softer, unified world with fewer distinctions.

I do not mean to resurrect uncritically the terminology subjectivity and objectivity. The dangers and difficulties that have been associated with the terms by feminist theorists and others apply most appropriately to the subjects and objects of empiricism. Even the feminists discussed here who endeavor to save a concept of objectivity use the terms in a manner derived from empiricism, but a more promising perspective exists. None of the feminist theory I have encountered looks carefully and critically at modern dialectical usage of the terms. It is true that dialectics in the late twentieth century is freighted with political implications that are not particularly feminist, and perhaps not particularly desirable on their own terms. It is nearly impossible to look at Hegelian and Marxian epistemology without the pressure to accept the political substance of Marxism or socialism. That is the project of the rest of this book. The terminology of subjectivity and objectivity has been used in a politically promising manner in modern dialectical theory, but the specific politics of Marxism or Hegelianism do not need to come along for the ride.

I offer a comparison of empiricist subjects and objects, and dialectical subjects and objects, to demonstrate the difficulties wrought by the former and the promise lying hidden in the latter. The dangers of empiricist objectivity and subjectivity will be analyzed in two chapters on liberal empirical thought, as exemplified in the work of John Stuart Mill. I have chosen Mill in part because of his importance as a modern liberal theorist. (For example, as recently as the 1960s Gertrude Himmelfarb could worry that *On Liberty* enjoyed too much influence among the youth of the day.) In part also I have focused on Mill because he was a self-avowed feminist, indeed one of the first outspoken (or in any event published) liberal feminists. He was articulate enough as a feminist to cause many who admire him for his liberal thought to attempt to dissociate him from *The Subjection of Women.* They argue that it was the work of his wife, Harriet Taylor, or at best an ill-advised venture written when Mill was, regrettably, under her influence. Yet, I shall argue, *The Subjection of Women* bears the same methodological problems as his *System of Logic,* and is thus not an aberration but quite characteristic of Mill's thinking. The work is nonetheless deeply flawed as a feminist treatise, and *not* because Mill was only a half-hearted advocate of feminism. The book fails, in spite of Mill's sincere efforts because its empiricist methodology simply will not permit a coherent argument for political change as radical as feminism requires. *Empiricism* divides the world into static subjects and objects. Empiricism assumes that objective truth is to be gathered in the form of data in a world external to the subject who seeks knowledge. Subjectivity must be held in abeyance if the objective truth is to be gathered. Apart from the question of how passive objects can possibly make themselves known to passive subjects, this epistemology raises questions about how political change might possibly be justified. For any empirical justification for change must come from the empirical world, which already exists. How can one expect to find justification for what does not yet exist in the world as it does exist?

Getting down to specifics: how can one expect to find

empirical evidence that women are fit to participate in public life if women have never systematically participated in public life? Desiring significant political change, we are left with a choice between arguing from abstractions, such as justice, which calls for a rationalist rather than an empiricist posture, or arguing from a purely ideological position, not even pretending to justify political beliefs and preferences in other than idiosyncratic terms. The stalemate is inevitable in a world divided into subjects and objects, with expectations that proof must be empirical. The contradictions that undermine Mill's political argument in *The Subjection of Women* are emblematic of the epistemological difficulty under which liberalism labors. The empiricist epistemology of liberal theory is incapable of carrying an argument for anything but the most minimal political changes.

If, however, the theorist could see himself in the objects studied, could actually recognize the subjectivity of something outside himself, recognize himself as also object to the other, the epistemological stalemate that cripples liberal empiricism might dissolve. This interchangeability or interpenetrability of subject and object is characteristic of modern dialectical thought. The vocabulary of subjectivity and objectivity is retained, but the border that separates the two is not static and not impermeable. There is of course difficulty with simply advocating dialectics as a panacea, as the solution to feminist theory's search for a method. Apart from the general undesirability of advocating any abstract method that promises solutions to complicated political problems, there is the problematic of the political history of modern dialectics. Whose dialectic do I mean to offer feminists? I have said modern dialectics, so I don't intend to discuss Socrates or Plato. However, that is not much of a qualifier, if the choices of modern dialecticians range from Kant, Hegel, and Marx to a host of contemporary phenomenologists and critical theorists, such as Sartre, Husserl, Merleau-Ponty, Horkeimer, Althusser, and Habermas.[13] In fact I do not mean to adopt any preexisting theory that calls itself dialectical, but rather to extrapolate a different, dialectical conception of the relationship between subjects and objects, in order to demonstrate that it is possible to retain the traditional terminology while using the terms in a radically different manner from both the static empiricist method and the ideologically oriented "dialectical method" which is equally instrumental in its consequences. I seek in this work to isolate dialectical method from political substance.

Such an endeavor may be thought foolhardy. Why bother to separate—indeed, is it possible to separate—the political content from the epistemological structure of a theory? I need only point to Mill's work to begin to answer that objection. The political content Mill sought to convey was, I believe, heartfelt and genuinely feminist, given its historical context. The inconsistencies in the argument were the result of Mill's method. In a similar vein, take Hegel and Marx as two examples of dialectical method. Hegel was no radical, and substantively speaking there is much in the content of his work that can be regarded as bourgeois at best, monarchical, racist, nationalist, and patriarchal at worst. He has been held up as an example of conservative, misogynist thinking by nearly every feminist I can think of who has written about him. Yet Hegel influenced a generation of young German thinkers, who considered themselves radicals, including Karl Marx, who used Hegel's dialectical method, inverted, to demonstrate the inadequacies of their radicalism. Marx's theory was antibourgeois, antimonarchical, antireligious, antifamilial, and so perhaps even antipatriarchal.

Still, how can one argue that method has any influence on political substance if two apparently contradictory theories can both lay claim to dialectical method? The most obvious answer would point out that Hegel was a dialectical idealist and Marx a dialectical materialist, which may account for the difference in the political substance of their theories. Do idealism and materialism describe the method or substance of dialectics? These questions will be addressed in the chapters on Hegel and Marx. For now, consider the possibility that if dialectical idealism and dialectical materialism share some common methodological core and if Marx's and Hegel's political substance differs radically, then method and substance must be in some sense separable.

Dialectical method has the capacity to support a radical political stance without sacrificing a solid base in history or traditional philosophical categories. Taking Hegelian and Marxist dialectics as a point of departure, I shall demonstrate that Hegelian dialectics possesses more radical political potential and that Hegel's substantive theory is more progressive than it is usually regarded as being. Similarly, the radicalism of Marxian dialectics lies as much in its epistemology as in its political and economic analysis. That is, the difference between idealism and materialism is less significant than the relationship between subjectivity and objectivity in dialectical thought.

Focusing on the structural, epistemological aspect of dialectics, paring away Hegelian and Marxian political ideology, I seek to articulate a minimalist view of dialectics that amounts to (1) the perspective that subjectivity and objectivity are completely interpenetrable, a perspective that is made possible by (2) the assumed inseparability in dialectical thought of philosophy and history, theory and practice, and (3) the insistence that the unity made possible between subjects and objects, theory and history, is only so by means of recognition and experience of profound conflict between the two.

Dialectical method does not dissolve, does not deconstruct the conventional world, taking satisfaction in a reversal of traditional subject and object for its own sake, relocating the usual centers of intellectual focus to the fringes, seeking to center perspective in what is usually regarded as supplemental, not central. It does not seek to abolish the possibility of a center or ground, disdaining all structural or geographic vocabulary in relation to thought.[14] However, a dialectical view insists that subjectivity can be counted upon only when it has risked itself in interaction with what it is not: when it has risked its own negation. Boundaries are seen to exist between subject and object, but they are neither finite nor permanent and have meaning only when they have been understood as problematic, as profoundly uncertain. The stability of the known world remains only to the extent that it is constantly risked, undermined, and challenged. Women *are* objects, at moments to themselves, and to other women as well as to men. Men are *also* objects to women, to themselves and to other men. Likewise, men and women are subjects. This is not to argue that customs and institutions have not encouraged women to act and think passively, men actively, both sexually and on more general levels of social functioning. It is rather to suggest that the current state of affairs is never static, always capable of negation, hence transformation.

This epistemology is different from the theories of feminists even such as Keller and Harding, who do want to retain the vocabulary of subjectivity and objectivity, because it takes seriously the reality, the inevitability, the pain of conflict. It does not presuppose a unity to override tension between subject and object. There is no guarantee of harmony, nor is there a glorification of detachment. Both harmony and detachment are presumed necessary and unavoidable in the pursuit of a more complete understanding of the world. Presupposing unity is as inappropriate for an epistemology as presupposing a desired political outcome: the move turns epistemology into ideology. In fact, then, minimalist dialectics courts precisely the danger that Harding sought to avoid when she advocated combining "oppositional consciousness" or a standpoint epistemology with postmodernist thinking. The postmodernist epistemology maintains a concerted innocence, an irresponsibility for the political consequences of its stance, while the oppositional consciousness is self-consciously political, and so not really pure method. Minimalist dialectics is riskier because it is neither antihistorical nor self-consciously political. The method carries no guarantee of arriving at a politically desirable solution, and precisely for that reason its moments of insight are overpowering, coming in the wake of the willingness to risk everything. The *possibility* is there for a solidly grounded radical new insight, but there is no guarantee.

If objectivity signifies (in at least some of its usages) distance, detachment, isolation, then dialectics takes those moments seriously as moments that are incomplete but experienced as absolute. The feminist theorists who think seriously about objectivity in relation to subjectivity, isolation, detachment, and objectification, regard those stances in a negative light. I make the argument that these negative moments are not only necessary to any epistemology intended to include the perspective of the excluded, but that they are neither specifically male, nor entirely bad.

As long as there are human beings, they will experience moments of subjectivity *and* objectivity, activity and passivity, experience themselves as both self-contained and at the mercy of others. At present I am compelled to make do with rather superficial usages of the terms *subjectivity* and *objectivity*. The range of possible meanings will be explored in more detail at the beginning of chapter 5, on Hegel. I postpone discussion until then because the terms *subject* and *object* are central to understanding Hegel and Marx while Mill barely made use of them.

Do I assume a theory of nature with the statement "as long as there are human beings . . ."? If I do, it is as minimal as the dialectical method I advocate. I suggest only that there *is* a problem for all human beings, which can be described as having to do with the relationship between internality and externality. This may be referred to as a problem between mind and the tangible world, self and other, the objective world and our subjective experience of it. Human beings are not entirely at peace in the world and may spend most of their lifetime working in one way or another on the problem.[15] Men may experience the tension or unease in a somewhat different way than women. I believe, however, that the uneasiness exists for all: what is felt by the baby in her mother's womb to be undifferentiated unity might describe a primal awareness, but it hardly constitutes a model of living consciousness. The mother's awareness of the baby growing within her is more complex than can adequately be described by the term *undifferentiated unity.* Her very consciousness of the situation creates a complexity that gives rise to what I have been referring to as "subject-object tension." The baby is a part of her, from her, in her, and yet in a sense very abstract because the pregnant woman has not yet "met" her child or actually looked at it. The baby, even to the mother who is carrying it, is an unknown in terms of face, shape of body, state of health, alertness, color of eyes, hair, level of energy, basic personality. . . . everything we associate with a person. The fetus might at times also be regarded as something invading the mother's body, bringing the pregnant woman nightmares (which some psychologists regard as a healthy prerequisite to the ability to relate to the baby once it is born), and moments of real terror about what is happening to her body.

My point is that separation and the tension of being separate—living in one's own body and yet in some more abstract sense not being fully separated from other—begins with birth and does not end until death. Life *is* tension: the tension of physical separateness, punctuated by moments when some inner sense of self is lost to, or merged with, another. The loss of self to others may occur during a moment of intellectual communication, when one is lost in thought, listening to another, or reading; it may occur as a moment of love, either sexual unity or a less physical, more spiritual intimacy, sharing, enjoyment, appreciation of another person; it may occur as a moment of aesthetic pleasure, when one is lost in the beauty of a sunset, a work of art, a piece of music; it may occur as a religious moment. The problem is that the moments don't last, and most people feel the temptation to cling, to try to do *something* to prolong the moment of unusually blissful unself-consciousness. It is frustratingly impossible: the sun sets, the colors of the sky change, and the most sophisticated technology in the world won't truly bring back the moment. The sun rises, or a car horn honks, and the lovers are startled to their senses; the magic of their mutual gaze broken. Then, too, a more permanent loss of self, without the usually disappointing moment of return, would mean ceasing to function in the world.

A deconstructionist such as Irigaray might focus precisely upon the moments of transition rather than presenting moments of subjectivity and objectivity as complete and in some sense opposed moments of unself-consciousness and self-consciousness. However, the moments of transition themselves must presuppose some sort of tension, experienced *both* as stages of transition and as stages of more or less completeness. They may be experienced somewhat differently by the two sexes; they are undoubtedly experienced somewhat differently by each individual. They may be experienced differently by gay men, lesbians, heterosexuals; one's cultural or economic background may have something to do with shaping the experience of this life tension. In some sense, however, I regard the tension as universal. Dialectical method has the greatest capacity for describing that tension.

I must emphasize that I am not here advocating Marxism or Hegelianism as a substantive basis for feminist theory. I have few preconceptions about what the substance of feminist theory must or should offer. Women constitute more than half the human race; therefore, it seems ludicrous to expect a unified theory to express the universal needs of all women. Nobody expects all men to find a single voice with which to express their needs. Indeed, that is precisely why I think method rather than substance is the more pressing need for feminist theory. What is the structure of knowledge that will most effectively encourage political change? An effective approach should be in some sense universally appropriate to both men and women: capable of incorporating and integrating plural needs without denying differences; capable of embracing the future without abandoning or denying the past. The purpose of this book then is to find a philosophical structure for feminism, rather than to advocate a particular political substance.

If I decline to articulate a specific political program, I should also emphasize that I do not intend to write a political or intellectual history. I have chosen Mill, Hegel, and Marx to represent empiricism and two varieties of dialectics, and have extrapolated their theories from historical context in order to compare them and to arrive at some judgment about the promise of each approach for a feminist epistemology. They may provide a potential *structure* for whatever feminist substance emerges. The three theorists are appropriate for the comparative basis of this study because they wrote at approximately the same period, so historical context can be held as a constant, and because their lasting influence has had time to be established.

I do not concern myself with the successors to these founders of tradition. The relationship between Mill's nineteenth-century empiricism and the methods of modern social science does not come under scrutiny here; nor does the relationship between Hegel and any subsequent theological philosophy (Kierkegaard, for example), or Marx and more contemporary phenomenology, or existentialism. I see potential in minimalist dialectics for feminist theory because it is rooted in history and serious about political change. I am not interested in theories that turn dialectical interpenetrability of subjects and objects into a playful and politically irrelevant preoccupation with paradox or irony. I am concerned with articulating the basis for a methodology that dissolves barriers between self and other and yet retains some familiar delineations, a methodology that takes seriously the lessons of history and yet is capable of facilitating more rapid political and social change than liberal society has seen in the past century. I do not wish to begin from scratch, to build my own feminist epistemology. I am willing to utilize revolutionary work already done and to integrate the needs of feminism with the best of established political theory. With these caveats and restrictions, let us turn to a comparison of the methods of liberal empiricism, and idealist and materialist dialectics, exemplified by but not confined to the theories of John Stuart Mill, G. W. F. Hegel, and Karl Marx.

CHAPTER 3

JOHN STUART MILL—
THE SUBJECTION OF WOMEN

John Stuart Mill is a paradoxical figure. An enormously influential theorist of modern liberalism, his political writings range from advocacy of radical change to arrant elitism. He was an advocate of woman suffrage, arrested in London for distributing literature on birth control, and he wrote *The Subjection of Women,* an essay still read and respected as a classic tract on liberal feminism. Whatever the flaws in his theory on women—and they have been noted in detail by feminists and nonfeminists alike—Mill must still be respected for political courage, and for the singularity of purpose that empowers his pioneering essay with at least the credibility of good intention.

Still, *The Subjection of Women* is ultimately disappointing as a feminist treatise. It contains glaring contradictions that undermine both its political and its intellectual force. It begins, for example, with the proclamation that the nature of woman, if there is such a thing, is not something knowable, since "everything which is usual appears natural" (14) and concludes with the appeal that women's nature guarantees that, once emancipated, women will bestow stereotypically feminine benefits upon all of society. Contemporary feminist criticisms of Mill usually focus upon the political limitations of liberal feminism. Either liberalism itself is regarded as an insufficient vehicle for effective feminist political change or Mill's sincerity is questioned, the implication being that the inconsistencies in his essay reveal the seams of his own ambivalence: he wasn't as good and pure a feminist as he thought he was, and the shallowness of his political convictions translates into logical inconsistencies in his work.

I think the problems with Mill's *Subjection of Women* run

deeper and are more generally significant than either political ambivalence on the part of Mill personally or the insufficiency of liberal politics for feminism. While the work reflects a problem with liberalism in general and liberal feminism more specifically, the problem is not so much political as epistemological: a problem with expectations about what knowledge is. Indeed, I confess to an unfashionable attraction to some of the substantive tenets both of liberalism and of liberal feminism. Its pluralism and individualism can certainly be misused, to justify neglect of people who have been crippled by a history of oppression, for example. An overemphasis on individualism particularly can result in an understanding of group and class membership as shackles that may hamper life's options. Isolation, anomie, and alienation can be mistaken for freedom in liberal society. Still, in a less fearful environment than we now inhabit, there may be some genuine possibility of freedom in a society that values the individual.

One vision of liberal individualism as a potential life force might be the neonatal intensive care unit. All the equipment and personnel that medical science and technology can muster hover over a three- or four-pound premature baby fighting for its life. Few who have spoken to the doctors, nurses and technicians called to assist in the battle for the infant's life can doubt their emotional involvement, the passion for the life of that tiny individual soul, regardless (at least in that moment) of the baby's cultural or economic circumstances.

A romantic vision true enough, and one that in the wrong hands can be used to justify antifeminist views, such as a willingness to sacrifice the individuality and autonomy of a mother for that of her unborn fetus. I present my attraction to liberal individualism, however, in the hope that it will not be twisted into a justification for the social irresponsibility of modern liberal capitalism. Rather, I mean to suggest that my criticism of John Stuart Mill's liberal feminism arises from a sense of frustration: *The Subjection of Women* enrages me, as does something about liberal theory in general. It contains a certain epistemological smugness, or arrogance, that I find infuriating, and at odds with the content of the theory itself. I propose to confront that conflict between the substance and the structure of liberal theory and more specifically liberal feminism, in the work of John Stuart

Mill. I shall consider first *The Subjection of Women,* to determine the source of the difficulty with that work: how could something with such promise have gone so wrong? Is its problem that liberalism is indeed inadequate as a vehicle for political change? Is it that Mill can't think straight, or was insincere? Or if, as I surmise, feminist dissatisfaction with *Subjection of Women,* and with liberalism, really derives from something deeper than liberal rhetoric alone, what might be the source?

I. *THE SUBJECTION OF WOMEN*

Substantively speaking, *The Subjection of Women* begins on a promising note: Mill proposes a theory, which he claims to have held for as long as he could formulate an opinion, that "The legal subordination of one sex to the other ... is wrong in itself, and now one of the chief hindrances to human improvement; and that it ought to be replaced by a principle of perfect equality, admitting no power or privilege on the one side, nor disability on the other."[1] He proceeds in the first chapter to argue against the romanticism, or sentimentalism, of the nineteenth century, because it uncritically associates feminine nature with whatever it sees in women. His own age, he laments, has substituted instinct for reason and has not thought about why women have been so oppressed. He is critical of an intellectual and social milieu that institutionalizes as rational, legal, and finally natural, habits based upon primitive instincts. "Laws and systems of polity always begin by recognizing the relations they find already existing between individuals. They convert what was a mere physical fact into a legal right ..." (7). Thus custom, sanctified by law, appears to be natural: "Was there ever any domination which did not appear natural to those who possessed it? ... No less an intellect, and one which contributed no less to the progress of human thought, than Aristotle, held this opinion without doubt or misgiving" (13).

Aristotle's empirical approach may be demonstrated by the syllogism: Whatever exists is natural; whatever is natural is rational; therefore whatever exists is rational. Whatever exists empirically is thus granted, without warrant, the sanctity of both nature and rationality. Mill would expose the faulty logic behind such an association. There is no *reason* to assume that however women (or men) *appear,* as phenomena, is how they actually *are* and must be, by nature. Indeed, Mill suggests that the situation of women has uniquely defied the human capacity to change from what is to what might, or ought to, be. The subordination of women "is the primitive state of slavery lasting on, through successive mitigations and modifications occasioned by the same causes which have softened the general manners, and brought all human relations more under the control of justice and the influence of humanity . . ." (7). "The social subordination of women thus stands out as an isolated fact in modern social institutions; a solitary breach of what has become their fundamental law" (21).

How does Mill hope to rectify this situation? Initially, his suggestion is Platonic: he demands a more rational state of affairs and refuses to be shackled by what already exists. However, Mill's reading of Plato is somewhat eccentric. As presented by him, Plato appears to have been the original empiricist! His ideal state was not after all ideal, but modeled after the "Spartan experience" which "suggested to Plato, among many other of his doctrines, that of the social and political equality of the two sexes" (14). Of course that observation is not unique to Mill, but he seems ready to assert that Plato arrived at his vision of the Republic *inductively:* not, as the more conventional interpretation would have it, through reason that could then be supported by the Spartan experience.

Not surprisingly, Mill needs to present Plato as an empiricist if he wants to share in his ideas about women. For Mill himself is essentially an empiricist, and he has no inclination to argue for women on grounds of either abstract reason or justice. In fact, Mill simply suggests *trying* the equality of women to see how it works in practice. He proposes a *laissez faire* experiment: "It is only asked that the present boundaries and protective duties in favor of men should be recalled" (27). This experiment would provide the empirical evidence to enable society to decide whether women should be excluded from full participation or not. As things stand, "Experience cannot possibly have decided between two courses, so long as there has only been the experience of one" (21). Theory, without empirical evidence, is not to be relied upon. "If it be said that the doctrine of the equality of the sexes rests only on theory, it must be remembered that the contrary doctrine also has only theory to rest upon" (22).

Mill is thus backing away from an argument based on either reason or political conviction. He is trying to present an argument for an as yet untested state of affairs in purely empirical terms. He is withdrawing his own involvement in the matter and arguing that there simply is not enough data to make a decision about whether or not women should be regarded as the equals of men. He doesn't place faith in an abstraction such as the nature of women: "What is now called the nature of women is an eminently artificial thing—the result of forced repression in some directions, unnatural stimulation in others."

Mill does not yet (although he will in the next chapter) make any statements that might be regarded as acquiescing to the conventional views of women. For example, he has not yet said, as he will at the end of chapter 2, "Like a man when he chooses a profession, so, when a woman marries, it may in general be understood that she makes choice of the management of a household, and the bringing up of a family, as the first call upon her exertions, during as many years of her life as may be required for the purpose..." (48). Substantively, the first chapter seems inoffensive to a contemporary liberal feminist. Yet, consider more closely what is involved in Mill's *laissez faire* experiment. Who will make the decision about which situation works best? Who will decide whether women should continue to be regarded as the equals of men? When will enough time have elapsed to permit the decision to be made with confidence? Does Mill believe women will quickly find their niches in the world, once they are legally permitted to try anything? Does he believe women's talents and abilities will immediately become evident, just as now "nobody thinks it necessary to make a law that only a strong-armed man shall be a blacksmith. Freedom and competition suffice to make blacksmiths strong-armed men, because the weak-armed can earn more by engaging in occupations for which they are more fit" (19)? Such an ahistorical view is indeed characteristic of liberal thought, but Mill himself has just admitted that experience is cumulative and historical. He has made reference to "the modern conviction, the fruit of a thousand years of experience... that things in which the individual is the person directly interested, never go right but as they are left to his own discretion" (18). If he understands the power of a thousand years of accumulated experience, he ought to be able to anticipate that women, who have been excluded from competition with men for so long, who have been imprisoned in a "separate sphere," will simply not be able to sail into battle with men and win (or even tie). What can possibly be accomplished by such an experiment, except perhaps to establish that women are after all *unfit* to compete with men? Although surely Mill did not envision this substantive conclusion, his epistemological stance leads him precisely there. The problem can be glimpsed in his reference to men "studying" women. When he suggests the methodological limitations of men studying their wives it becomes evident who controls the social experiment in women's equality. The experiment exists not *for women* but in order to provide a sufficient data base by which men may arrive at a statistically significant decision about whether or not women are, after all, their equals:

> The most favorable use which a man can generally have for studying the character of a woman, is that of his own wife: for the opportunities are greater, and the cases of complete sympathy not so unspeakably rare. And in fact, this is the source from which any knowledge worth having on the subject has, I believe, generally come. But most men have not had the opportunity of studying in this way more than a single case: accordingly one can, to an almost laughable degree, infer what a man's wife is like, from his opinions about women in general .... (25)

This passage reveals Mill's assumptions about the accumulation of knowledge: he assumes the world to be static, containing passive objects and active subjects who study them. Whether or not he was conscious of the fact, Mill assumes that women must prove themselves to the satisfaction of men, who will judge their performance and decide whether the experiment in equality is working. One might argue that Mill is being politically shrewd and presenting a controversial position most delicately. In fact, I don't doubt the sincerity of Mill's conviction about the equality of women. His presentation in chapter 2 of women's legal bondage to men is unequivocal and should be some indication of his sincerity. My point is that in spite of his political convictions, his method and the epistemological assumptions that underlie it make it impossible for him to present an effective theory for political change.

In chapter 2 Mill outlines, with all the force and passion he can muster, the deplorable absence of legal rights for women. He comes close to arguing that "the personal is political" when he likens a wife's legal subservience to her husband to worse than abject slavery to a political sovereign. He notes that under the old laws of England a man could murder his wife with impunity, whereas if a woman should kill her husband she was charged with petty *treason* and could be punished more cruelly than if she had committed high treason against the state: the penalty was burning to death. How can such a powerful statement conclude with the stereotypical observation that when a woman marries she chooses the profession of wife and mother?

I believe Mill's commitment to an empiricist methodology is precisely what creates the contradictions. His brand of empiricism, which may be regarded as representative of Anglo-American empiricism to the present day, assumes a boundary that divides tangible empirical objects, to be studied from the outside and defined by their static boundaries, from active subjects who study them. The logical difficulties with such a stance will be explored in some detail further on (see pages 113–117). The point here is simply to demonstrate that Mill's epistemology is at odds with his political convictions. Empiricism is an insufficient vehicle for getting him where he wants to go politically for two reasons: (1) the empirical evidence for women's successful participation in public life simply didn't exist at the time when he wrote, and indeed may never exist, if one wants to argue that beginning several thousand years late is definitive proof of women's inferiority, and (2) Mill's empiricism permits women to be locked into a role as objects—the data to be studied, the political problem.

His dichotomized view of the world carries implications for others besides women. Even in the rather stridently feminist second chapter there are gratuitous indictments of working-class men, and it is apparent that Mill feels quite comfortable assuming that he understands what people are like from the way he perceives them to behave. He had earlier expressed disgust at the fact that "The clodhopper exercises or is to exercise, his share of the power equally with the highest nobleman" (12). Now he claims,

> The vilest malefactor has some wretched woman tied to him, against whom he can commit any atrocity except killing her, and, if tolerantly cautious, can do that without much danger of the legal penalty. And how many thousands are there among these lowest classes in every country, who, without being in a legal sense malefactors in any other respect, because in every other quarter their aggressions meet with resistance, indulge the utmost habitual excesses of bodily violence towards the unhappy wife.... (35)

The capitulation to stereotypes based upon superficial observation is no quirk in Mill's work. It goes right to the heart of what is disturbing about *The Subjection of Women* and, I shall argue, about liberal theory in general. The problem is not simply a haughty attitude with regard to the victims of liberal society. The problem as I see it is that the liberal epistemological stance, exemplified by Mill, divides the world into subjects and objects and doesn't consider the possibility that the objects themselves may have subjective existence. This static, dichotomist epistemology actually encourages stereotypical thinking or, put more technically, encourages mistaking the world as it appears at any particular moment from a privileged "legitimate" perspective for a permanent and objective state of affairs. We can observe Mill's dependence upon a static empiricist worldview in the last two chapters of *The Subjection of Women* and observe, as well, the political manifestations of such a view.

In chapter 3 Mill considers whether women themselves are capable of contributing as much in the way of genius as men to society, and in chapter 4, what society might stand to gain from a full utilization of women's talents. Both chapters rely upon empirical evidence about women. In both, we witness the collapse of the hopefulness of Mill's early agnosticism about feminine nature.

Chapter 3 begins with the acknowledgment that the empirical evidence on women's ability to participate fully in public life is simply not yet in. The concept of nature begins to intrude in a vague way when Mill declares, "Let us first make entire abstraction of all psychological considerations tending to show, that any of the mental differences supposed to exist between women and men are but the *natural* effect of the differences in their education and circumstances, and indicate no radical difference, far less radical inferiority, of *nature*" (53, emphasis added). *Nature* is used in this sentence twice, once to refer to the effects of education and circumstances, and again to refer to something like innate qualities. The second sense is of course the one often used to lock women into characteristics that seem unchangeable, and as Mill himself acknowledges, "inferior." But what can the "natural effect" of education and circumstances mean? The context suggests that Mill intends *natural* in this sense to imply "inevitable," and here particularly *logically* inevitable or necessary. Rather than draw premature conclusions let us simply note that the term *nature* has made an appearance. Mill continues by proposing to consider women empirically, "as they already are, or as they are known to have been; and the capacities which they have already shown. What they have done, that, at least, if nothing else, it is proved that they can do" (54). In spite of the weight of evidence against their possessing equal literary, artistic, scientific, and political genius with men, Mill is determined to utilize empirical evidence.

He believes the evidence justifies the observation that "looking at women as they are known in experience, it may be said of them, with more truth than belongs to most other generalisations on the subject, that the general bent of their talents is towards the practical" (57). Fair enough: one common generalization about women is that they are practical rather than speculative, a quality that is certainly valuable. However, no sooner has Mill stated that this useful quality is empirically verifiable than once again the abstraction of nature intrudes. He uses it again in a loose sense, not quite to refer to the whole immutable makeup of a woman's body, mind, and soul, but rather in a partial sense: "Let us consider the special nature of the mental capacities most characteristic of a woman of talent." He doesn't acknowledge that he *is* indeed using a concept of nature rather than the purely empirical evidence he stated he was going to use, and that he seems comfortable with facile generalizations about what women are intellectually fit for. Mill celebrates the difference between women and men but never considers the political implications of such a celebration. For if women have acquired their talents from circumstance rather than from nature, when their circumstance changes (which is what Mill seems to want to accomplish by writing his treatise), presumably their talents would also change. If he is serious about women's valuable characteristics being a part of their nature, why bother to argue for change?

Mill plunges on, finding that "the special nature of the mental capacities" of a woman of talent are "all of a kind which fits them for practice, and makes them tend towards it." He finds a "gravitation of women's minds to the present, to the real, to the actual fact." He finds that "A woman seldom runs wild after an abstraction." He is delighted that these qualities are such a useful counterbalance to the male penchant for abstraction, speculation and theory. Mill never uses the term *nature* to refer to masculine traits. Still, being a speculative male thinker carries its disadvantages, it seems: "The principal and most characteristic aberration of speculative minds as such, consists precisely in the deficiency of this lively perception and ever-present sense of objective fact.... Women's thoughts are thus as useful in giving reality to those of thinking men, as men's thoughts in giving width and largeness to those of women" (59). My point here is not to undermine what Mill is consciously trying to do in this chapter. My guess is that he really means that women are the way they are because of historical circumstances, not by nature. But he isn't cognizant of how often and in what ways he uses the term, or of the limitations it places upon his argument for change.

In fact, *neither* an argument from nature *nor* an argument from history (empirical evidence) will enable Mill to argue for the equality of women. If women are a product of their environment (Mill's celebrated "environmentalism"), then their talents result from their history of oppression, which Mill seeks to change. If women are the way they are by nature, then presumably political changes would not fundamentally affect that nature, and women would continue to play the less than central role they have played in the history of both ideas and action. Mill believes he is basing his argument upon the empirical evidence at hand, establishing that the way women are is after all enough to commend them to equality. I shall turn in a moment to the culmination of this line of argument. Before that, however, consider what is involved in his argument thus far.

Mill is suggesting that women as they are have already demonstrated worthy qualities that should qualify them for full participation in public life, but his perspective is entirely, subjectively, and yet unconsciously male. Women must prove to men, or rather Mill will help them by demonstrating to men, that their qualities are "good enough" to warrant inclusion in all walks of life. For example, he offers that "hardly anything can be of greater value to a man of theory and speculation who employs himself not in collecting materials of knowledge by observation, but in working them up by processes of thought into comprehensive truths of science and laws of conduct, than to carry on his speculating in the companionship, and under criticism of a really superior woman" (59). What if we grant Mill this statement as a political gambit? His audience is, after all, male, and it is men whom he must convince about women's qualifications for emancipation. But it is precisely in his failure to question that point that Mill demonstrates that he *himself* can't think beyond women as objects of his study. What limits his perspective is his assumption that the world consists of static subjects and objects. His own epistemological stance allows him to believe that women actually *are* as they appear *to him* to be. He assumes that he can reasonably and accurately base an argument upon his observations.

If women can be "freed" by men or "made the equals of" men, if "how they are" is useful to men or makes an argument for equality sound ludicrous, women are still regarded as passive, external objects in relation to the active men, the subjects who make decisions about their fate. His blindness to the limitations of his epistemology permits him to glide from woman's nature to environmental influences without recognizing the contradictions between the two. From his point of view, women's *nature* is external to men. Women's *behavior*, the result of women's history, environmental influences, etc., is *also* assumed to be external to men. Both aspects "belong" to women in a self-contained sense. Women's nature and women's behavior are thus both regarded as objects: objective to, outside of, different from the man who studies women. The difference between an argument from nature or from environment doesn't amount to much because both terms refer to something thoroughly external. Mill's relation to women's nature *and* behavior is identical; neither really involves him. No wonder his use of the term *nature* is so ambiguous, so confusing.

The tendency to regard women as objects is in full flower in the final chapter, which opens with the question, "Would mankind be at all better off if women were free? If not, why disturb their minds, and attempt to make a social revolution in the name of an abstract right?" (79) Again, it is probably kindest to Mill to regard his zealous utilitarianism here as a political maneuver: Why should men be convinced to change women's circumstances unless they believe it will be to their advantage to do so? But Mill is a man who believes in reason; he means this essay to be more than a political pamphlet. He believes he is making sense in some more universal way. His utilitarianism seeks to foreclose the need for an argument in the name of abstract right. He will not presume to define abstract justice or nature. He simply wants to present the empirical facts and let his readers decide. So he proceeds to demonstrate what he believes are the advantages that would accrue to men, should women be respected as equals. However, focusing his argument on empirical evidence, ignoring questions about the origins of women's characteristics, projects an unwarranted permanence onto the data and amounts to an unacknowledged assumption of women's nature.

His list of the utilitarian benefits to society that would result from the emancipation of women begins with his suggestion that the "mass of mental faculties available for the higher service of humanity" would double if women were to be educated and taken seriously. The sympathetic reader might be inclined to protest at this point: "At least thinking in terms of society is better than thinking only in terms of benefit to men! And after all, Mill means to include women in society." My point is that thinking in terms of benefit to society is a euphemism for thinking in terms of benefit to men because Mill cannot, given his epistemology, consider that women might have active needs and preferences that could change society. Mill wants predictable results from liberating women. This means that he doesn't really wish to free women but rather to change their role according to his own specifications. Women remain objects to be manipulated by Mill, here, specifically for what he regards as their benefit. Mill can't let go, he apparently can't take a chance on letting women define the terms of both their needs and the needs of society.

Following his list of the social advantages of freeing women, Mill turns to a discussion of the cultural advantages to men. Here the one-sidedness of his perspective is glaring. He applauds "the influence of mothers on the early character of their sons, and the desire of young men to recommend themselves to young women," which "have in all recorded times been important agencies in the formation of character" (84). He believes that "the moral influence of women has had two modes of operation": a softening influence, as well as an inspirational influence urging men towards "courage, and the military virtues," which result from "the desire which men felt of being admired by women." He adds, "The chivalrous ideal is the acme of the influence of women's sentiments on the moral cultivation of mankind" (85). In sum, "The influence of women counts for a great deal in two of the most marked features of modern European life—its aversion to war, and its addiction to philanthropy" (87).

Again, it is important to remember that while there may be objectionable substantive aspects to Mill's views, that is not the central thrust of my criticism. For example, it is evident that Mill is considering only women and men of a particular, enlightened class. We saw his callous treatment of working-class men; here it is obvious that Mill is thinking only about educated women, and only about the value of their freedom for educated men. One might even argue that he is advocating full participation of an elite group of women in political life in order to counteract the rising influence of uneducated working-class men upon the politics of his day. The notion of bolstering a besieged elite with the inclusion of "sisters"—the women of elite ranks—rather than permitting one's class to be overrun by barbarians from the lower classes is not without historical precedent. A critical reading of the fifth book of the *Republic* has Plato creating an elite guardian class of both men and women but demonstrating little regard for the members of the bronze class. The American Progressive party at the turn of the twentieth century was also more supportive of woman suffrage than the lower classes and immigrants tended to be. The same interpretation may be offered there. In both fifth-century Athens and late nineteenth- and early twentieth-century America, as well in as the England of Mill's day, massive social and economic upheavals threatened to dislocate once secure social classes. It can be argued that educated women were being used against uneducated men by the leading political minds of their day, not particularly for the women's benefit but rather for the benefit of an upper class.

I am less interested in the validity of that social interpretation of the motivations for women's freedom than with the structure of the argument for emancipation. Sticking with Mill's case, his epistemological stance is what is problematic for women, *whether or not we would regard his political intentions as admirable.* Mill discusses women as he would any empirical objects. They sit still to be studied; they "are" or "are not" a certain way. This means that even if he should succeed in convincing his male cohorts to act upon his political suggestion, to repeal the existing laws prohibiting women from pursuing certain occupations, for example, women would still be regarded as objects, still have to prove that their freedom is merited in male terms, still be tempted to live up to the faith men have placed in them.

In addition to the inevitable political limitation of this epistemological stance, there are logical difficulties that make the empiricist stance simply self-contradictory. Mill relies on the empirical evidence he finds but does not consider it as something changing and evolving, something with a history. If the womanly characteristics he utilizes are simply empirical facts with no history and if, as it seems, he expects them to remain unchanged *after* women are freed, then he is tacitly arguing from the standpoint of a feminine nature.

An empiricist method cannot provide a perspective that justifies political change because it provides no means for getting beyond an existing state of affairs. Attempting to explain the viability of change by drawing upon the empirical evidence at hand leaves one with only two choices: either the way things are is the way they will continue to be, which is no argument for change at all, or the way things are is the result of a particular history—in the case of women, an oppressive history—which is precisely what one is attempting to change, and so the empirical evidence in isolation carries no weight. If what one finds in the present will change in the future, it has little bearing on the projected future state of affairs.

II. TOWARD MILL'S *SYSTEM OF LOGIC*

Perhaps Mill is simply not thinking clearly in his argument on behalf of women. Perhaps political fervor kept him from seeing the contradictions in his argument. Surely this short, logically contradictory essay on a most controversial political topic cannot be regarded as representative of the best of empirical theory. Let us turn, then, to a more representative and well-respected example of Mill's epistemology. If the same difficulties can be found, perhaps there is a case to be made that the logic of empiricism itself carries certain contradictions.

Mill's *A System of Logic* will serve as a purer example of the logic of empiricism. It was highly respected when first published and eagerly devoured by English students of philosophy and politics. Sir Leslie Stephen, who has written a three-volume history of utilitarianism[2] (and who was also Virginia Woolf's father), noted that "Mill's *System of Logic* may be regarded as the most important manifesto of Utilitarian philosophy. . . . Indeed, I can testify from personal observation that it became a kind of sacred book for students who claimed to be genuine liberals."[3] Bertrand Russell remarked, "I first read Mill's *Logic* at the age of eighteen, and at that time I had a very strong bias in his favor. . . ."[4] Russell notes that although his influence on the younger generation of scholars was enormous, *A System of Logic* did not mark a radical departure from the English logic of its day. "His influence in politics and in forming opinion on moral issues was very great, and to my mind, wholly good. . . . Mill's first important book was his *Logic,* which no doubt presented itself as a plea for experimental rather than a priori methods, and, as such, was useful, though not very original. . . . Everything that Mill has to say in his *Logic* about matters other than inductive inference is perfunctory and conventional."[5]

A note of explanation is necessary before proceeding to an

analysis of *A System of Logic*. Because Mill was, and still is, taken very seriously as a spokesman of modern liberal thought, he is an appropriate representative of both the logic and the politics of liberalism. A range of scholars testifies to his importance as a symbol of nineteenth-century liberal thought, now embodied in the Anglo-American legal tradition. Gertrude Himmelfarb, for example, notes, "Mill represents in the Anglo-American world what Nietzsche does in the continental tradition: the apogee of 'modernity.' It is no wonder *On Liberty* is so enduringly contemporary." And "What public philosophy we have is that which Mill bequeathed to us."[6] In a similar vein, Roger Scruton remarks that "Mill's doctrine of liberty has survived in essence to our own day. His influence passed through Sedgwick and Herbert Spencer to provide what has become liberal orthodoxy in jurisprudence."[7]

Because Mill's work can be regarded as a form of liberal orthodoxy, because he is still regarded as a thinker who has shaped the sacred principles of liberalism (such as the first amendment to the American constitution), and because I am arguing here that his *System of Logic* is indeed compatible with his theory in general, and methodologically flawed, it is necessary to proceed carefully and respectfully. The section that begins here is a review of recent scholarship on Mill, as introduction to chapter 4, in which Mill's *System of Logic* is discussed in detail. Some readers may find the discussion of Mill excessive, but because he is so well respected, and so fiercely defended, I feel constrained to include a full and careful discussion, and to commiserate with the reader. This section may be slow going, but it is warranted by the importance of addressing the problems with the logic of liberalism.

Although Mill is still revered, it is also commonly acknowledged that his theory is beset by contradictions. Scholars usually focus upon two dimensions to explain these contradictions, the political and the psychological, but do not question that Mill's method may itself be less than consistent and workable. The conflicts plaguing his work are attributed not to his method but to his intense and ambivalent relationship with his father; to intellectual loyalties divided between his father and his wife Harriet Taylor; or to strong political convictions that may have overridden his methodological consistency.

My argument that the empirical method Mill claims to

adhere to is insufficient for a theory of political change demands that I establish that the problems plaguing Mill's work are "larger" than Mill himself. I must demonstrate that inadequacies inherent in the empirical method supersede conflicts he may have had with his father, as well as conflicts between his political and his intellectual commitments. Empiricism simply will not provide the basis for a theory of political change. *That* inherent methodological inadequacy is what Mill runs up against in *The Subjection of Women,* and it is glaring in his *System of Logic.*

There is agreement, then, that *System of Logic* is flawed by inconsistency: Mill appears to be arguing in the first part for a purely inductive method, and in the second for a deductivism to which he doesn't quite want to admit. He is seeking a compromise between inductivism and deductivism. The source of his need for compromise is said to be either political or psychological: either *A System of Logic* reflects conflicts in Mill's emotional life or it is more of a political treatise than one would expect it to be. Bertrand Russell makes out the traditional case for Mill's confusion in *A System of Logic:*

> The substructure of his opinions remained always that which had been laid down for him in youth by the dominating personality of his father, but the theories which he built upon his substructure were very largely such as it could not support.... The new storeys which he added under the influence of Carlyle and Mrs. Taylor, were intellectually insecure. To put the matter another way: morals and intellect were perpetually at war in his thought, morals being incarnate in Mrs. Taylor, and intellect in his father. If the one was too soft, the other was too harsh. The amalgam which resulted was practically beneficent, but theoretically somewhat incoherent."[8]

That is, Harriet Taylor pushed Mill toward political and ethical involvements that were not supportable in terms of James Mill's purer intellectual method. The conflict between politics and method in Mill's work is personified by conflicting loyalties to his wife and his father.

Other scholars have noted, without bringing in psychological motivations, that Mill sought to reconcile the major intellectual trends of his day: English empiricism and German rationalism. Why would it be so important for Mill to reconcile conflicting philosophical trends? Perhaps rather than a conflict between politics and method, the symbolic conflict between Mill's father and wife took the form of a more purely intellectual conflict that he felt he urgently needed to resolve: rationalism representing his father's theory and empiricism representing Mrs. Taylor.[9] Nonetheless, let us consider what the dominating intellectual traditions of his day stood for and the possibility that Mill had an intellectual, and not only an emotional, stake in finding a compromise.

Scholars not intrigued by psychological explanations for the conflicts tugging at Mill find *political* explanations for the intellectual tensions in his work. For example, R. P. Anschutz, in the Schneewind collection, suggests that Mill was tempted by the rationalist method, but that because he associated it with conservative politics he could not embrace the "intuitionism" wholeheartedly.[10] While Mill was tempted by the "Germano-Coleridgeans," everything in his personal intellectual background —particularly the importance of Jeremy Bentham and the utilitarians—was stridently empiricist. Perhaps Coleridge and German philosophy served as a way to free Mill from the influence of his father's circle; except that he never quite got free, either because of the strength of his father's influence or because he genuinely abhorred what he regarded as the conservative political implications of German philosophy. The problem, Mill believed, was that the rationalist conviction that truth lay in the nature and "properties" of "things-in-themselves" led the German metaphysicians to accept the universality, the necessity, the inevitability of what already exists. As Mill remarks in his essay on Coleridge, "They committed the very common error of mistaking the state of things with which they had always been familiar, for the universal and natural condition of mankind."[11] This "intuitive" or rationalist school represented political conservatism and philosophical determinism to Mill because it seemed to him that the universals the Germans found lurking beneath empirical surfaces could be found only by making "what is" the object of philosophical inquiry. Furthermore, if only existing phenomena could contain the universals, and universality implies philosophical necessity, then whatever exists *must* exist because it is the only basis for universality. Hence there is no possibility for change, an observation that sent Mill back to the empiricism of Bentham and Locke and, by association, his father.[12] Mill (the younger) remarked, in response to the Coleridgeans,

> We here content ourselves with a bare statement of our opinion. It is that the truth, on this much debated question, lies with the school of Locke and Bentham. The nature and laws of things in themselves, or of the hidden causes which are the objects of experience, appear to us radically inaccessible to the human faculties. We see no ground for believing that anything can be the object of our knowledge except our experience, and what can be inferred from our experience by the analogies of experience itself....[13]

Alan Ryan is another who believes that Mill was struggling to find a method to justify political change, and that the "doctrine of philosophical necessity" was anathema to him. Mill saw empiricism as an epistemology that permitted a "doctrine of free will." "Free will" implied that people could change, which in turn justified reform politics. Again, I am moved to note that Mill's rejection of "philosophical necessity" in favor of a doctrine of free will contains psychological parallels in his life. Mill was the product of his father's educational experiment, inspired by Benthamite utilitarianism, to prove that with the proper system of behavioral rewards and punishments any child—even the dullest—could be made to perform intellectually for the benefit of society. Mill had had an emotional breakdown as a young man as he struggled (ambivalently) to free himself from being wholly the product of his father's upbringing, entirely without a will (and a life) of his own.

Ryan is not particularly interested in the psychological conflicts that may be reflected in *A System of Logic.* He is more concerned with the logical impossibility Mill might face as he endeavors to bridge the gap between the political promise of a doctrine of free will and the intellectual rigor of a doctrine of philosophical necessity, or causality. Ryan notes, "Absolute free will is not compatible with a theory of causality." That is, there may be an inherent conflict between empiricism and rationalism, or between an inductive and a deductive stance conventionally viewed. Mill acknowledges a tension between the schools of Bentham and Coleridge, and even between Locke and Aristotle on the one hand and Kant, Coleridge and the German philosophers on the other. He sees the one mode of thought as a salutary balance to the other, rather than as posing a potentially insurmountable logical difficulty. Ryan regards *A System of Logic* as a "reformer's book," with political prescriptions close to the surface; but he sees a difficulty that was not faced squarely by Mill. "At the foundation of the *Logic* is the pervasiveness of causation; if everything we do has its sufficient causes, then how could we ever do anything that we do not do?"[14]

Mill would like to have been able to rely upon empiricism as the basis of his logic, in Ryan's view, because he believed it to be more amenable to political change, less grounded in rationalistic assumptions, such as the existence of universal causation. He was not, however, willing to relinquish completely the certainty of a rationalist, deductive system, and this left him endeavoring to reconcile two philosophical stances that may not be reconcilable. He regarded empiricism as a path away from the logical constrictions of rationalism, and yet a pure empiricism must relinquish the belief that causes are knowable. This logical problem is difficult enough, at least in the linear terms that characterized Mill's thought. There is further irony, however, because the same argument that Mill made about the inherent conservatism of rationalism can also be made about a "pure" empiricism. For if the only basis of knowledge is what exists, how can we even imagine what doesn't yet exist? How can we ground an argument for what doesn't exist in anything except, perhaps, imagination? Empiricism has its own built-in conservatism; it provides no way out of what is seen or experienced in sensuous terms. We saw Mill up against this difficulty in *The Subjection of Women*. How could empiricism justify a different role for women, if there is no empirical evidence that such a change would work?

One question remains before launching into a critical analysis of Mill's *System of Logic*. I have attempted to establish the significance of comparing the method in *A System of Logic* and

The Subjection of Women in order to demonstrate that the inconsistencies in *The Subjection of Women* are the result of the empiricist method itself, rather than inadequate political or psychological commitment to feminism on Mill's part. I have presented enough of the literature to demonstrate the importance Mill has retained as a spokesman for modern liberalism. What if Mill's brand of empiricism is not emblematic of contemporary empiricism, even if his political thinking is still representative of modern liberal thought? In one sense, if my thesis is correct and method places some limitations on the content of political thought, such a criticism cannot hold. Method and political content are separable, but not *that* separable: if Mill's political content is recognizable and relevant in late twentieth-century liberal society, then his method should be also. However, because I am about to consider Mill's empirical method, independently of the political content of his work, let me at least consider the possibility that empiricism has advanced beyond the state of Mill's conceptualization. Is it still relevant to focus upon John Stuart Mill as an empirical philosopher?

On the one hand, of course empiricism has changed since the mid-nineteenth century. Willard Van Orman Quine, writing a century after Mill, is perhaps more representative of current "state-of-the-art" empirical philosophy. He has also been quoted by contemporary feminist philosophers of science[15] as a philosopher who has avoided the pitfall of dichotomist thinking. His essay "Two Dogmas of Empiricism" argues against a dichotomy between analytic and synthetic truths and against reducing all meaningful statements to "some logical construct upon terms which refer to immediate experience."[16] Eliminating the distinction between analytic and synthetic statements, and eliminating the distinction between the linguistic and factual content of a statement certainly undermines the centrality of belief in the physical world for this sort of empiricism. Quine states, "As an empiricist I continue to think of the conceptual scheme of science as a tool, ultimately, for predicting future experience in the light of past experience. Physical objects are conceptually imported into the situation as convenient intermediaries—not by definition in terms of experience, but simply as irreducible posits comparable, epistemologically, to the gods of Homer" (44).

Quine regards this as a step towards pragmatism, as well as one towards blurring the boundary between speculative metaphysics and natural science.

This is surely a loosening of the rigid worldview of orthodox nineteenth-century empiricism, but it is still plagued by problems for which I seek answers with minimalist dialectics. It relinquishes rather than confronts the problem of the relationship between subject and object. Quine maintains the impossibility of establishing a rigid boundary between the physical world and what we can say about the physical world, but he argues in essence: "Let's act as though the physical world exists as it appears, with the understanding that such a stance is a useful explanation, rather than The Truth." He distinguishes this stance, for example, from Hume's skeptical empiricism by his adherence to the irreducibility of the world to single terms, or even to single statements.

> The idea of defining a symbol in use was, as remarked, an advance over the impossible term-by-term empiricism of Locke and Hume. The statement, rather than the term, came with Frege to be recognized as the unit accountable to an empiricist critique. But what I am now urging is that even in taking the statement as a unit we have drawn our grid too firmly. The unit of empirical significance is the *whole* of science. (42)

I am interested in exploring precisely the relationship between the world and what we can say about it. It is true that Quine's argument demonstrates that discomfort with the traditional empirical world of fragments and dichotomies is not an exclusive characteristic of feminist philosophy: his empiricism is indeed more compatible with the concerns of contemporary feminist epistemology than is traditional empiricism. While his argument demonstrates that the same epistemological problems confront men as women, it still leaves me unsettled with regard to the relationship between mind and the world.

There is feminist theory that more directly confronts the problem of how knowledge can result from the relationship between inner and outer, in a manner that comes closer to addressing the questions I raise in this book. I take as given a certain universal tension between subjective experience and objective reality and call for an epistemology that best describes that tension. The problem with Mill's brand of empiricism is that it views subjectivity and objectivity as irreconcilably separate, implying that nothing exists to draw them together, not even a tension between them. Mill's traditional empiricism founders on the question of how knowledge is possible at all. Evelyn Fox Keller, as we saw, traced efforts to bridge the gap between subjectivity and objectivity to the birth of empiricism in Bacon's philosophy. Whether the data or the scientist is active or passive has been acknowledged as a problem for empiricists but seldom adequately addressed by them. Keller and Christine Grontkowski take on the border between inner and outer once again in their provocative essay, "The Mind's Eye."[17]

How can empiricism work? How has it worked throughout history? These are the questions implicit in Keller and Grontkowski's essay. They focus upon the prevalence of vision and light as metaphors for knowledge in Western philosophy, and upon the eye as the principal organ for accumulating knowledge. The authors trace vision as a metaphor for knowledge to Plato's philosophy: "All three components of the visual system—eye, the sun and light—are used by Plato, both metaphorically and directly to establish the characteristics of intelligibility" (211). They remind us that Plato's word for the Forms, the essence of knowledge, is εἶδος, things that are seen.[18]

Keller associates the conviction of modern science "that nature is knowable" with the Platonic emphasis on vision and suggests that two conditions are prerequisite to such knowledge: "The first is the separation of subject from object, i.e. the distinction between the individual who perceives and the object which is perceived. The second is the move away from the conditions of perception, i.e. the separation of knowledge from the unreliability of the senses, or so to speak, the dematerialization of knowledge" (212). The dissociation of knowledge from the bodily senses was begun by Plato but not completed until Descartes. Vision as the metaphor for knowledge permits detachment, even though the eye is certainly a part of the body. Of all the human sense organs, the eye is best suited for distance and abstraction:

"Vision is that sense which places the world at greatest remove; it is also that sense which is uniquely capable of functioning outside of time. It lends itself to a static conception of eternal truths. Although itself one of the senses, by virtue of its apparent incorporeality, it is that sense which most readily promotes the illusion of disengagement and objectification" (213).

If vision and light are still the ways we most naturally conceive of knowledge ("The 'cool light of reason' establishes, in a single move, worldly distance and divine communion" [213]), then the eye as the mediator between mind and world brings us right to the question of the activity or passivity of the senses. Plato thought the eye emitted its own stream of light; modern optical theory presents us with a passive eye, receiving light. Plato's theory, though physiologically erroneous, permitted an image of knowledge that involved a coupling of inner and outer. Now the image of vision and light is still a dominant metaphor for knowledge, but if the eye is thoroughly passive, there is a real problem with how one acquires knowledge. Descartes offered a radical withdrawal from the physical world, a mistrust of the sense organs. Cartesian knowledge is the result of an active, subjective intellect, even while Descartes utilized light and vision as metaphors for the mind's activity. To Descartes, "light" connotes active reason and a sort of divine inspiration. "The inborn light receives its metaphysical dignity and stability by being totally and in a markedly Augustinian manner derived from divinity" (214). In other words, Descartes divorced body from mind, sight from vision, without acknowledging that sight is a passive sense. As Keller and Grontkowski remark: "It would seem, at this juncture, that we either accept the conclusion that knowledge itself is passive, or we abandon the visual metaphor. Not so, Descartes provided us with another alternative. He enabled us to retain *both* the conception of knowledge as active, and the use of the visual metaphor by severing the connection between the 'seeing' of the intellect and physical seeing—by severing, finally, the mind from the body" (215).

Knowledge cannot result from the mere passive recording of data: it demands at minimum the active compilation and evaluation of accumulated material. Still, vision, a passive sense, remains our central metaphor for knowledge. Vision is the sense most appropriate for conceptualizing objective knowledge, in that we expect it to be detached, unengaged. Keller and Grontkowski suggest that a certain "fudging" of the metaphor is necessary to include the active response to seeing that makes knowing possible. Hence, the emergence of "inner light," the vision of the "mind's eye," in order to retain the detachment of vision, without admitting the utter passivity of sight. This model of knowledge persists as the paradigm of scientific objectivity to this day: "The dual paradigm behind the promise of the visual—clarity and communion—survives as the root aspiration behind the dual tenets of modern science. In *objectifiability* the world is severed from the observer, illuminated as it were, by the sense that could operate, it was thought, without contaminating. In *knowability*, communion is re-established, mediated by a now-submerged but still evident dimension of the same sense" (218).

I think liberal science is happier with passivity and less eager to take on the mantle of masculine activity than Keller and Grontkowski believe. Vision prevails so strongly as a metaphor for empirical knowledge precisely because scientists (or at any rate, social scientists) prefer to think that the knowledge they accumulate in the form of data *is* acquired passively, objectively— with active subjectivity held in abeyance. One of the implications for this epistemological stance is a lack of responsibility for one's theory: "My data made me do it." Human pride, which Keller and Grontkowski believe prohibits an entirely passive view of knowledge (see 215) is eclipsed in liberal practice by the desire to escape involvement. The desire for detachment—both epistemological and social—is powerful enough to ensure that the necessary active moments are denied and avoided as much as possible in the sort of empiricism valued in the liberal social sciences. The struggle, then, between activity and passivity, which takes the form of a struggle between subjectivity and objectivity, is what characterizes modern empiricism. Not the distance between the two, but the denial of the very role of activity, hence subjectivity, is what I find so problematic about empiricism. I shall present a more careful discussion of the meanings of subjectivity and objectivity, in relation to passivity and activity, in chapter 5. Before that, however, I turn to Mill's *System of Logic*, to demonstrate that it founders precisely on Mill's difficulty with the activity of the mind. Mill prefers to depict the scientist or logician as the passive recipient of data. He runs into the difficulties outlined by Keller and Grontkowski: a thoroughly passive stance is quite simply incompatible with the accumulation of knowledge. He considers the possibility of an "inner eye" in his attempt to make scientific experiments analogous to the observation of empirical data. However, his ultimate unwillingness to admit to the active role of intellect brings his logical system down in a hail of contradictions. These contradictions, although acknowledged by his philosophical successors, bedevil empiricism to the present day. For to acknowledge a flaw is not the same thing as to exorcise it.

CHAPTER 4

JOHN STUART MILL—A SYSTEM OF LOGIC

In *A System of Logic,* John Stuart Mill goes to great lengths to establish the inductive basis of all knowledge, and then runs into the problem anticipated by Keller and Grontkowski: if all knowledge is the result of passive, piece-by-piece accumulation of data, how is the mind to make use of it? Indeed, how does it come to constitute knowledge at all? He presents an image of logic in the opening pages, in which subjects are separated from objects and knowledge from the knower, who in turn is a mind separated from a body. That is, Mill begins with the most disembodied, fragmented view of the world imaginable. Logic is regarded as a form of knowledge—"the science of science itself"[1]—and it seems that Mill would favor a world where all knowledge is self-evident, involving no active intervention at all on the part of the philosopher or scientist. He expends the greater part of his effort establishing the inductive basis of all knowledge and dismissing deductivism as metaphysical nonsense. As we shall see, he must go farther and farther out on a limb to maintain his stance, until the limb finally snaps, and some role for deductive thought must be acknowledged.

Inductivism is more passive than deductivism. It is the stance that makes use of physical sight: the world "presents" itself to the human eye, which absorbs the data. Deductivism, in contrast, is a more active stance requiring logical intervention of the mind's eye. Mill indicates in the opening pages that the human mind possesses an innate capacity for logical thought, which precludes even the need to communicate: "If there were but one rational being in the universe, that being might be a perfect logician; and the science and art of logic would be the same for that one person as for the whole human race" (1:5).

Mill is not interested in metaphysics, or the origins of knowledge in the abstract, but rather with knowledge of the material world, and so he must deal with the relationship between mind and that world. He *does* address the mind/body question early in the book. Far from dividing one from the other, as a feminist might expect a liberal empiricist to do, Mill proclaims that there is no basis for any division at all. "One of the sources of confusion... is the division commonly made of feelings into Bodily and Mental. Philosophically speaking, there is no foundation at all for this distinction..." (1:56). He then claims that all "sensations" are states of "the sentient mind, not states of the body," and, furthermore, that the mind is passive and the body active. "For as our conception of a body is that of an unknown exciting cause of sensations, so our conception of mind is that of an unknown recipient, or percipient of them; and not of them alone, but of all our other feelings. As body is the mysterious something which excites the mind to feel, so mind is the mysterious something which feels, and thinks" (1:67). Mill thus presupposes an answer to the dilemma of mind and body, even though he has just argued that there is no way to distinguish between them. The mind, he now says, is completely passive in relation to the body, and also divided from it.

His dismissal of both body and mind as "mysterious" suggests that Mill would prefer to avoid the inconvenience of *both* body and mind in the pursuit of knowledge. It is as though he harbors the secret longing that the objective truths of the world make themselves known even without the existence of human beings to receive them. This seems outlandish only until we remember Mill's truly bizarre relationship with his father, whose theory amounted to the dismissal of any possibility of an inner life, particularly for his son, who complained of being at war with his own physical body. It is not surprising that at this very juncture the son sees fit to bring his father into *A System of Logic*.[2]

All of which we are aware of, even in our own minds, is (in the words of Mr. [James] Mill) a certain "thread of consciousness," a series of feelings, that is, of sensations, thoughts, emotions, and volitions, more or less numerous and complicated. There is a something I call Myself, or by another form of expression, my mind, which I consider as distinct from these conceptions, thoughts, etc.: a something which I conceive to be not the thoughts, but the being that has the thoughts, and which I can conceive as existing for ever in a state of quiescence, without any thoughts at all. But what this being is, although it is myself, I have no knowledge, other than the series of its states of consciousness. (1:68)

The younger Mill's conclusion, which bears a remarkable resemblance to his attribution, in the opening pages of his *Autobiography*, of everything he is to his father, is: "I know nothing about myself, save my capacities of feeling or being conscious (including, of course, thinking or willing): and were I to learn anything new concerning my own nature, I cannot with my present faculties conceive this new information to be anything else, than that I have some additional capacities, as yet unknown to me, of feeling, thinking, or willing" (1:68).

The significant point to be made is that in Mill's world the logician is a passive, egoless being, receiving sensations from the outer world through the medium of the body, which converts experiences into sensations—thoughts and feelings—for the utilization of the mind. Far from seeing mind as dichotomized from body and physical world, Mill can barely distinguish a border between self and other. The mechanisms for accumulating knowledge are at best murky. He is eager to thrust responsibility for truth upon the self-evidence of the world itself. Considerable effort is expended upon establishing the inductive basis of all knowledge, and he even presents the astonishing argument that mathematics is an "inductive science." The basis for all things known is the empirical world: Mill dismisses "ratiocination" (deductive logic) as a relic from a superstitious past, belonging to the obsolete realm of metaphysics.

This maxim ... when considered as a principle of reasoning, appears suited to a system of metaphysics once indeed generally received, but which for the last two centuries has been considered as finally abandoned, though there have not been wanting, in our own day, attempts at its revival. (1:196)

Mill's view of the history of knowledge is thoroughly linear: once something is known it becomes a permanent part of a statically viewed body of common knowledge. New knowledge added to what is already "known" may provide a fuller, more complete truth, but there is little likelihood of a qualitative transformation of knowledge. Knowledge is historical only in the sense that it is remorselessly cumulative. Historical context adds nothing to the substance of what is known: if something is "true" it is valid in some sense for all time. Mill's linear, cumulative perspective is evident in statements such as ". . . what can be learnt from names, is only what somebody who used the names, knew before . . ." (1:199). Or, "No reasoning from generals to particulars can, as such, prove anything: since from a general principle you cannot infer any particulars, but those which the principle itself assumes as known" (1:205). Generalizations are only records of observations made in the past. "All inference is from particulars to particulars: General propositions are merely registers of such inferences already made, and short formulae for making more . . ." (1:216). Generalizations are sometimes useful, serving as a form of philosophical shorthand, but they have no reality and often impose a detour.

Syllogisms, then, must be viewed as mere recordkeeping in the service of induction, with data compiled cumulatively over time. Even the traditional example of an (English) syllogistic proposition, "The Duke of Wellington is mortal," is not, after all, derived from the generalization that "All men are mortal," because how do we know that all men are mortal? "Of course, from observation. Now, all which man can observe are individual cases. From these all general truths must be drawn, and into these they may be again resolved: for a general truth is but an aggregate of particular truths" (1:208). Arriving at a general truth, after accumulating sufficient particular cases, that is, arriving at the general propositions for syllogisms, is a feat performed once and for all:

> The inductions may be made once for all: a single careful interrogation of experience may suffice, and the result may be registered in the form of a general proposition, which is committed to memory or to writing, and from which afterwards we have only to syllogize. The particulars of our experiments may then be dismissed from memory, in which

it would be impossible to retain so great a multitude of details; while the knowledge which those details afforded for future use, and which would otherwise be lost as soon as the observations were forgotten, or as their record became too bulky for reference, is retained in a commodious and immediately available shape by means of general language. (1:223, 224)

I quote in such detail because the general frame of mind that a century later invented the computer is in full evidence here. This *is* the logic of liberalism; this *is* fully articulated empiricism. Generalizations have nothing to do with reasoning, nor does an active, intervening human mind. The mind is capable of extinguishing its subjectivity. Operating at its most efficient, it merely accumulates and stores data, to be retrieved when needed. What Mill only dreamed of has now, through technology, become a reality that can do away with the need for any generalizations, for any deductive thinking. We have invented computer memories capable of retaining gargantuan databases, whereas Mill could only wistfully imagine that "If we had sufficiently capacious memories, and a sufficient power of maintaining order among a huge mass of details, the reasoning could go on without any general propositions; they are mere formulae for inferring particulars from particulars" (1:236).

The shorthand of generalization may in fact prove an obstacle to the simplest, most straightforward path to truth. In such cases Mill would simply abandon abstraction altogether:

I cannot perceive why it should be impossible to journey from one place to another unless we "march up a hill and then march down again." It may be the safest road, and there may be a resting place at the top of the hill, affording a commanding view of the surrounding country; but for the mere purpose of arriving at our journey's end, our taking that road is perfectly optional; it is a question of time, trouble, and danger. (1:210)

The extreme to which Mill takes his professed belief in the universality of induction is apparent when he tackles the logical basis of mathematics. There he argues that even mathematical truths have no meaning as abstractions. There are, for example, no "ideal" lines or circles in geometry, only real ones. The very concept of length without breadth (an "ideal line") is meaningless because it has never actually been observed. Mill would use mathematics as the test case for his conviction that all knowledge is based upon experience. Mathematics, and in particular geometry, plays an important part in his critique of deduction because mathematics has for so long been regarded a prototype of deductive thinking. Nobody denies that mathematics is an "exact science," therefore, if Mill is able to demonstrate that it is, like all knowledge, grounded in experience, he will have gone a long way towards appropriating a "real" science with which to lend authority to empirical method. Mill insists, quite straightforwardly, that the "ground of our belief in axioms," the "evidence on which they must rest," is observation. Axioms are "experimental truths; generalizations from observation. The proposition, Two straight lines cannot enclose a space—or in other words, two straight lines which have once met, do not meet again, but continue to diverge —is an induction from the evidence of our sense" (1:258).

As Mill attempts to demonstrate that mathematics is grounded in the empirical world, he finds himself relinquishing the very certainty associated with mathematical logic, conventionally conceived as deductive. Instead of "empirical mathematics" lending certainty to induction, mathematics is itself undermined: it is no more "exact" than any other science that relies upon observation as its basis of analysis. The "necessities" of geometry are illusory in that while any conclusion may indeed follow "necessarily" from any supposition, if the supposition be false, so then will be the conclusion. The assumptions and suppositions upon which mathematical truths are supposedly based, Mill scoffs, are "so far from being necessary . . . they are not even true" (1:253). Thus, by arguing that mathematics derives from induction, Mill forgoes the very certainty that initially attracted him to the science of numbers.

His treatment of mathematics appears an eccentric interlude and cannot fail to raise questions about what on earth Mill thought he was doing. Did he really intend to argue that mathematical truth is based upon experience? Why? The only reason could be to establish the certainty of inductive logic. Why then give way to the usual *uncertainty* of induction? It is clear that the discussion was not carelessly introduced because Mill goes on to anticipate objections and to prepare answers for hypothetical opponents. For example, he tries to head off the possible objection that geometrical truths cannot possibly be the result of experiment by anticipating more common counterexamples of inference: that a stone will sink in water is not deducible merely by looking at the stone but must be the result of observing what happens when it is placed in water. In contrast, no amount of experimentation will lead to geometrical axioms and so opponents will conclude, geometrical truth must be the result of abstract deduction. Mill's response is startling for its obvious distortion of the meaning of both *experiment* and *observation.* He suggests that geometrical forms are actually seen.... but in the imagination! The liberties he takes with the concepts are so astonishing that Mill has to be quoted at length to be believed:

> One of the characteristic properties of geometrical forms—
> [is] their capacity of being painted in the imagination with a
> distinctness equal to reality: in other words, the exact resem-
> blance of our ideas of form to the sensations which suggest
> them...makes those pictures just as fit subjects of geometri-
> cal experimentation as the realities themselves.... The foun-
> dations of geometry would therefore be laid in direct experi-
> ence, even if the experiments (which in this case consist
> merely in attentive contemplation) were practiced solely
> upon what we call our ideas, that is, upon the diagrams in
> our minds, and not upon outward objects. For all systems of
> experimentation we take some objects to serve as represen-
> tatives of all which resemble them; and in the present case
> the conditions which qualify are completely fulfilled by an
> object existing only in our fancy.... I contend, that we do
> not believe this truth on the ground of the imaginary intu-
> ition simply, but because we know that the imaginary lines
> exactly resemble real ones, and that we may conclude from
> them to real ones with quite as much certainty as we could
> conclude from one real line to another. (1:261)

Mill considers that he has answered the objection that a geometrical axiom cannot be the result of an experiment with the rejoinder that the experiment does take place, if only in the imagination of the geometer!

ဇ๗

Mill thus exemplifies in his lengthy treatise on logic the problems Keller and Grontkowski attribute to the history of science in general. He seeks to establish that the observable, empirical world is the ultimate basis of all knowledge. Such a view, however, only stimulates questions about the relationship of body to mind, of what can be seen and the physical organ of sight. Mill acknowledges the problem but dismisses it as insoluable because not subject to examination. He goes to great lengths to establish that all knowledge is based upon induction and denies the relevance of any generalizations by likening them to scenic walks: mere detours that serve no purpose. Rather than relying upon the certainty usually afforded by belief in the empirical world, Mill falters on the question of activity and passivity. How is the scientist to "gather" knowledge from the world? Gathering facts must call for some activity of the mind, but Mill is far more comfortable with passivity. Rather than actually placing his empirical scientist actively in the world, he imagines him alone in a private laboratory, performing experiments on lines and circles, except that the experiments take place in the scientist's head. Mill has moved from observation of the real world to working with the mind's eye. We still don't know how he proposes to gather data because the empirical world no longer seems important to his withdrawn empiricist, who no longer passively absorbs data but rather actively experiments with intangible representations of the tangible world.[3] The only certainty is Mill's uncertainty about the relationship between inner and outer, subjectivity and objectivity, activity and passivity. His dichotomization of the world thus does not take any conventional male form. He is no more comfortable with an active, aggressive stance towards the objective world than with a passive one.

    If Mill insists that the mind adds nothing to what it perceives when it makes a generalization, can his definition of induction possibly constitute more than mere counting and the cataloguing of observations? How does he move from the collection of separate facts, which are the raw materials of induction to new understanding? What allows him to argue that induction permits the logician to move from "facts" to generalization? What permits him to define induction as "Generalization from Experience" (1:316)?

In the third chapter of his section on induction he introduces an axiom that, he believes, permits inductive logic to move from the description and accumulation of data to the ability to explain and predict. That axiom is "The Uniformity of the Course of Nature." The universe "is so constituted that whatever is true in any one case, is true in all cases of a certain description; the only difficulty is, to find *what* description" (1:316). This assumption, or axiom, is central to inductive logic. "Whatever be the most proper mode of expressing it, the proposition that the course of nature is uniform, is the fundamental principle, or general axiom of Induction" (1:317).

How can Mill remain consistent with what he has argued about the essentially particularistic nature of truth and the superficiality of generalization, while at the same time introducing an ungrounded axiom into his system? Doesn't this abstract generalization contradict his argument that all knowledge is grounded in observation? The only way out is to establish that the axiom of the "uniformity of nature" must also be the result of induction. Sure enough, Mill argues just that: "I hold it to be itself an instance of induction, and induction by no means of the most obvious kind. Far from being the first induction we make, it is one of the last, or at all events one of those which are latest in attaining strict philosophical accuracy. . . . the truth is, that this great generalization is itself founded on prior generalizations" (1:317).

Mill's linear, cumulative view of intellectual history permits him to suggest that at a certain unnamed point in the past enough evidence was amassed to permit a generalization that would hold for all future discoveries, simply because the empirical evidence was so compelling. He does not consider that the generalization once drawn and put into operation would change the course and method of all future thought: it would undermine the primacy of induction by placing an *a priori* generalization, no matter what the source, at the basis of all future thought. Mill actually recounts the history of the "discovery" that nature follows uniform laws. He tells us that before the discovery only primitive generalizations were possible. The more sophisticated laws had to await the axiom that gives form to the knowledge that nature behaves predictably. The law of the uniformity of nature was that breakthrough, the result of accumulated crude inductions. "We should never have thought of affirming that all phenomena take place according to general laws, if we had not first arrived, in the case of a great multitude of phenomena, at some knowledge of the laws themselves; which could be done no otherwise than by induction" (1:318).

This is an oddly concrete view of intellectual history. When was the discovery of the uniformity of nature finally clinched? Was there a specific event? A date? Mill is not forthcoming on that score.

The axiom of the uniformity of nature permits Mill to present logic in a utilitarian light. Metaphysicians in the past may have indulged in speculation about the essence of knowledge and in generalizations for their own sake, but Mill wants *usable* knowledge. What is known about the world allows us to predict the future course of events, which is, of course, potentially useful. The law of the uniformity of nature is the basis for the law of universal causation, which Mill claims is the "main pillar of inductive science." Everything in nature must have an identifiable cause and effect. He insists that there *is* universal causality, but that this is no more metaphysical an imposition than anything else he has advanced: one need only look at the empirical world to see that everything has a cause and an effect. If we cannot see it, "We may not have found out what this concurrence of circumstances may be; but we never doubt that there is such a one" (1:339). This sounds more like an incantation of faith, but never mind. Mill simply insists that all knowledge is inductive, based upon the observation of facts, which, it has been empirically discovered, operate under two laws: the law of the uniformity of nature, and the law of universal causation.

Let us overlook what appears to be the glaring intrusion of active deductive assumptions on his passive inductive world, and focus instead upon the distinction he makes, or more accurately does not make, between observation and experimentation, investigation with the physical eye and with the mind's eye.

Direct observation in Mill's schema is a *passive* epistemological stance: the eye absorbs data and relays observations to
the mind. Experimentation is an essentially *active* way of attaining knowledge: the experimentalist manipulates the world he
studies, and as Mill has already suggested, "interrogates nature"
actively. Yet Mill confounds the distinction he himself articulates
and places the two modes on a single continuum, with experimentation presented as simply a more sophisticated form of
observation. "The first and most obvious distinction between
Observation and Experiment is, that the latter is an immense
extension of the former" (1:386). His description of the mechanics of experimentation demonstrates how active an epistemological mode it really is. He refers to "produc[ing] a phenomenon
artificially," "introducing one well-defined circumstance after
another into the experiment," and notes that experimentation
"enables us to obtain innumerable combinations of circumstances which are not found in nature" (1:386). Yet the distinction between experiment and observation fades as experimentation pushes its way to the forefront of Mill's argument. It
eventually replaces observation itself as the preferred mode of
investigation, but Mill refuses to admit that experimentation
may be in conflict with direct observation.

He is actually moving from an epistemology generated in
the world (induction) to one generated in the mind (deduction),
but the shift is not acknowledged. Ultimately experimentation
replaces observation, but Mill regards it as an advance rather
than a momentous shift in epistemological approach. Mill argues
so enthusiastically that experiments are a vast improvement over
direct observation that observation, privileged at the outset as
the one avenue to reliable knowledge, is soon utterly eclipsed
and discredited. "Observation, in short, without experiment
(supposing no aid from deduction) can ascertain sequences and
coexistence, but cannot prove causation" (1:391).

This perspective marks the reversal of the methodology
Mill had been presenting. In a sleight-of-hand equivalent to his
contention that geometry is a science based upon observation of
the actual world as imagined by the mathematician, experiments
are here presented not as artificial worlds, or intellectual con-
trivances, but as more accurate assemblages of reality than the

real world itself. Mill does not even entertain the idea that an experiment must be seen as a mental construct, or that it might not be an accurate replication of what exists in the world. It makes no difference whether the philosopher starts with his own ideas or with the empirical world!

> We may have recourse... either to observation, or to experiment; we may either *find* an instance in nature, suited to our purposes, or, by an artificial arrangement of circumstances, *make* one. There is... no difference in kind, no real logical distinction, between the two processes of investigation. (1:385)

What, then, has become of the inductive discovery of the uniformity of nature? Mill's newfound admiration for experimentation undermines his argument about the inductive basis of proof for the axiom of the uniformity of nature.

By the end of the first volume the distinction between deductive and inductive reasoning has utterly collapsed. Nor is that all. Mill concludes that volume with a chapter titled "The Deductive Method," which asserts that the experimental method has its limitations. It is unsuitable for more complex data, hence useless for social science. Mill had already jettisoned observation in favor of the greater reliability of experimentation, but that method is now deemed unsuitable as well for studying the complexities of human behavior. Only one possibility remains for understanding in the social sciences: deductivism! "Two, therefore, of the three possible methods for the study of phenomena resulting from the composition of many causes being, from the very nature of the case, inefficient and illusory; there remains only the third—that which considers the causes separately, and computes the effect from the balance of the different tendencies which produce it: in short, the deductive, or a priori method" (1:463).

In sum, Mill has entirely reversed what he originally claimed to be the basis of all knowledge, but without acknowledging, or even seeing what he has done. He has moved from the proclamation that all knowledge is inductive, passive, based on observation, to a stand where knowledge is more properly deductive, based upon active manipulation of natural phenomena. Rather than admit the inevitability of an active, aggressive intellectual stance, Mill shifts terminology. In the beginning of his treatise observation was presented as the only basis of knowledge, but Mill needed a generalization to be able to make use of observations. He then suggested the axiom of the uniformity of nature, which led to the law of universal causation. All of this was still perceived by him to be inductive. Experimentation then displaced observation as the principal means of obtaining data, but still no conflict between experimentation on the one hand and inductive observation on the other was considered. In the second volume Mill argues for deductivism as the basis of knowledge but still maintains that deductivism is simply a form of inductivism. Again, he shifts terminology as he moves through the treatise but doesn't see that he is also shifting the very ground of his epistemology.

ટ&

What, finally, is the purpose of this treatise on induction that is not really a treatise on induction? Why should a contemporary reader concern herself with a self-contradictory discourse that seems, in spite of its reputation, to be a private dialogue with a handful of English philosophers and political thinkers, one of whom is the father of the author himself? To begin to answer the question, it must be understood that Mill wrote *A System of Logic* with an eye to establishing the basis for a social science. The object of *A System of Logic* is to make possible a "science of mankind," and the final book, "The Logic of the Moral Sciences," is devoted to this end.

The measure of an exact science is that it makes prediction possible, although Mill admits that predicting human behavior is nearly impossible, given the intricacy and complexity of the causal determinants. There are too many variables ever to be certain of having taken them all into account. Still, Mill believes, "approximate generalizations make it possible to make predictions which will *almost* always be verified, and general propositions which are almost always true" (2:418). He is optimistic that general laws governing human behavior are ultimately accessible to science, permitting the possibility of a "Science of Human Nature."

Mill thus finally arrives at a proposal for a methodology for the social sciences. Given a thousand pages of equivocation on the meaning of induction and deduction, it turns out, not surprisingly, to be Mill's own brand of inductive deduction. He presents two versions of his method, both with titles speaking eloquently to confusion and ambivalence. He presents first the "Physical Method," subtitled the "Concrete Deductive" method, and modeled after the physical sciences, specifically physics. Secondly, he offers the "Historical Method," subtitled the "Inverse Deductive" method.

The concrete deductive, or physical, method divides the social world into distinct behavior patterns and analyzes each separately; the historical method attempts to integrate the components into a general "Science of Society." The physical method makes use of the Deductive Method described at the close of volume 1; the Historical Method inverts it. For example, the Physical Method might study the aspects of human behavior that are concerned with profits and losses, constructing the science called "Political Economy" (2:481). The dismemberment of human behavior into discrete disciplines, Mill considers to be deductive. "Verification" is the concrete aspect of the method.

When subject matter becomes very complex, reasoning *a priori,* and verification *a posteriori* may not follow a neat order, but rather work together however they will. "Nothing more results than a disturbance in the order of precedence of the two processes, sometimes amounting to its actual inversion: insomuch that instead of deducing our conclusions by reasoning, and verifying them by observation, we in some cases begin by obtaining them conjecturally from specific experience, and afterwards connect them with the principles of human nature by a priori reasonings, which reasonings are thus a real Verification" (2:476).

The Concrete Deductive Method, then, amounts to a combination, in whatever order is most helpful, of abstract reasoning and concrete verification. When the reasoning comes first Mill bestows upon it the title "concrete deductive." When the observation or verification comes first he calls it "inverse deductive." Even if this sounds perfectly reasonable, it hardly warrants the title exact science, and the very use of the categories deduction and induction seems gratuitous, as though Mill were involved in a private dialogue, a tug of war over the names of logical methods, and anxious to emerge from the struggle bearing the names of the methods he desires for his *System of Logic.*

A combination of the concrete and the abstract *does* seem inevitable as a method for attaining the truth about anything. In attempting to fit "deduction" and "induction" together into one indistinguishable blur, Mill is fleeing an inevitable conflict between the two, which makes the relationship between abstract and concrete much more complicated than Mill is willing to acknowledge. He relinquishes the opportunity to explore the distinctions between mind and body, subjectivity and objectivity, perception and object early in his treatise. The "metaphysics" he sought to avoid have now returned to haunt his closing pages. Whether or not Mill wants to admit it, induction and deduction *do* clash, even if only momentarily. He is so eager to find a consensus between them that he never fully acknowledges the conflict, and so cannot reap the rewards of conflict resolved. He loses both concepts in the blur of his effort to keep them from destroying one another. In the end, it makes little difference whether he calls his social science deductive or inductive: he has reduced them both to an indistinguishable greyness, a blandness that deprives his work of life.

இ

John Stuart Mill's method in *A System of Logic* thus reflects some of the problems with empiricism, and with scientific objectivity associated by feminist scholars with the history of science. He seeks certainty by means of objectivity, and he desires to locate the basis of all knowledge in the external, physical, visible world. He neglects subjectivity, neglects even the activity of the mind that would allow it to gather necessary data from the world. Yet the very activity with which Mill is so uncomfortable is also associated with a male stance toward the world by Keller and Grontkowski.

So we have an irony: Mill's *System of Logic* reflects certain anticipated male problems with a dichotomously perceived world. And yet, his work is also thoroughly undermined by an avoidance of dichotomies, and avoidance of conflict. Indeed, it echoes the problems that I have associated with contemporary feminist theory. Whenever a contradiction rears its threatening head, he immediately leaps to resolve it: induction and deduction are not in conflict, but are rather part of a continuum. This may be true, and it sounds like an observation feminist "theorists of unity" would welcome. My complaint is that he assumes the continuity rather than facing up to the possible conflicts between an epistemology that regards the empirical world as its starting point and one that "begins" with the mind of the observer. Mill is so eager to avoid conflict that he grasps prematurely at whatever unity appears closest to hand, which is all too often illusory. A unity embraced because all conflict is feared is no basis for building an epistemology. It is a camouflage, a dreamlike fantasy about the world.

I believe that there is a *human* problem with the relationship between the mind and the world. The question of what goes on inside us and what goes on outside us *is* a problem, causes tension, and characterizes a conflict inherent in the human condition. Feminists have brought to our attention the problems caused by *fear* of unity, by too ready an impulse to dichotomize, to dwell upon the disjointedness of inside and outside. I argue that the problem of avoiding conflict, tension, and distance is just as dangerous, if our task is to understand ourselves and the world as fully as we can.

This excursion through *A System of Logic* has demonstrated that Mill, like the archetypical male scientist, minimizes the problems of "objective knowledge" by overlooking how problematic is the border between mind and the world, by refusing to consider important differences between an active and a passive stance towards the world. Ironically, Mill, like many contemporary feminists, also minimizes how problematic that border is by refusing to consider the important differences between an active and a passive stance and to acknowledge that each in its own way may be necessary at times. Prematurely grasping at "unity" simply doesn't work. Acknowledging conflict may be uncomfortable, even dangerous, but necessary in order to develop awareness of oneself and one's cognitive and emotional functioning in the world. If too much conflict is destructive, if dichotomies are analogous to a death wish, so too is the wish for an end to all conflict. What is needed is an epistemology with which to face the human problem of being-in-the-world, with neither detachment nor romanticism.

I have argued that the problems with *The Subjection of Women* run deeper than political, that they are more pervasive than anything having to do with John Stuart Mill himself. The contradictions that plague that work have less to do with Mill's ambivalence about the emancipation of women, or with the political inadequacies of liberalism per se, than with epistemological flaws. Mill *is* a fair example of someone trying to argue for political change using liberal theory as a basis. The epistemological assumptions of liberal theory short-circuit its political promise. Mill tried to make an empirical argument on behalf of women, tried to avoid abstract arguments from nature or justice.The empirical evidence simply would not take him where he wanted to go. He needed something else: belief in the *active* capacity of intellect. To move beyond empirical evidence, Mill needed to believe in imagination. In fact he made certain assumptions at the very beginning of his treatise on women that involved the workings of a more active mind, but he soon buried them or (conveniently) forgot that he had made them and proceeded in the belief that he was actually advancing a thoroughly empirical argument.

I described the first part of *Subjection of Women* as Platonic and the second part as Aristotelian. Mill concluded with tacit generalizations about women's nature, arguing that "how women are" provides a trustworthy basis from which to argue for the utility of their full participation in all spheres of life. Instead of the terms Platonic and Aristotelian (and in spite of Mill's attempt in *The Subjection of Women* to make Plato over into an inductive philosopher), think now in terms of deductivism in the first part of *The Subjection of Women* and inductivism in the second. The same epistemological problems can be seen to plague *A System of Logic*. Mill insists in both *The Subjection of Women* and *A System of Logic* that he is making an inductivist argument, one based entirely on "actual facts" in the world, depending upon neither *a priori* reasoning nor any sort of abstraction. He shuns the mountaintop vista, but in fact he *is* tacitly operating from assumptions and generalizations all along, yet taking no responsibility for them. The facts, he believes, "speak for themselves."

For example, in the first part of *The Subjection of Women,* Mill seems to be arguing deductively. He states that empirical facts are no basis for coming to conclusions about women or feminine nature. The nature of women is subject to proper education and nurture. This part of Mill's argument is very much like Plato's in the fifth book of the *Republic.* Mill does not admit to deductivism here. Nonetheless, the argument is essentially deductivist, and indeed rationalist, in that the abstract possibilities for women are considered more important than women's empirical history. Mill insists instead that he is making an inductivist argument: he couches his argument about the unforeseeable possibilities for women in terms of a *laissez faire* experiment—"let's just see what they can do"—forgetting the deductivist grounds upon which the experiment is based. He is trying to argue that the empirical evidence could be found, given the proper environment. It is a deductivist argument for change, disguised as an inductivist argument, and is a recapitulation of Mill's discussion of experiments in *A System of Logic.*. Only empirical data will bring conclusive evidence about what women are capable of, and that data must be actively sought. He believes that the empirical evidence sought by experimental method has nothing to do with hypotheses and assumptions, the "interrogation" of the world that shaped the experiment and might actively shape the results. Mill focuses solely on the empirical outcome generated by the experiment. That is, he simply denies the role of input and focuses on the outcome. The social scientist according to Mill is entirely passive.

In the second part of *Subjection of Women* Mill also believes he is offering only the facts. In this part he does not suggest accumulating sufficient data on women through experimental means, but utilizes the data that already exist—"women as they already are and are known to have been." He does not acknowledge that the facts he offers are meaningless unless he is willing to admit that they constitute a concept of women's nature. For unless "women as they are" can resist the influence of changed political circumstances, nothing can be established about what will happen as the result of liberating women. Thus in the first part of the book Mill is actually making a deductivist, or rationalist, argument ("women's nature is unknowable from the available evidence"), but he diverts attention from it by focusing on the evidence that *could* be gathered about women if they were permitted to test their powers in a number of circumstances. In the second part he really *is* making an inductivist argument based upon the facts at hand about women, but the facts again don't serve his political purpose, unless they also describe something immutable, something bigger, more abstract than merely discrete facts—in a word, a nature of women.

The epistemological confusion in *The Subjection of Women* parallels that in *A System of Logic*. The effort in both works is to diminish, to the greatest extent possible, the active role of the philosopher, logician, social scientist, and to ground knowledge in a world of objective facts. The problem is that the facts don't do anything by themselves: *they* really *are* passive. Unless the social theorist is willing actively to intervene, objective evidence just lies there: it constitutes no basis for a political argument of any sort. If the methodological difficulties in *A System of Logic* and *The Subjection of Women* are parallel, so are the substantive conclusions. In *A System of Logic* Mill argues for a hegemony of intellect in any society, the assumption being that the most rationally trained society is the most "advanced." In *The Subjection of Women* it is clear from Mill's discussion in the final chapter that educated women of certain moral habits are really the ones he is thinking about. They are the ones who stand to double the intellectual capabilities of society and serve as inspiration for the young men.

What renders Mill's method in both *The Subjection of Women* and *A System of Logic* inadequate as a vehicle for explaining and justifying political change is the static relationship it assumes between subjects and objects. That aspect of *Subjection of Women* has already been discussed. In *A System of Logic* Mill is hampered as well by his view of the world as a mass of static data. He sees only truths *or* falsehoods, knowledge that is linear and cumulative: the more data, the more truth. In his world, subjectivity is minimized. Although the words subjectivity and objectivity are hardly mentioned in either work, in both Mill does everything he can to remove the active idiosyncratic presence of the one who seeks knowledge, and to place the basis of knowledge in a tangible world, outside himself. The facts are there to be gathered by anyone who possesses a rational mind (although given one thousand pages of flamboyant self-contradiction in the *Logic,* one wonders what "rational" could possibly mean to Mill). There is a sterility to Mill's conception of knowledge: it has nothing to do with the particular human being who is engaged in its pursuit.

At the same time that the subjective role of the "scientist" is denied, his effect on what he studies is also denied. Hence in *The Subjection of Women,* while women seemed to be released to do whatever they wish to compete with men, to prove themselves, the implication that they are part of an experiment controlled and judged by men is invisible. The conclusion of *A System of Logic* contains the same problem: the advanced cultures of the world are the ones that are intellectually developed. Mill's standards of intellectual development are thoroughly subjective—they are his own—and not acknowledged as such. Presumably he will judge which cultures are indeed advanced.

The vocabulary of subjectivity and objectivity has been introduced for a specific reason. We discussed the problems feminists have experienced with the terms; some have argued that they reflect a dichotomized worldview that will inevitably isolate women from men, nation from nation, emotion from rationality, private from public life. The terms subjectivity and objectivity and the outlook they reflect have been presumed destructive to harmony, community, and intimacy in the world, and probably reflect a singularly male perspective.

Although Mill doesn't make use of the terms, I think the central problem with *A System of Logic* is the dichotomization of internal and external, mind and world, subjective and objective, in a way that is recognizable to the feminists concerned about dichotomization and objectification. Mill's methodology stands as an example of precisely the problems that have concerned contemporary feminist theorists. The pretense of objectivity is everywhere, while subjective involvement is denied.

Each time Mill edges up on the likelihood of an assumption or any active responsible role for the observer he balks, finding a way to express his fervent hope that no social scientist need contaminate his data with his own personality or political preferences. The acrobatics called for in order to preserve this illusion become ever more spectacular as *A System of Logic* drones on. The contradiction in the title "Concrete Deductive Method" is sufficient indication of the impossibility of Mill's quest.

Whatever grievance I might have against Mill is not that subjectivity and objectivity represent an entirely false dichotomy, or that the world is after all unified. I believe there is a problem with the relationship between subjectivity and objectivity, with the relationship between mind and the external world, and Mill's gyrations reflect his struggle *not* to acknowledge that any such problem exists. Splitting the world into static subjects and objects is the only way he can avoid addressing the conflict between the two perspectives. The contradictions in Mill's treatise reflect a denial of a conflict that cannot be avoided. Ironically enough, while the wish for consensus causes Mill to split the world, to keep inner and outer as far apart as possible, that same wish causes feminist theorists to leap at the universality of women's more unified, less dichotomized perspective. I think denial of the problem between mind and the world, self and other, consciousness and history, subjectivity and objectivity, is as dangerous to history and philosophy as any psychological denial is to the individual. The repressed is bound to return, and the conflict had better be acknowledged and looked at carefully, before consensus can be considered at all.

Dialectical theory, represented by but not limited to Hegel and Marx, offers a dramatically different perspective on the relationship between mind and the world, and one with more promise than Mill provides for a theory of political change, of feminist change. If Hegelian and Marxian dialectics circumvents the logical difficulties Mill encountered, acknowledges a problem between thought and action, and still makes it possible to act, to change the world, then it is worth looking into. If nothing else, it may be useful in conserving effort and preventing the further isolation of feminists, an isolation that is driving them to an attempt to rewrite all philosophy and metaphysics specifically for feminist theory.

CHAPTER 5

HEGELIAN DIALECTICS

I. HEGELIAN OBJECTIVITY AND SUBJECTIVITY

In this and the chapter to follow, we turn to an investigation of Hegelian and Marxian dialectics. The point is not to champion Hegel and Marx as saviors of feminist theory. Rather the effort is to liberate the structure of dialectical method from the particular substance of Hegel's and Marx's theories and to assess the utility of that structure itself for the feminist project. My argument is that two things distinguish dialectical epistemology from Mill's brand of empiricism: (1) the assumption that subjectivity and objectivity are not static concepts but are interpenetrable and mutually self-defining, and (2) the assumption that everything in the world is constantly changing and developing, which permits the interpenetration of subjectivity and objectivity. That is, dialectical method is fundamentally historical in outlook.

Hegelian and Marxian dialectics are not identical; indeed Marx considered himself to be responding to Hegelian dialectics and moving beyond it. He inverted Hegel's epistemological priorities, "stood Hegel on his feet," and tried to ground the Hegelian method in the material world. Hegel saw history as the movement of ideas; for Marx the movement of history is human activity. My project here is to consider whether that methodological core is of use toward the construction of an epistemology for feminism. Minimalist dialectics is proposed as a methodology that avoids the dangers of static empiricist objectivity as well as the specific substance of Hegelian and Marxian theory—for neither Hegel nor Marx was a feminist, and much of their substantive concerns can be regarded as antithetical to feminism.

In part also my project is to demonstrate that constructing an epistemology for feminism does not entail beginning from scratch. The purpose of considering and comparing existing methodologies, male methodologies, is to attempt to build a feminist theory that is not severed from the entire history of political thought (admittedly in this context, Western political thought). The terms or the building blocks for feminist epistemology already exist. Men and women do, from a certain perspective, live in the same metaphysical universe, and women need not invent an entirely new vocabulary or an entirely new philosophical system in order to be heard and understood. Utilizing, even appropriating, concepts used mostly by men actually may be politically compelling, demanding as it does that "the tradition" in Western political thought sit up and take notice. Feminist theory is not entirely new, not composed of a vocabulary and concepts that are incomprehensible to conventional political theorists. The "regulars" can hear feminists because feminists *do* speak their language. They have no excuse for ignoring us or pretending they don't understand.

With that political project in mind, it seems pertinent to lay out, as briefly as possible, the philosophical history that preceded the emergence of Hegelian and Marxian dialectics, and then to consider in some detail the structure and substance of the dialectical method.

Dialectical thought represents the first modern effort to reconcile the apparent incompatibility between the external world of materiality and the internal world of thought. Immanuel Kant's dialectic, which is more accurately called "idealist scepticism," marks the first effort at such a philosophy of unity, or philosophy of identity as the Hegelian dialectic is often referred to. Kant argued that knowledge would be impossible if thought and objects were not somehow integrally related. Without prior possession of some concept of "object," he reasoned, there could be no way to recognize objects in the world. If there is a link between English empiricism and the German dialectics that began with Kant, it is provided by David Hume. His empiricist scepticism may be regarded as an acknowledgement of the limitations of empiricist theory: if anything exists "beneath" what appears empirically, it is inaccessible to the human mind, and we might as well forget it. All knowledge *might as well* be regarded as empirical, with the acknowledgment that we are relinquishing claims to any deeper awareness of how the world or the universe works.[1]

Kant was influenced by Hume's theory. He too believed that human beings can know about only what appears to them: about *phenomena* (from the Greek φαίνω, appear). He also believed that there was more to know than that: there are essences— *noumena*. Everyone senses that the real truths lie beneath surface appearances. All thinking people hold ambitions to get at those deeper layers of truth, and because of the limitations inherent in human intellectual capabilities are doomed to be frustrated in their quest for absolute knowledge. Kant's stance is thus a form of idealist scepticism because he assumes that there is a point at which human knowledge reaches its limits. Yet he does not doubt that there is, indeed, an essential aspect to everything. He thus departs from Hume's sceptical contention that even if there were essences (universals, or noumena), they could not figure into a theory of knowledge because they would be inaccessible. The empiricist turns his back on essences if they are so tenaciously inaccessible. If phenomena are the only accessible form of truth, the question of essences, of a noumenal aspect to anything, is simply spurious.

Kant's theory diverged from this empiricism, but it also parted company with the traditional rationalist position. He agreed with Hume that phenomena are the basis of all knowledge, even while he assumed the existence of noumena as an aspect of the mind itself. The essences that he assumed to exist cannot ultimately be separated from their phenomenal forms. Thus metaphysical questions were not legitimate to Kant: "pure reason" is an illusion.[2] Kant may be regarded as the first modern philosopher to try to reconcile the epistemological dichotomies of the empiricist world. Everything has *both* an essential, or ideal, and an objective, or concrete, aspect. Our innate sense about the existence of absolutes is what permits us to understand anything about the objective world of concrete particulars. However, in spite of Kant's belief in the ultimate inseparability of essence and existence, his theory still assumes a divided world. His assumption that truths exist once and for all, but are tied to the empirical world, overlooks the reality of history, which belongs to the phenomenal world. If Kant would link essence and appearance, he must acknowledge that essences also change, responding in some way to appearances.

Thus the questions about activity and passivity concerning the relationship between mind and matter, the process of attaining knowledge, remain unaddressed in Kant's philosophy. Does the activity of the mind affect the world it perceives? Does the existence of *a priori* categories in the mind mean that recognition of the phenomenal world is primarily passive? Kant had done away with the notion that the mind is a blank page, but how does the "newly defined" mind actually get at the phenomena in the world? His philosophy was still constrained by the limitations of a static epistemology. He was the first to see subjectivity and objectivity as two aspects of the same reality, one with a face to the world, the other always turned away, like the dark side of the moon.[3]

It was Hegel who proposed a way out of the dichotomous aspect of even that view. Hegel saw the two aspects of reality as existing within one another, pushing or being pushed alternatively to the surface, to the realm of experience. For Hegel, knowledge of the objective or phenomenal aspect of anything is impossible without access to the noumenal or subjective aspect. The two aspects present themselves as moments in time, rather than as finite "sides." He thus rejects the limitations Kant places on the possibility of knowledge: without knowledge of both noumena *and* phenomena there is no knowledge at all. Hegel's perspective on the relationship between essence and existence is thus fundamentally historical. He argued that the world presents knowledge historically, developing in conjunction with the world as a series of perspectives, alternately subjective and objective. The experience of one disappears into the other, actually begets the other as knowledge through time becomes ever more "complete."

The terms *subjectivity* and *objectivity* take on new importance and new meaning in Hegel's epistemology. In a sense, the centrality of the terms for dialectical thought are a clue to the potential relevance of dialectical methodology for feminist theory. The terms in a variety of forms have, with disastrous political results, been applied to women, and in general to groups that have not had access to power and influence in liberal capitalist society. Women and people of color have been objectified. They have been made sexual objects or subjects of social scientific inquiry: "the woman problem," "the race problem," "the Jewish question." The assumption is that these groups *are* the problem—*not* that they themselves may *have* a problem with dominant culture, as that would call for the admission that they are subjects capable of thought and action. Objects in this sense are passive; subjects are active. Yet at the same time that women have a problem because they are a problem—are regarded as objects by objective scientific observers—they are also accused of being too subjective (as indeed are most men of color). Women don't think "straight," they are incapable of "hard-headed" logic. They allow their feelings to wander (circular, full of curves and switchbacks), to become mixed with perception, which compromises their ability to observe in a detached, straightforward, objective manner. Women are idiosyncratic and operate on the basis of unfathomable inner motivations, instead of responding to objects outside them. They are soft and internal; men are hard, straight, and external.[4]

Close examination of the dialectical use of subjectivity and objectivity, in contrast to the empiricist usage, will demonstrate the possibility of retaining the terms in a manner that does not divide the world, does not sever inside from outside, rationality from passion, thought from action. I begin with Hegel because the political substance of his theory seems from a feminist standpoint to be so unpromising. Examination of his use of the terms will demonstrate potential that goes beyond the specific substance he gave them and even perhaps beyond his control over the implications of his method. We begin with the etymology and ordinary usage of the terms subjectivity and objectivity.

What do subjectivity and objectivity mean? The Oxford English Dictionary (*OED*) devotes pages to the words. Both come from the Latin: *Object* translates literally as something "thrown in or at," and *subject* means something "thrown beneath." The first two listings for *object* are "a statement thrown in or introduced in opposition," and "something 'thrown' or put in the way so as to interrupt or obstruct the course of a person or thing; an obstacle; a hindrance"; the third listing is literally a "material thing": "something placed before the eyes, or presented to the sight or other sense, an individual thing seen or perceived." This is the sense in which an object is empirical: available to human experience (from the Greek ἐμπειρία, experience).

The *OED* also lists two senses in which objects are both external to, and passive: "That to which action, thought or feeling is directed; the thing (or person) to which something is done... the end to which effort is directed; the thing aimed at...." The term is correlated (or contrasted) to the "knowing subject" in the sense that an object is "something external to the mind; the non-ego as related to, or distinguished from, the ego." Finally, the *OED* lists a grammatical sense of object: "A substantive word, phrase, or clause, immediately dependent on, or 'governed by' a verb as expressing, in the case of the verb, action, the person or thing to which the action is directed."

In sum, object means pretty much what we would expect it to: something external—material, or tangible, or perceptible; something passive, receiving action. It has associations with something egoless, unthinking, inactive.

Subject is a little more complicated. It is derived from Latin, but also has associations with the Aristotelian ὑποκείμενον, something lying beneath, used in Greek as a subject of discourse, rather than ὑποχείρ, political subject. There are also specialized uses of the term *subject:* scientific, medical, physiological, and pathological uses, and a special derivation from Kant's use of the word.

The original usages were political: someone under the dominion of a monarch or prince, and then one "bound to" any superior "by an obligation to pay allegiance, service, or tribute." Third, in this group of definitions, a person (and, rarely, a thing) "that is in the control or under the dominion of another; one who owes obedience to another." The original meaning of *subject* was thus passive, not active. It referred to someone under somebody else's control. The modern philosophical usage has come to mean someone active, which is compatible with the grammatical sense: the agent of the verb in a sentence. Philosophically, this becomes a "conscious or thinking subject; the mind as the 'subject' in which ideas inhere. That to which all mental representations or operations are attributed; the thinking or cognizing agent; the self or ego." This is a word with an interesting history. It has meanings that are nearly contradictory: a political subject lying beneath and owing tribute to a ruler, and a thinking, active agent: an ego.

Kant provided philosophical respectability for subjectivity as a necessary aspect of truth. The *OED* cites the Kantian subject as "subjective existences: either parcel of the understanding or ideas which the understanding knows by itself alone." The Kantian meaning slides into a usage that is most unscientific, however: "Pertaining or peculiar to an individual subject or his mental operations; depending upon one's individuality or idiosyncracy; personal, individual." This association with idiosyncracy or individualism is in turn related to the physiological and pathological usage: "Due to internal causes and indiscoverable by oneself alone; said of sensations, symptoms, etc." A contradictory collection of meanings. How has it come to be used in contemporary ordinary language?

Ordinary language usage echoes the etymology of the words. In the modern age, scientific objectivity calls for facts, data, evidence from the empirical world, while subjectivity has been associated with feelings and perceptions originating in the mind or heart of a human subject. Objectivity implies necessity; subjectivity implies the idiosyncracy of an agent. Objective truths, then, originate with empirical data in the material world; subjectivity originates in the mind of the thinker.

Using the terms objectivity and subjectivity to signify where a truth originates—in this case inside or outside the mind—soon becomes troublesome. For example, if an objective truth is a necessary truth, how is the necessity recognized? Does it present itself, inevitably, to a subject? We must assume that the subject who "receives" the truth is a human subject, an agent, and prone to idiosyncracy in terms of the dichotomy just presented. However, idiosyncracy usually implies neither passivity nor predictable activity. It is not easily associated with the idea of a passive recipient to undeniable truth, or with predictable (or rational?) activity, which would necessitate the subject recognizing the truth as such.

No sooner, then, have we introduced the terms *subjectivity* and *objectivity* to inform us about the origin of a type of truth—inside or outside the mind—than we have the problem of how inside and outside interact with one another. We are immediately presented with a problem of activity and passivity. This line of thinking may also present some question about whether it makes sense to refer to subjective thoughts as true at all. What are the standards for evaluating what is "subjectively true"? If subjectivity refers to idiosyncracy, or at least acknowledges the validity of experience as such, unreflected upon by any standards other than one's own, must every experience be regarded as equally valid, hence equally true? And doesn't this violate the ordinary meaning of truth?

Even granting that subjective thoughts (whether true or not) originate in the mind of the agent while objective truths originate in the world outside, what are we to do with logical truth? In the terms just presented, logical truths are neither objective nor subjective. Although they seem to originate in the mind of the philosopher or the logician, they are not idiosyncratic but the essence of philosophical necessity. Logical truth is independent of both the tangible world of objects and the idiosyncratic world of subjects; hence logic is a sense in which an objective, "necessary" truth is independent of the world of tangible objects. Logicians seldom use the terms *objectivity* and *subjectivity* in association with truth. *Analytic* and *synthetic* are the terms favored in the context of logic, and may be useful in providing a perspective that frees us momentarily from the confines of objectivity and subjectivity. However, the problem of how to think about the relationship between the mind and the world persists, no matter what terms we use. For when the analytic *a priori* truths of conventional logic are regarded as possessing a necessary relation with the world of objects, we have the puzzle of "synthetic *a priori*" truths, the concept Kant invented and sought to explain. How is it that we recognize truth in the world at all is the question answered by the synthetic a priori.

It may be helpful to think of the terms *subjectivity* and *objectivity* as representing different perspectives on the same problem—the problem of the mind's relation to the world—and only by the most determined concentration can the distinctness of their perspectives be maintained, so ready are they to collapse into one another. They are like the two images of a child's wiggle-picture: the slightest movement of hand or eye presents the contrary image. This problem was evident when we noticed how quickly the distinction between the terms gave rise to a question about their relationship to one another, the problem of "activity and passivity."

The difficulty of separating the terms is not limited to the epistemological sense of subjectivity and objectivity. In at least two additional senses of the terms, we encounter similar difficulties. The grammatical model parallels the epistemological one in that a subject is active and an object "receives the action," is passive. That seems simple enough when a conventional verb of action is used: the dog bit the man. Simply supplying the verb *know,* however, is enough to evoke all the epistemological problems encountered earlier: the subject knows the object, but how? Does the object lie there passively while the subject attacks it, or devours it, investigates it, or circles around it sniffing? At what point during these possible acts does the subject decide that it knows the object? Must the object contribute something to make itself known to the subject? For example, perhaps a theory must "make sense" to a person (subject) before that person can be said to know the theory. Or a person (object) must "look familiar" to another person (subject) before the subject person can be said to know the object person. Even granting that "to know" is an active verb of the same sort as "to hit," the epistemological question still remains: is what is known objective truth, by reference to the object known, or "subjective truth" because the subject is the one who knows? Put another way, is what the subject knows objective or subjective? Separating the two concepts seems a fleeting and abstract endeavor; no sooner is a verb supplied than the two become interdependent.

A vivid example of the confusion of the two senses of the terms appears when we consider the concept of "objective proof," the sort associated with scientific method. Objective proof relies upon the assumption that there is a world of objects, independent of any particular observers. The objective truth to be gathered in such a world remains objective only so long as the observation does not interfere with it. The imposition of the scientists' preconceptions or idiosyncracies is enough to "contaminate" the perception of data. How then can the subject gather the data? Perhaps the subject or the sense perceptions of the subject must remain *passive* in order to "receive" the data, in which case ... what? Are the objects then the active terms, presenting themselves to the subjects? Scientific objectivity on an empirical model would thus depend upon interaction between active objects and passive subjects, which is impossible by grammatical definition. Even more bizarre is the possibility that empirical truth, which relies upon the assumed separability of subject and object, forecloses the possibility that *either* subject or object can possibly be active in relation to the other.

Now consider the political sense of the terms. A "political subject" has already been mentioned. One thinks conventionally of "the king's subjects," and even of "the subjects of a state" without necessarily invoking the mystical Hegelian subject. Object also has a modern political sense, encountered more often in the form of objectification. Perhaps a "political object" exists only as a departure from a more natural state of some sort—political subjectivity? In other words, perhaps there are no political objects as such but only political subjects and the political *problem* of objectification.

Still the problem of activity and passivity remains. Are political subjects active? It doesn't seem that subjects in the political sense are as active as they are in the grammatical sense. They are *subjected* to political rule. If being objectified has something to do with being made a thing, an object, and therefore passive, what is the relationship between (passive) political subjects and (passive) political objects?

Indeed, there are ways in which subjects and objects are used that defy the grammatical and epistemological conventions regarding subjects as active, and objects as passive. Political subjects usually seem to be passive subjects. There is also the passive sense of "being subject to," e.g. an undesired event. A "subject of study" is also a passive subject. Likewise, one can "object to" something quite vigorously, i.e. actively. What is the relationship between, for example, an "object of one's inquiry," or even an "object to be studied," and the aforementioned Aristotelian subject of study? In sum, a cluster of usages composes a nucleus of meaning: epistemological, grammatical, and political subjectivity and objectivity. The relationship between active and passive uses of the terms creates some difficulty in understanding the relationship between all three cases.

∂&

When Hegel uses the terms subject and object, all of the senses outlined above seem inappropriate. His use of the terminology is specialized, as though he were inventing new uses for the terms, a new way of thinking that defies more ordinary usage, although Kantian subjectivity may be regarded as a precursor to Hegelian subjectivity. A subject is abstract to begin with, and must pass through an objective stage before it properly knows itself as subjectivity. That knowledge of itself is in turn recognized as incomplete, and the subject continues its path of development through a series of moments of loss and recapture of objective self. Finally an all-inclusive merging of subjects and objects in universal self-consciousness is achieved. This is "absolute knowledge" or "absolute universality," or "the idea."

A closer look at Hegel's use of the terminology is a priority here. Focusing on the terms *subjectivity* and *objectivity* may permit discussion of his ideas about the growth of knowledge and self in a manner that permits comparison with the vocabulary of liberal empiricism. It is difficult to talk about Hegel's epistemology without making use of the terms *subject* and *object,* but equally difficult to use those terms in a conventional way: for Hegel the terms have distinct identities only by virtue of their participation in a process in which they become the opposite of what they were. During the process, the moments of subjectivity and objectivity become manifest. In an initial "moment" of abstraction, only an empty shell of awareness exists. This moment, which Hegel calls subjective, resembles the empiricist view of objectivity: where subject and object are distinct and appearances are regarded as "reality." The next Hegelian moment involves loss of the boundaries between subject and object. Engagement, involvement, or activity characterizes this stage of knowledge. "Knower" (or subject) is lost, merged with the object of knowledge, without the perspective that comes from detachment. From an empiricist standpoint, it would be appropriate to regard such a moment as subjective, for subjectivity *is* loss of awareness of oneself as an entity, with the likelihood that one's idiosyncratic needs will distort perception of the data. The empiricist standpoint assumes the perspective of a human subject who is either aware of the border between self and object and keeps personal preferences in check (in an objective moment) or who is unaware of it and cannot control the intrusion of personal preferences (in a subjective moment).

For Hegel, a moment in which the initially abstract subject loses itself to the objective world in order to "actualize" or "realize" its desires may be called a moment of objectivity. Calling such a moment objective does not imply that it is truer than the initial subjective moment, or that it is complete in any sense. Hegel's initial moment of subjectivity was abstract because it remained uninvolved in the concrete world; it was a moment of impulse but also of impulse separated from actuality. His second moment involves the experience of limits, of the finitude of the objective world. One's subjective impulse is tested; the reality of the objective world may render actualization of the impulse impossible. Only by risking all do impulses have a chance of becoming realized. The risk involved is simply that when one begins to act one has no control over the exact outcome of one's action. Hence subjective impulses must be relinquished to the objective world.

A third moment involves reflection upon the action, upon the worldly test of initial impulse. This moment appears to involve withdrawal from the world of objects, a separation between subject and the objective world, while the subject reflects, but in Hegelian terms, it is *not* an objective moment. It is another moment in which the subject is drawn in upon itself: a subjective moment. For Hegel, the subjective moment is abstract in the sense that it is unengaged. The objective moment is concrete in the sense that it involves the integration of subject and objective world: it is real.

It may be useful to try to understand Hegel's sense of objective and subjective moments by using the terms *abstract* and *concrete,* but once again the endeavor leads one into conflict with conventional definitions of subjectivity and objectivity. In ordinary (empiricist) terms, moments of objectivity are moments of separation between subject and object, while subjective moments are moments when the subject is "lost" in the object, i.e. without perspective. Moments of empiricist objectivity are thus more abstract than moments of empiricist subjectivity. For the empiricist, the word *objectivity* takes its meaning from the reliability of the tangible world of objects, detached from subjective perception. Hegelian objectivity, on the other hand, takes its meaning from the moment when objects dominate, that is, when the subject is lost to the world of objects. *Abstract* in both the Hegelian and empiricist senses means detached from the world of objects, but abstract is a characteristic of objectivity for the empiricist and subjectivity for Hegel. *Abstract* implies truth to the empiricist, and incompleteness to Hegel.

For Hegel, knowledge will not be complete until it achieves its culminating historical moment of absolute knowledge, which is the integration of subjectivity and objectivity. Objective and subjective, abstract and concrete, are simply terms describing moments on the journey toward truth. Truth itself is neither subjective nor objective, neither abstract nor concrete.

Understanding Hegelian subjectivity and objectivity is further complicated because unlike empiricists Hegel does not ground his philosophy in human experience (an aspect of Hegel's thought of which Marx is critical), so there is no single perspective assumed. Rather people, actions, events and ideas constitute all of world history, which is progressing (even with apparently chaotic moments and setbacks) toward a culmination of absolute understanding and self-conscious spiritual unity. It is not the people, or even one person, who will "be" or "possess" this understanding. Because human beings are not the central subjects in Hegelian thought, there is real difficulty knowing what verbs to use when writing about Hegelian theory. The grammatical definitions of subject and object discussed earlier do not have obvious applicability in Hegelian thought because the interpenetrability of subjectivity and objectivity means that subjects will all have moments when they are "putting in their time" as objects, and vice versa. Because people are not the only subjects, and all subjects are also momentarily objects, things ordinarily regarded as nonactive have their moments of activity. This creates the familiar but rather eccentric Hegelian grammar. The difficulty is not simply that abstractions and objects are regarded as possessing the capacity for action, but there are sentences in Hegel's writing in which there is also no conventional recipient of action, let alone conventional active subject.

Consider a sample of verbs used in conjunction with various Hegelian concepts in *Philosophy of Right* (emphasis added):

The particular *is contained in* the universal. (§6)

Insofar as intelligence *thinks,* its object and content *remains* something universal, while its own behavior *consists* of a universal activity. (§13)

By *resolving,* the will *posits itself* as the will of a specific individual and as a will *separating itself off* against another individual. (§13)

When reflection *is brought to bear* on impulses, they are *imaged,* estimated, compared, with one another.... (§20)

The will *is* then universal because all restriction and all particular individuality *have been absorbed* into it.... (§24)

The universal ... *overlaps* its object, *penetrates* its particular determination through and through and therein *remains* identical with itself. (§24)[5]

What is odd about these sentences is not so much that abstractions are regarded as active while objects conventionally understood are given the capacity for subjectivity. Rather there are no conventional actors or recipients of action at all. Both subjects and objects are enormously abstract, and yet there is a sense of urgency, even high drama. Various intangibles are "contained," "separated off," "brought to bear," "absorbed," "overlapped," and "penetrated." The language is almost sexual,[6] and yet the participants in this romance are "the universal," "the particular," "the will," "reflection" and "intelligence." The reader who relishes a happy ending to a love story may be gratified when "the universal," after "penetrating" the particular "through and through," decides, like a gentleman, to "remain."

The point is that it is difficult to do justice to Hegel's concepts without using his language structure and his terms. The only way, for example, one can understand what universality is, is to see universality in action, as it were, to look for what Hegel says universality does, and in relation to what. One cannot understand *the will* as a thing, or as a static abstract concept, but must look at what Hegel says will *does.*

II. MASTER AND SERVANT

Why should a feminist care about Hegel's overly specialized views of the terminology? Surely feminist theory does not need to adopt ready-made concepts, especially ones not even in keeping with ordinary usage? Contemporary feminist thought has backed away from dualisms and dichotomies, and objectification has been considered one of the chief culprits. However, objectification and objectivity are not the same words. If objectivity and objective truth are suspect categories to feminists, the problem may be guilt by linguistic association. To avoid the very concept of objectivity because women have been its victims is to surrender far too much. Likewise, the acceptance of subjectivity as somehow less destructive to feminist theory is equally limiting and worthy of question. Indeed, to accept one term as more appropriate to women while rejecting the other is a dichotomizing move in itself, whose dangers are both political and philosophical. Politically speaking, to accept an epistemologically one-sided view of femininity is to lock women into a history that has been regarded as oppressive. If the inability to be objective is associated with the inability to participate in public and political life, then to accept the term *subjective* as more descriptive of women is to acquiesce in that exclusion. Furthermore, agreeing that women may be characterized as more subjective than men leads to the question of a specifically feminine nature. How did women get to be more subjective? Is it a cause or a result of centuries of exclusion from public life? If it is a cause, it may be a characteristic of "feminine nature," in which case further investigation into this nature is appropriate. If it is a result of oppression and exclusion throughout millennia, it is nothing to celebrate and would presumably change, given a change in women's social and political situation.

Presenting a dilemma along these lines is, of course, overly simplistic. It is unlikely that causality works in such a linear fashion. One way to avoid the thorny and probably unsolvable question of a feminine nature is a compromise hypothesis: women have been excluded from public life for any number of reasons, none of which is particularly important now, but which have created certain tendencies among women, different than those among men. Women have *become* more subjectivistic, meaning inner, idiosyncratically responsive, less inclined to be detached, and so forth. Then, surely, those tendencies, associated with women, became an excuse for further exclusion until the question of feminine nature became a moot point. Such a line of reasoning can support the viewpoint now fashionable among some feminists that no matter how women became more subjective than men, subjectivity is a valuable and underrated aspect of life: perhaps even better than the detached, rationalist or materialist objectivity. Therefore, it should be recognized and incorporated into our public as well as private values. There is, however, something philosophically unsatisfactory about such a line of thinking. It *accepts* a dichotomized view of subjectivity and objectivity without looking carefully at what the terms mean or what the more complex relationships between them might be.

If the question of nature is avoided simply by saying "it doesn't matter anymore," feminist theory runs a risk of shallowness. True, the question of human nature and a "state of nature" are no longer central to political theory in general. Since the nineteenth century the concept of nature has been subsumed by a mode of thinking steeped in the material world. Nature is regarded as an abstraction. Marx, for example, uses "species life" to refer to an essential human life, but life to Marx is a historical product. Human beings are essentially productive (creative), social, and conscious beings, but Marx does not believe that those characteristics constitute human nature. Likewise, Hannah Arendt refers to the "human condition" and explicitly denies that she means to refer to a human nature. She also insists that there are particular aspects to life that are essentially human. If the most powerful theoretical minds of the modern age do not refer to nature, at least in the sense of origins, or something immutable about human life, why should feminist theorists not also be able to avoid the term?

There is one obvious reason why feminist theory *should* address the question of nature, and it is political more than philosophical. The assumption of a feminine nature is one of the most powerful arguments against the possibility of radical change in the role women have played in history. "How did women get oppressed in the first place?" is a question that invariably evokes responses from the standpoint of nature: women were encumbered with childbearing and still are; men are physically bigger and stronger, etc. John Stuart Mill, as we saw, tried unsuccessfully to dismiss the importance of nature and particularly feminine nature. His conclusions, however, were grounded in the implicit assumption of immutable feminine characteristics. Feminists must confront questions about the origins of women's oppression without becoming chained to an abstract concept of an unchangeable human nature.

I believe that dialectical thinking, in both its Hegelian and its Marxian forms, provides a way of dealing with these difficult questions without the danger of dichotomization or of destructive labeling. The terms *subjectivity* and *objectivity* have meaning in dialectical thought, and at the same time are not ultimately separable from one another. They are more properly regarded as moments, aspects of the same phenomenon, each of which is descriptive and meaningful, but only in relation to the other. Objectivity is not an entity: it describes a relationship between people and the world. So does subjectivity. The terms are useful for addressing the problematical relationship between mind and the physical world. Through dialectical thought the world is seen as both pluralistic and unified. The choice is not between a world with no distinctions at all and a world of dichotomies. Rather a dialectically conceived world is one where anyone who looks carefully and thoughtfully can see *both* the connections and the distinctions, the intangibility and the tangibility of thought and life, and will recognize the inconclusiveness of a detached, Archimedean perspective. This method for looking upon the world from within it makes it impossible to imprison nature in a primitive past. Nature *is* people and therefore develops along with people and the rest of the material world. This permits, for example, removal of nature from the realm of the primitive and reestablishment of the term as an aspect of human history, even perhaps as the goal of human history.

In *Philosophy of Right* Hegel refers to the liberation of the individual as a "hard struggle against pure subjectivity of demeanor, against the immediacy of desire, against the empty subjectivity of feeling and the caprice of inclination" (§187). I take this "hard struggle" to be the essence of dialectical method. One must struggle against both the sense that the external world is outside of or opposed to the self, and also against the limitations, the finitude of merely subjective perception. Understanding has to do with a continual overcoming of what has already been accepted. There are no final truths about anything during this struggle. There is no authority of settled questions: one grows and gains knowledge only by continually risking oneself and what one knows.

To begin to see the possibilities of dialectics as a way of systematically deconstructing *and* reconstructing the obvious, consider Hegel's classic discussion of master and servant in *Phenomenology of Mind.*[7] Hegel's passages in "Master and Servant" are both dramatic and starkly schematic on the growth of self-knowledge and the relationship between self and world. He regards the quest for freedom, which *is* knowledge, as a "life and death" struggle. Is he referring to a combative, divisive approach to the world, a perspective hardly compatible with feminism? Is his philosophy a grand example of knowledge as heroics, as conquest? Such a view ignores another aspect of Hegel's theory. "Master and Servant" is a discussion of the inevitable dissolution of ego, which is a necessary prerequisite to growth, knowledge, freedom. It is a discussion of the ultimate impossibility of finite boundaries between one individual and another. It is, finally, a discussion of the impossibility of the persistence of inequality in any human relationship.

The border between self and other is so problematic in Hegelian thought that in the opening paragraphs of "Master and Servant" it seems barely to matter whether the struggle that takes place concerns two separate individuals or one. The first sentence of the section on master and servant seems to indicate that what is to follow is indeed about *two* "self-consciousnesses," two subjects, two people: "Self-consciousness exists in itself and for itself, in that, and by the fact that it exists for another self-consciousness; that is to say, it *is* only by being acknowledged or 'recognized.'"[8] One "exists" only if one is recognized by another.

The description of the "double self-consciousness" that follows creates a sense of wonder about whether Hegel is really referring to an internal dialogue with self or a confrontation between two people: "Self-consciousness has before it another self-consciousness; it has come outside itself. This has a double significance. First, it has lost its own self—because it finds itself as an *other* being; second, it has thereby sublimated that other, for it does not regard the other as essentially real, but sees its own self in the other" (399). Perhaps the other is another human being, who appears unreal only to the self. Is the other outside the self? Is Hegel talking about two people? In part it seems so: one is temporarily lost to another and must find some way back to a sense of self. "It must set itself to suspend the other independent being, in order thereby to become certain of itself as true being," but "secondly it thereupon proceeds to suspend its own self, for this other is itself" (400).

"Suspending the other" might sound like dominance or violence, but I think that such a conclusion is superficial. Think instead of this encounter in psychoanalytic terms: as identification and introjection. Even more dramatically, think of the encounter as falling in love: the desire both to "lose oneself" to the loved one and to make the loved one part of oneself. In some way, the beauty and the frustration of love is the desire of two souls to merge with one another, regardless of the actual physical impossibility. In spite of the desire to lose oneself in the person one loves, if such "loss" actually occurs the relationship isn't considered "love" so much as psychosis. True enough, in the early stages of love the other may be idealized: qualities may be projected that may in fact be one's ideal image of oneself. We also assume, however, that at some point one must "get hold of oneself," return to a sense of oneself as distinct from the loved one. That is not the end of love but the end of idealization or infatuation and the beginning, perhaps, of a love that can survive in the world. Consider, then, the process of losing oneself in infatuation and then "suspending the other." The imagery need not be regarded as violent, although it does involve the temporary destruction of ego boundaries.

From this perspective Hegel *is* talking about two people. Up to this point, however, the discussion has been one-sided. The second subject has really been treated as an object, used by the first subject, in a "game" of the development of the first self. There is no thought that the object might possess its own life and subjectivity. The encounter is "safe" in the sense that any subjectivity on the part of the other is not really engaged; one might as well be projecting one's love onto a blank screen or a lifeless object such as property. In Hegel's dialectic, however, the encounter becomes human, and dangerous, because the interaction between human subjects is invariably mutual. Each attempts both to "get outside of itself" and to "get hold of itself." Only through an encounter with another active human subject can such a test of self-consciousness, such dialectical loss and regaining of self, take place.

> This action on the part of one has itself the double signifi-
> cance of being at once its own action and the action of the
> other as well. For this other is likewise independent, shut up
> within itself, and there is nothing in it which is not there
> through itself. . . . The process then is absolutely the double
> process of both self-consciousnesses. (400)

The idea that one really knows oneself only through recognition of another human being, that is, the "double self-consciousness," is endemic to dialectical thought. The world of material objects is insufficient for the task of providing mutuality of recognition. Although in dialectical thought the borders of material objects are "open" in the sense that they can be infused with human will and provide in return the experience of being in the world, they cannot provide recognition that contributes to the development of human self-consciousness. Unlike the case of an encounter with an inanimate object, the other human self-consciousness *is actually a subject.* The two self-consciousnesses *appear* as objects to each other in the initial moment of their encounter, but such a misconception is destined to change as self-conscious subjectivity asserts itself: "But the other is also a self-consciousness; an individual makes its appearance in antithesis to an individual" (401).

An unreflected, untested sense of self is without truth. Without risking continuity of self and other, self-consciousness has no viability. Before encountering another subject, "each is indeed certain of its own self, but not of the other, and hence its own certainty of itself is still without truth" (402). Truth, as regards human beings, can never be self-contained but requires mutual recognition. Without the loss of pure self-containment, "its truth would be merely that its own individual existence for itself would be shown to it to be an independent object." With mutual recognition, however, comes the awareness that "as the other is for it, so it is for the other" (402).

"Mutual recognition" is not a benign look of acknowledgement from another human being. The interaction between two individuals must on some level be threatening before it can be anything else. Before the borders between people can dissolve, they must be acknowledged. There can be no hasty assumption of the possibility of communication, no romantic merging of souls without recognition of a problem. People are individuals, and they strive to be more than that. Unity comes only with risk. This is a different conception of the relationship between subject and object, or self and other, than either rigid individualism or subjectivist denial of any problem about borders between people. The very existence of an other is initially regarded as threatening. With characteristic drama, Hegel argues that the struggle for self-certainty must be experienced as a life-and-death struggle. One's "certainty of self" is threatened from without by the existence of another subject and also from one's own objective bodily existence. Each tests self against the other.

> The process of bringing all this out involves a two-fold action—action on the part of the other and action on the part of itself. In so far as it is the other's action each aims at the destruction and death of the other. But in this there is implicated also the second kind of action, self-activity; for each implies that it risks its own life. The relation of both self-consciousnesses is in this way so constituted that they prove themselves and each other through a life-and-death struggle. (402)

Hegel continues in this vein, perhaps sounding like a territorializing, sword-rattling male: "The individual who has not staked his life, may, no doubt, be recognized as a person; but he has not attained the truth of this recognition as in independent self-consciousness. In the same way, each must aim at the death of the other, as it risks its own life thereby; for that other is to it of no more worth than itself; the other's reality is presented to the former as an external other, as outside itself; it must cancel that externality" (403). Is he really talking about physical combat? Does this language of combat confirm feminist suspicions about all male theory as inherently dichotomizing, objectifying, and imperialistic? How can a theorist who presents self-knowledge as combat have anything to contribute to feminist theory?

If we allow Hegel his rhetorical style and contain our impulse to be offended by the imagery of warfare, it is possible to see the high drama of his desperate attempt to capture for a moment a fleeting and elusive reality. The arrogance of the empiricist claim that the objective world stands still for examination is impossible for Hegel: without challenging the certainty of the boundaries of one's own ego, there is no possibility of truth. "There is nothing present but what might be taken as a vanishing moment—that self-consciousness is merely pure existence, being-for-itself" (403).

The argument Hegel is making is not about victory over an object, or another human being. It is not an arrogantly self-confident argument about the inevitability of truth. If there is a "victory" in this drama, it is over the self. Hegel is writing about the fragility of self and the dependence of human beings upon one another for self-knowledge, for "mutual recognition." Life and knowledge are serious endeavors that must be worked at. He insists in these pages that the goal is not to die in struggle, or to kill the other. One's survival does not depend upon the death of the other. However, the language of life and death can be understood if we appreciate how seriously Hegel takes the struggle. "Self-consciousness becomes aware that *life* is as essential to it as pure self-consciousness" (404). Not only must one stay alive; life—corporeal, physical life—is inseparable from consciousness. One lives in the world; one's ideas are of the world; both life and thought are achieved through engagement. One must become involved with what one wants to know about. The lofty distance of the "objective observer" has no place in Hegel's thought.

Testing one's defenses, risking obliteration of the internal world that one naturally constructs in order to maintain some emotional stability, challenging one's view of the world: all this must take place before it is possible to know one's real strength as a human being. This should not be confused with the procedures of fashionable "encounter groups," flirtation with and subtle adjustment to a safely confined worldview. Hegel's account is not about creating a drama, a hullabaloo about every emotional discomfort that may arise in a physically safe, probably boring existence. Hegel's life-and-death struggle cast as a psychological drama is a call for challenge to one's very approach to the world. The discussion of master and servant, if read as a metaphor for a struggle for consciousness, is about freedom from the shackles of one particular fix on the world. One's worldview must be shaken to its roots and rebuilt, perhaps reincorporating aspects of its former self, altered, or seen in a new light, but one must also dare to live with a new perspective. Perhaps a Freudian theorist would call such a struggle a revolt against the internalized perspective of one's parents: a revolt against the superego. It is a call to rebellion in the name of self. This is not to suggest that Hegel had in mind precisely a psychological struggle between, for example, the mentality of a parent and a child. However, even if one accepts that he was thinking of an "actual" master and servant, the liberation achieved by Hegel's servant is spiritual or emotional before it is physical or political; the defeat of the master is a defeat in terms of self-certainty.

Up to this point, we have been talking rather abstractly about an encounter between two self-consciousnesses. The implications for feminism may be better understood when we consider Hegel's explicit discussion of the actual master and servant. The impossibility of detached, objective consciousness provides the basis for Hegel's argument that mastery over another human being is ultimately a contradiction in terms.

Our probable first impression of the relationship between a master and a servant is that the master lives an apparently independent existence. He dominates his servant and, even more, is conscious of his control. The servant works in a world of objects, acting as a mediator between that world and the master. She does the physical work. "The master . . . who has interposed the servant between [the object] and himself, thereby relates himself merely to the dependence of the thing, and enjoys it without qualification and without reserve. The aspect of its independence he leaves to the servant, who labors upon it" (405).

From another perspective, it is the master who is dependent upon the servant, in the sense that the servant, whom the master regards as an object, confirms the master's existence as a subject. This is no earth-shattering observation: often people attempt to confirm themselves at the expense of others. However, confirmation of self by default of the other is bound to fail. It doesn't work well, psychologically speaking, because it renders one's sense of self-esteem dependent upon someone else's misfortune. It brings, at best, temporary relief from anxiety and always leaves one enslaved to the fortunes of another. It is, in fact, an avoidance of confrontation with the self. The master has assumed, in an unreflective way, that he is the "independent self-consciousness," while the servant is dependent.

In Hegelian terms, such rudimentary, untested consciousness will not prevail for two reasons. First, as in Hegel's other descriptions of the initial moment of self-certainty, it simply has no truth before it is tested in the objective world. The servant *is* that objective world to the master. "Each is indeed certain of its own self—but not of the other, and hence its own certainty of itself is still without truth" (402). The master is not master in any final way; his mastery must continue to grow and develop through challenge and reaffirmation, or it will die. He has been using the servant as an object and confirming his own independent subjectivity in that way. However, a human being needs another human being for recognition. Being the master calls for confirmation from another human being, but the human being from whom the master most urgently requires recognition in order to confirm his mastery is the servant, whom he has been treating as an object rather than as a human being. Only two possibilities are available to the master: (1) if the servant is *not* a human being with "its" own subjectivity, but rather an object, "it" is incapable of recognizing the master as master, hence the master is unsure of himself as master, and (2) if the servant *is* a human being, capable of providing recognition, then there is by definition mutuality, and the relation between master and servant is not a matter of definition or a foregone conclusion. Rather, the master really has a battle on his hands. His mastery must be challenged to the core before it can be confirmed. In either event (and of course the second is the true one), absolute mastery is a logical impossibility. The acknowledged humanness of the servant is a constant threat to the absolute subjectivity of the master. Furthermore, Hegel argues, this really puts the servant in the position of independence, or control of the relationship.

> It is evident that the object *servant* does not correspond to its notion; for, just where the master has effectively achieved rule, he really finds that something has come about quite different from an independent consciousness. It is not an independent, but rather a dependent consciousness that he has achieved.... The truth of the independent consciousness is accordingly the consciousness of the servant.... Just as the position of the master showed its essential nature to be the reverse of what it wants to be, so, too, the position of the servant will, when completed, pass into the opposite of what it immediately is: being a consciousness repressed within itself, it will enter into itself, and change around into real and true independence. (406, 407)

Hegel concludes his treatment of the master and servant with a more detailed look at the aspects of the servant's existence, which give him the capacity for independence: anxiety, and shaping and fashioning. Both phenomena operate by means of fear, which permeates the core of the servant's existence and forces her to find that last kernel of self-consciousness that can be depended upon to sustain life. It is also the mechanism that activates the struggle for freedom.

Anxiety in this context is the conscious experience of fear of death. This is a loss of control, a loss of the experience of subjectivity, a loss of self. One is aware of oneself only as an object; another person is the subject, the active defining force in one's world. In political terms, the objectification of the oppressed is a familiar enough theme in terms of members of a dominant culture not recognizing the humanity of the oppressed. The really destructive aspect, however, is the *self* definition of a member of an oppressed group in terms of the dominant group or culture. People of color, for example, may experience reality as whatever they believe white people define it to be and may denigrate their own experience as unworthy. Women may regard male experience as reality and deny that what happens to women and among women is legitimate experience on its own terms. Only a man, or a white person as the case may be, can legitimize an event or an experience.[9] In the Hegelian dialectic, the experience of loss of self, that anxiety, is prerequisite to the experience of freedom. It is a source of life and strength from which the master has forever excluded himself.[10]

One additional aspect of Hegel's discussion of master and servant makes evident the particular appropriateness of his discussion for people who have been excluded from "rationality" and decision making in history—that is, for women and minorities. The basis of true independent self-consciousness in these passages is physical, not abstract. Work in the material world is what provides the basis of the servant's freedom: "Through work and labor . . . this consciousness of the servant comes to itself" (408). The master is the one who has interposed the objects in the material world between himself and the servant. By that very act of making the material world into the servant's chains, the master provides a means by which the servant can find her own subjectivity, hence her own independence. The servant is, to begin with, in mortal fear for her life at the hands of the master. Her survival depends on doing the work (the concrete, physical work) the master bids her do. In working for the master through the mediation of the physical world, the servant is forced into direct confrontation with the physical world itself, while the master, in the same move that forces the servant into direct intercourse with the material world, deprives himself of both the necessity of such interaction and the confirmation of selfhood that accompanies mastery of the objective world. The physical reward of the fruits of the servant's labor is actually a pale reflection of the psychological (or metaphysical?) strength acquired in the experience of physical effectiveness. The servant is *forced* to work on the physical world, and forced to discover her own agency, effectiveness, subjectivity in relation to the world of objects. The master merely desires something, while the servant must produce it for the master. The master's desire is abstract, and he does nothing to make it concrete. The servant's activity bequeaths upon her the benefits of actually making the abstract concrete.

The servant is able to see in concrete form the infusion of subjective energy into an object, which then, independent of the master, permits the servant awareness of self as both object and subject. This involves overcoming fear of the object as an alien, external reality confronting her. In other words, it is not a foregone conclusion that the servant can perform the work she intends to do. In being cast back upon herself, summoning the courage to shape and mold the objective world, the servant "destroys this extraneous alien negative in the element of permanence and thereby becomes aware of being objectively for [her]self" (408).

By confronting both the objective world and her own fears about her capacity to influence that world, the servant is in a position to confirm her own subjectivity in a manner foreclosed to the master. "Thus precisely in labor where there seemed to be merely some outsider's mind and ideas involved, the servant becomes aware, through this rediscovery of himself by himself, of having and being a mind of his own" (409).

The fear that is the necessary prerequisite to freedom is the result of the servant's relationship with the master. The servant is forced back upon herself, has no alternative but to experience the desperation of having nothing left to lose. She must find herself or perish. The fear, the experience of desperation must be total: "If it has endured not absolute fear but merely some slight anxiety, the negative reality has remained external to it, its substance has not been through and through infected thereby. Since the entire content of its natural consciousness has not tottered and shaken, it is still inherently a determinate mode of being; having a 'mind of its own' (*der eigene sinn*) is simply stubbornness (*eigensinn*), a type of freedom which does not get beyond the attitude of the servant" (409).

The desperate fear at the hand of the master and the objective world is accessible only *to the servant;* it is not a possibility for the master. The political implications of such a perspective are enormous: ultimately oppression of another human being is impossible. The experience of servitude is itself the origin of the obliteration of the master. By definition, a human being possesses subjectivity, which cannot be destroyed; but the existence of the objective world is necessary in order to make that subjectivity viable. Treating another person as an object is enough to ensure that one's own subjectivity will be threatened in relation to that person. Subjectivity and objectivity are both necessary moments; freedom does not consist of the elimination of objectivity, or the arbitrariness of subjective impulse. To the extent that the "border" between subjectivity and objectivity is dynamic and permeable, the struggle can also take place internally, as a psychological battle.

There is danger, of course, that this argument may be used as an excuse for all sorts of actual, material oppression. It might be used to argue that actual enslavement pales in relation to the opportunities for psychological freedom provided by oppression itself. It almost sounds as though one should be grateful for being oppressed, for therein lies the only opportunity for freedom. I think such an interpretation is a distortion both of Hegel and of dialectical method. What makes Hegel a dialectician and not simply an idealist is that his method, if not his goals, incorporates the material world. He needs the material world for his dialectic to work: for history, spirit, the idea to have form. The materialism of Hegel's dialectic is apparent in the "Master and Servant" when he refers to the importance of "shaping and fashioning": working on the world. The importance of material actuality is evident in the introduction to *The Philosophy of History*[11] where he declares the chaos of unreflected history to be the prerequisite to reason. That the Owl of Minerva takes flight only at dusk indicates Hegel's belief that action must precede wisdom. In *Philosophy of Right,* his discussion of property in "Abstract Right" makes it apparent that soul and body are not separable. Spirit needs a corporeal, material vessel: "When I am alive, my soul (the concept and, to use a higher term, the free entity), and my body are not separated; my body is the embodiment of my freedom and it is with my body that I feel.... If another does violence to my body, he does violence to me" (§48). To use his discussion of master and servant as an apology for physical oppression is an outright distortion of the Hegelian dialectic.

III. MARRIAGE AND FAMILY

Hegel's section on "Master and Servant" is well known, and has been regarded as possessing radical potential by Marxists, if not by feminist scholars. My question is whether there is a relationship between the political substance of these particular passages and Hegel's dialectical method in general. The epistemological dimension of "Master and Servant" that seemed promising was the fragility of any one perspective on truth; the person who seeks knowledge must challenge herself, make herself vulnerable to the perspective of another before self-consciousness and truth are possible. The need for mutual recognition made possible the conclusion that masters are ultimately more dependent upon their servants for self-knowledge than vice versa.

Hegel's notion of truth includes the imposition of one's subjectivity on the world and threat to the subjective power from the objective world. Subjectivity is a *part* of Hegel's concept of absolute or universal truth. Regardless of whether Hegel's ends are hegemonic, his method toward those ends holds promise for feminist theory because the concept of objectivity is both challenged and retained. Neither subjectivity nor objectivity may be dispensed with in the search for truth. In this respect, the passages in "Master and Servant" are not unique in Hegel's work. There runs throughout, even in those passages that are less substantively or politically promising, the same dynamic.

Philosophy of Right is an example of Hegel's more conservative thought: on the surface at least, a justification for the bourgeois state and its supporting institution, the patriarchal family. It should thus serve as an appropriate test of the hypothesis that dialectical method itself is promising, independent of content. That is, if there is anything in *Philosophy of Right* that can be salvaged for feminist thought, it may instruct us about how, more precisely, dialectical method creates or contains its own radical potential, in spite of Hegel's political intentions.

In the introduction Hegel takes the reader carefully through the phases of dialectical thought, in preparation for his discussion of the development of human will. His project is to understand how human beings live in the world together, each with a particular will that is not necessarily compatible with the will of any other. His concern is with how individuals are bound together in civil society and ultimately in the state. The self must develop at the same time that society seems determined to restrict the growth of the self. Self seeks "infinity" while the social world must restrict the individual's will. The individual ego grows as a result of its confrontation with the need for restriction: "The ego determines itself in so far as it is the relating of negativity to itself" (§7).

The imperative to challenge borders and boundaries, to strive after infinity in the face of the finite objective world, is regarded by Hegel as the "ultimate spring of all activity, life and consciousness" (§7). Life itself may be described as a process in which finitude is challenged, in which the subjectivity of self and the objectivity of the world are pitted against one another. The clash between self and the world, the quest to overcome finitude and still live in the world may be considered the central dynamic running throughout all of Hegel's writings.

This is a complicated way of saying that in Hegelian thought a subject is not completely a subject until it has tested its will in the actual (objective) world—not just in imagination. For example, a baby is a subject and possesses voracious will. An adult has presumably learned something more about the restrictions the world places upon individual will. Thus it is the adult's will that we take more seriously. The intensity of the infant's demands constitutes a subjectivity appropriate for its age but still thoroughly undeveloped in terms of our understanding of human subjectivity. The initial subjectivity must get beyond its immature "formality." The will "determines itself" by "the process of translating subjective purpose into objectivity through the use of its own activity and some external means" (§8). Neither objectivity, which has something to do with the external world, nor subjectivity, which has something to do with the self, is complete as a description of the truth of the world. Rather, truth results from the interaction between the two. Moments of self-consciousness, truth, or universality occur when the subject has itself for an object. "This—the concept of the free will—is the universal which overlaps its object, penetrates its particular determination through and through and therein remains identical with itself" (§24).

For Hegel the external world is not static; subjects and objects do not dwell in "places," one inside, the other outside, nor are they terms that *describe* inside and outside places. For Hegel they have meaning only in relation to one another in a world where inside and outside are in constant flux. Thus the problem of whether one is active and the other passive, which we encountered with the more ordinary (empirical) usages of the words, makes no sense when contemplating Hegel's thought. Both are active, each capable of subsuming the other, hence both also passive. The question of which "dominates" and our sense that probably subjectivity dominates, is a question that concerns only "ends" in Hegelian thought. In the long run, his thought may be considered "subjectivist" in the conventional sense that intangibles—spirit, idea, understanding—dominate. Hegel, of course, would deny that his philosophy is subjectivist: the culmination of philosophy in "universal knowledge" or "absolute idea" signifies not subjectivism but the integration of subjectivity with objectivity, which, as discussed earlier, more closely resembles the Hegelian concept of objectivity.

Substantively *Philosophy of Right* is a description of the development of the individual subject in relation to the bourgeois state. The first part of the work on "Abstract Right" is a description of "arbitrary will." This will is abstract because it is a moment of subjectivity untested in the world. Subjectivity at this stage is a simple assertion of ego. It is the infant's "I want": abstract in Hegel's terms because the assertion comes from within, oblivious to the possibilities and limitations of the objective (external, concrete) world. That initial abstract subjectivity Hegel calls "personality," and personality, he says, is the "universal" form of subjectivity: one's subjective awareness of the need for more than "mere" subjectivity. It encompasses a quest for "infinitude," for freedom, and at the same time reflects awareness of actual "finitude." Personality is a starting point: a contradiction that must be played out. Private property is a necessary aspect that permits abstract will, or personality, to take a concrete form in the world. "Since my will, as the will of a person, and so as a single will, becomes objective to me in property, property acquires the character of private property; and common property of such a nature that it may be owned by separate

persons acquires the character of an inherently dissoluble partnership in which the retention of my share is explicitly a matter
of my arbitrary preference" (§46). He even goes so far as to criticize Plato's ideal state because it "violates the right of personality by forbidding the holding of private property" (§46).

According to Hegel, willing and attaining property are necessary for the development of personality because they involve
"recognizability by others" (§51). However, this is no simplistic
argument that "you are what you own." In Hegelian thought,
really making a thing one's own involves its relinquishment.
Property is used as an expression of one's will or subjectivity, but
one must then demonstrate that one's will is shackled to no particularity. To relinquish one's property is to demonstrate one's
freedom. In order to attain freedom, human subjectivity must
transcend the particularity of property; ownership of property is
no more static than anything else in Hegel's epistemology.
Accordingly, there are three stages of ownership: taking possession, use, and alienation or relinquishment. "These three are
respectively the positive, negative, and infinite judgements of the
will on the thing" (§46). While Hegel believes that the activity of
the will involves at least the temporary possession of property,
the will's freedom *from* property is actually the goal of all life
and history. Ultimately property is finite, a fetter: not a source of
freedom except through the use to which it is put by will or
human personality. If freedom involves not being hampered by
finitude, human will must transcend the particularity of property.

What Hegel has described, even with its significant depar-
tures from "simple" bourgeois individualism, is still focused
upon the liberal individual—on the liberal subject conventionally understood. Isolation is the perspective assumed in the section
on abstract right. The physical world is at the individual's dispos-
al. He exerts will in quest of freedom. The next stage in the
development of will is the recognition that the external world
also includes the wills of other human beings. Its sphere, "morality," is composed of the interaction within this complex network
of subjectivities: "The external subjectivity which is thus identical with me is the will of others" (§122). Morality is the working
together of the multiplicity of subjective wills. Morality results
from the understanding that true or universal will involves the

will of others. The discussion culminates in the third part of *Philosophy of Right*—"Ethical Life"—where Hegel describes the converging needs of the individual and society embodied in the laws of the state.

The section on "Ethical Life" contains Hegel's famous discussion of marriage and the family. Feminist scholars have often emphasized the conservative aspects of the discussion, for Hegel asserts that a property-owning bourgeois family, where the wife is responsible for household matters and the husband for the affairs of state, is both rational and "ethical," with the implication that it is inevitable. Such a description cannot really be considered a distortion of Hegel's argument. He states, for example:

> The difference in the physical characteristics of the two sexes has a rational basis and consequently acquires an intellectual and ethical significance . . . (§165) Thus one sex is mind in its self-diremption into explicit personal self-subsistence and the knowledge and volition of free universality, i.e. the self-consciousness of conceptual thought and the volition of the objective final end. The other sex is mind maintaining itself in unity as knowledge and volition of the substantive, but knowledge and volition in the form of concrete individuality and feeling. In relation to eternality, the former is powerful and active, the latter passive and subjective. It follows that man has his actual substantive life in the state, in learning, and so forth, as well as in labour and struggle with the external world. . . . Woman, on the other hand, has her substantive destiny in the family, and to be imbued with family piety is her ethical frame of mind. (§166)[12]

Ironically, many contemporary feminists would agree with this conceptualization of the important differences between men and women in spite of its obvious implications for the confirmation of patriarchy. My effort is not to salvage or justify the content of such a passage (and others like it). I have profound disagreements with any theorist's claim to know the "substantive" or ethical destiny of women or anybody else. I intend to establish that such conclusions are not only unwarranted by but actually impossible within the framework of Hegelian dialectic. Given what we have learned about the inseparability of subjectivity and objectivity in a dialectical conception of the development of absolute knowledge, given what we know about the role of unpredictability and conflict between the two before any unity is possible, can Hegel, with consistency to his own method, argue for separate destinies for men and women?

As a preface to such an analysis, it should be noted that some of Hegel's observations about love, marriage, and the making of a family concern the unity of two separate (and apparently equally human) beings, which substantively undermines the one-sided domination of a patriarch in the family. For example:

> The family, as the immediate substantiality of mind, is specifically characterized by love, which is mind's feeling of its own unity. Hence in a family, one's frame of mind is to have self-consciousness of one's individuality within this unity as the absolute essence of oneself, with the result that one is in it not as an independent person, but as a member. (§158)

Further:

> The ethical aspect of marriage consists in the parties' consciousness of this unity as their substantive aim, and so in their love, trust, and common sharing of their entire existence as individuals. (§163)

Marriage involves the unity of individuals: the mutual dissolution of the borders between human beings. Is patriarchy possible under such conditions? We have arrived at the epistemological level of Hegel's discussion of marriage and family. How does such dissolution of ego boundaries occur?

The interaction between the two partners in a marriage follows the by now familiar dialectical path of loss and reacquisition of subjectivity in an ever enriched spiral. The merging of two separate identities into one might sound like the height of spirituality. However, in Hegelian dialectic it presupposes conflict between subjectivity and objectivity. The dialectical problem Hegel addresses is that two souls in love actually live in separate (physical, objective) bodies. The spiritual unity of love must have its origins in a physical moment of desire. "Marriage, as the immediate type of ethical relationship, contains first, the moment of physical life" (§161). Only from the physical can the spiritual emerge. Ultimately, separation of mind from body is impossible, hence Plato's argument (in the *Symposium* and elsewhere) that spiritual love is finer than physical love is wrongheaded. "It is a further abstraction still to separate the divine, or the substantive, from its body, and then to stamp it, together with the feeling and consciousness of mental unity as what is falsely called 'Platonic' love. This separation is in keeping with the monastic doctrine which characterizes the moment of physical life as purely negative and which, precisely by thus separating the physical from the mental, endows the former with infinite importance" (§163).

Consider Hegel's description of marriage and the family in terms of the range of meanings of subjectivity and objectivity offered in section I of this chapter. Marriage begins with a subjective moment in the sense of inner motivation understood as caprice: choice of "the particular inclinations of... two persons... or... the foresight and contrivance of the parents and so forth" (§162). However, the meaning of marriage as more than caprice (or subjectivity) soon becomes evident. Marriage has a rational (objective) aspect that begins to emerge as the recognition of the limits to what appeared to be free choice. In choosing each other both partners freely consent to surrender their natural (and immature) "freedom," which is really untested individual subjectivity. Recognition of the limits of selfhood is a moment of objectivity. Objectivity in this sense can be understood as external and physical: something that forces subjectivity to achieve some perspective on its limitations. Objectivity in this instance takes the form of the awareness of an other who is a subject outside oneself (as in "Master and Servant"). The subjective choice to face the objective limitation of one's will and personality creates the possibility that love, which seems in the beginning to be subjective and capricious, also has an objective—that is rational and necessary—dimension. Marriage is both profoundly personal and universal. "Its *objective* source lies in the free consent of the persons, especially in their consent to make themselves one person, to renounce their natural and individual personality to this unity of one with the other" (§162).

What had initially appeared to be choice is now understood

as caprice, arbitrariness: an immature will, rather than freedom. Real freedom is the choice to renounce one's isolation as subject, to dare to lose oneself to another: "a self-restriction, but in fact... their liberation, because in it they attain their substantive self-consciousness." Marriage is thus an "objectively appointed end" (§162), which means Hegel considers it rationally necessary, an "ethical duty." Equally necessary is the fact that it begins in subjective choice, which is transcended. Hegel is writing not about an externally imposed objectivity, but about the emergence of objectivity from subjectivity.

The reference to ethical duty has most often been read as an acquiescence to the constraints of traditional civil (bourgeois) society. That interpretation seems limited in the context of Hegel's own contention that the legal ceremony itself is only the formal confirmation of something that follows the choice of two people for each other. That choice is merely confirmed, objectified by the legal ceremony, which is the culmination, rather than the beginning of the marital relationship.

> It is in the actual conclusion of a marriage, i.e. in the wedding, that the essence of the tie is expressed and established beyond dispute as something ethical raised above the contingency of feeling and private inclination. (§164)

The ceremony may be formal, but if it remains "an external formality," it becomes meaningless. The marriage ceremony itself must be understood as the integration of subjective and objective. Only if the partners actively understand their choice and commitment can a civil ceremony perform its task of objectifying the subjective aspects of marriage. If the external ceremony is used as a substitute for or prerequisite to the more important subjective commitment, "it [the formal ceremony] appears as something not merely indifferent to the true nature of marriage, but actually alien to it. The heart is constrained by the law to attach a value to the formal ceremony ... [which] appears to bring disunion into their loving disposition and, like an alien intruder, to thwart the inwardness of their union..." (§164).

The dialectical basis of marriage calls for complete mutuality between partners. Although at the time Hegel wrote it was still customary for parents to choose mates for their children, Hegel did not believe that such outside influence could produce real union.[13] Both partners must consent freely. This aspect of Hegel's theory of marriage implies that women are after all human beings in some of the same important ways that men are: they must possess the capacity for choice, rationality and will. Hegel argues for a mutual surrender of two personalities in marriage. The unity that results is a far cry from the surrender, during the nineteenth century, of a woman's legal personality to a man's in the liberal marriage contract. For Hegel, "Marriage results from the free surrender by both sexes of the personality—a personality in every possible way unique in each of the parties" (§168).

Which is the correct reading of Hegel, then? Is he an apologist for bourgeois patriarchy, or does his dialectical method call for an egalitarian choice to merge souls and bodies in marriage? Can Hegel really mean that both men and women have free choice? Substantively, he certainly seems enmeshed in unreflected generalizations about women, grounded in the "empirical evidence" of his time. What is the relationship between the structure of dialectical method and the substance of Hegelian thought? Does it lead to patriarchal bourgeois marriage? Or, is that a conventional prejudice on the part of Hegel, rather than a legitimate result of his methodology? Are Hegel's substantive beliefs about patriarchy and separate domains for men and women in fact unwarranted from the standpoint of dialectical method?

Two aspects of his own method undermine Hegel's ability to forecast the "ethical destiny" of women.... or men: (1) If appearances are only the first moment in a process in which truth emerges through the negation and transcendence of initial appearances, then the significance of what Hegel himself observed about women is cast into doubt, and (2) the dialectical assumption that the boundary between subject and object is not finite and must be challenged to be understood suggests a potential identity between men and women on some essential level as the opposition between the sexes is confronted and transcended. Men can know themselves only to the extent that they are *also* capable of understanding themselves as "like" women. Masculinity and femininity can be understood only in relation to each other. Men and women do not belong to different species but reflect different aspects of the same whole, and because they need each other for both physical life and spiritual understanding, they cannot be regarded as static entities, complete unto themselves. All attempts to know what men and women are ultimately like, or what purposes they are intended for, must be relinquished. Men and women must be regarded as "in process": becoming, or progressing toward a "destination." It is thus more appropriate to think of men and women as constituting a continuum, which is itself constantly changing within history.

Still, it must be remembered that two people can achieve true unity only if there really is a recognized problem about all such merging. If there is no recognition and acknowledgement of initial conflict, if there is no developing recognition of conflict in the course of marriage itself, there is no possibility of resolution or unity. In dialectical thought the appearance of unity or compatibility is not to be trusted without having been tested. Conflict must be sought out and overcome before unity is achieved. This should not be mistaken for an invitation to create artificial chaos; it is rather the belief that order can be understood only in the wake of chaos, that disorder is an inevitable and necessary step in the long, difficult process of achieving knowledge.

Does that necessarily translate into heterosexual bourgeois marriage? An epistemological commitment to order through conflict *must* relinquish its hold on conventional expectations. For example, it might initially be argued that opposition between the sexes is what must be overcome before the unity of marriage can result. What could be more "given" and more apparently dialectical than the fact that people (as well as animals) are divided into two sexes that don't quite understand each other's physical and biological experiences and yet are members of the same species? Human beings divided into both sexes are very much alike and also very different. How perfectly Hegelian! One can envision Hegel seizing upon what appears to be obvious: the necessity of union between the "opposite" sexes for the perpetuation of the human race and world history. What makes unity believable is negation and negation of negation, or the overcoming of conflict.

However, if the source of conflict is not given to be specifically biological or social, if it is described in the more abstract terms *subjectivity* and *objectivity,* which are not "fixed" in the world but rather the prototype of conflict and unity, then who can say what specific substance "opposition" or "negation" must entail? Is the "basic" contradiction really the existence of the male and female of each species? Are male and female to be defined biologically? Hegel certainly slips from biology to social roles (from sex to gender) with perhaps unwarranted facility, but should he be regarded as an expert on the specifics of the relationship between physiology and social structure? Might a man and woman from the same social class, for example, be more alike than a couple of women from very different backgrounds? Heterosexual love is the only possible convergence of oppositions in Hegelian dialectic, though its "naturalness" is undermined by the contention of some contemporary feminists that the two sexes constitute a continuum, rather than an opposition.[14]

Can it be possible that homosexual and lesbian couples actually live with, or embody enough opposition, enough potential for negation, to be the beneficiaries of the self-knowledge that is the promise of dialectical conflict? Perhaps couples from different races as well as sexes would provide the ultimate conflict, with the ultimate possibility for union? Hegel would no doubt be aghast, but remaining true to dialectical method calls for moments when expectations and control must simply be relinquished, in the faith that some order will emerge without external intervention. Neither we nor Hegel can know what order will arise before we have relinquished our hold on the familiar. Hegel betrays his own dialectical method in his premature reach for substantive conclusions. His statement, for example, that "the family, as person, has its real external existence in property; and it is only when this property takes the form of capital that it becomes the embodiment of the substantial personality of the family" (§169) is an example of hasty, undialectical presumptuousness.

The true enemy of dialectical method is the inability to live with anxiety, that is, with the absence of certitude. The betrayal of a dialectical perspective always shows itself in a preference for premature closure. The failure of the teacher to practice what he preaches is not sufficient in itself to vitiate the teaching, however. Were it otherwise, not only Hegel but Marx, Freud, and the vast majority of thinkers and parents, as well as teachers, could be dismissed out of hand. Few of us have the capacity or the nerve to practice exactly what we preach; it is, however, important to keep trying.

IV. DIALECTICAL METHOD AND FEMINIST EPISTEMOLOGY

Let us begin to think about the practical contribution this understanding of dialectical method might make toward constructing a feminist epistemology. Dialectical knowledge is a *process,* calling for challenge to the stability of all the subject regards as secure. The authority of the knowing subject in dialectical theory is never final. Any knowledge at all calls for the subject's own experience undergoing challenge. One who presumes to have knowledge must have experienced *passivity* in relation to the object of knowledge: literally surrendered all presupposition, indeed traded places with the original object. What is initially perceived as passive object must also be experienced as having its own subjective power or *activity.* Likewise, the relationship between subject as "inner" and object as "outer" must be placed under challenge. A subject initially certain of its own activity perceives the objective world as outer as well as passive. In dialectical method the relationship between inner and outer is to be questioned; the tendency to assume that the active subject is the center of its own epistemological world, challenged. Objects also must be seen as subjects with their own centrality, their own inner motivations. This dynamic stance effectively prohibits declaring anything permanently outside, a problem: whether epistemological or political.

Translated into the terms of social science: an "expert"— man or woman—sets out to study "the woman problem" in American history. The initial moment of endeavor marks the expert as subject, while women are thereby regarded as the problem, the object to be studied. The empiricist investigator would gather data, accumulate historical, sociological, demographical material, voting behavior statistics, descriptions about participation in public life, attitudes about women participating in informal political groups, public office, business, the professions, whatever was deemed salient to the study. However, in this empirical approach, the relationship between expert (subject) and problem (object) is never threatened. There is never a moment when the empiricist experiences the startling, undermining awareness that *he or she is the problem.* There would never be a moment when reality would be understood as the life of the subjects of study, where the social scientist would be regarded as the oddity, the problem to be dealt with. "Why are these people intruding with tape recorders and questionnaires? What can they be up to?" ask the real subjects. The subjects begin to understand that if they act, they can relieve the experts of their livelihood, end public funding for social scientific studies, and guarantee that the intruders will not interrupt their lives again.

The dialectician in contrast to the empiricist must necessarily experience such a reversal, and *not* merely as an expert's idle reverie engendering the comfortable feeling that his or her heart is in the right place. The dialectician would experience a crisis of faith, doubting to the soul of her being the legitimacy of her enterprise, of her life's work. One hopes that a sense of stability returns to the dialectician, who has learned and changed as a result of her experience, but the positive moment, the happy ending, is not guaranteed. The crisis feels absolute. The experience of metaphysical death is the return ticket to a sense of stability, now strengthened by the experience of the problems of the other. One knows that one has walked in another's shoes, but a smug "conclusion" or self-confidence about one's understanding of another is not what results. There is no end point: only a moment of fully experienced understanding.

This encounter with the other is experienced not only in terms of a reversal of the initial active and passive roles of subject-scientist and object-problem. It also involves reversing perspective on who or what is inside and what is outside. The initial perspective of the "expert-subject" was assumed and accepted uncritically, like the initial moment of Hegelian unreflected subjectivity. The second moment was the loss of that position to the perspective of the world of the object: an "objective moment" in Hegelian terms. In that second moment, the initial perspective of the subject is gone; there is no longer a place to stand. In a third moment, the original position of the subject-expert might reappear, understood differently because of the experienced loss, but there are no guarantees.

This is a hard and earnest call for introspection in the pursuit of knowledge. Knowledge that is the result of this sort of experience would have to be qualitatively different from that gathered by a cool-headed objective observer. Epistemologically and politically, there would be no static objects and no objectification because all who purport to know anything would know themselves as both subject and object. In rather crude psychological terms, nobody could possibly claim knowledge of anything, anybody, any group with whom he or she had not experienced identification. Again, it must be emphasized that this identification does not refer to romanticized distant "identification with the oppressed," which has been a self-indulgence of the privileged in American society. Rather, it involves an experience of unease that lingers, informing all future perspectives. Taking as point of departure Hegel's discussion of master and servant: you must be scared to death that you *are* what you study before you can claim any knowledge about it.

If this appears to be an overemphasis on the terrifying dissolution of borders between subject and object in dialectical epistemology, it should now be emphasized that the destruction of boundaries is not to be equated with knowledge for the dialectician. Unlike some strains of contemporary feminist theory, it is not merely the acknowledgement of one's subjectivity that constitutes the basis for legitimate knowledge. There *is* tension, along with conflict and moments of division, between subjects and objects in dialectical epistemology. The epistemological structure is traditional, securely grounded in the sense that the relationship between inner and outer, mind and material world, forms the parameters of human knowledge. The relationship may be problematic, but it refers to something. Boundaries are not "assumed away" in a move suggesting that peace and understanding will come to the world when all dichotomies are eliminated, the most fundamental being the dichotomy between mind and matter. The dialectical position begins with an acknowledgment of a problem between the subjective and objective positions and faces down the conflict, concentrates its epistemological energy on the dichotomy itself. In the process, the dichotomy disappears, and everything appears to change. There is, however, no guarantee that the dichotomy will not reappear. In dialectical epistemology the feminist who is confident that women think more subjectively than men would have to confront the barrier she has assumed to exist between women and men and experience herself as a dichotomist, objectifying thinker before she could be certain of the truth of her own position, of her own subjectivity. Likewise, the social scientific expert would have to experience the subjectivist in himself. Only through the acknowledgement of difference and exchange of positions is true understanding of self and other possible. Only such an acknowledged conflict can begin to break down the boundaries between perspectives. The dialectical position incorporates both the deconstructionist and the subjectivist feminist positions as moments in the process of the growth of dialectical knowledge.

CHAPTER 6

MARXIAN DIALECTICS

I. DIALECTICAL MATERIALISM AND NATURE

Thus far the Hegelian dialectic has been presented as a dynamic that may hold promise as a basis upon which to forge a feminist epistemology. The promise is twofold. On the one hand, dialectics provides a way to challenge the static existence of the objective world, conventionally understood as external and passive. The complacency and integrity of the knowing subject is confronted; borders between self and other are constantly challenged, and knowledge is based upon the (temporary) experience of loss of self. The promise of dialectics is the reintegration of history with consciousness. If the first aspect of dialectical method is its radical subjectivism, the second aspect is the dialectician's recognition of history as an objective dimension that makes a one-sided idealism impossible. Not just any interpretation of history is possible: there is the assumption in dialectical thought that an objective world *does* exist, that events *do* occur, even though knowledge depends upon acknowledged human subjectivity as an agent of interpretation. Dialectical method is thus critical of traditional objectivity, focusing attention on the usually neglected importance of subjectivity, although *not,* however, relinquishing objectivity completely. Particular structures and tradition are challenged, yet not entirely abandoned.

Objective moments involve a role for subjectivity, without reducing truth to subjectivism. Dialectics is a methodology for a theory of political and historical change that retains sufficiently traditional aspects of truth to permit inclusion of feminist theory in the history of Western political thought. It permits recognition of the compatibility of feminist theory and political theory more generally and forestalls the exile of feminist theory to the outer reaches of radical theory and epistemology.

Why should a feminist care how traditional theory regards feminist theory? If feminist theory is beholden to either methods or substance of traditional theory, it will never become a viable political influence. Still, willfully avoiding anything having to do with the terms and methods of traditional theory excludes feminists from a battery of well-articulated methods and a recognizable vocabulary.

The concern not to abandon potentially useful methods is articulated by Sandra Harding, in her proposal to incorporate both a feminist standpoint epistemology and a poststructuralist epistemology. Her successor science, characterized by a feminist standpoint epistemology, is an effort to preserve the vocabulary of conventional science, to address the tradition in its own language but with a new and explicit political agenda. The poststructuralist aspect of Harding's proposal is the hedge against entrapment in the confines of traditional epistemology. I raised doubt about whether poststructuralism is compatible with conventional epistemology. Dialectics, in my view, incorporates the very contradiction that I believe Harding underestimates. In dialectics there is explicit belief in moments of conventional truth, but that truth is arrived at, earned through relinquishment of ego and obliteration of conventional boundaries between subject and object, experienced as chaos.

My belief that traditional theory may have something to offer feminist theory—at least epistemologically—does not include enthusiasm for adopting ready-made political concerns and "pasting" feminist political needs onto them. I argue only that including women in the same metaphysical universe as men is not necessarily counterproductive to the formulation of a feminist epistemology. It is thus necessary to distinguish, if possible, dialectical method from the substance of dialectical theory. In this context, a distinction must be drawn between Hegelian and Marxian dialectics. To begin with, of course, there is the difference between Hegel's idealism and Marx's materialism. This difference is associated with the difference between Hegel's conservativism and Marx's radicalism, and it has certainly been associated with Marx's more favorable rating among feminists. I believe, however, that focus on either materialism or idealism in an effort to manipulate substantive outcome is a betrayal of dialectical method itself. Dialectics must incorporate fully both a materialist and an idealist perspective. Indeed, what is radical about dialectical epistemology is its incorporation of both idealism and materialism, which takes the form of an interplay between subjectivity and objectivity. From this perspective, both Hegel and Marx abandon what is epistemologically radical and politically promising about dialectics when they stress either idealism or materialism as starting or end points.

What makes Marx's theory appear more promising to feminist theory than Hegel's? Feminists have focused on Marx's materialism as the foundation of his radical potential. Consider the opening pages of *The German Ideology*. Marx moves from a diatribe against young Hegelian idealists for beginning with abstractions, to the proclamation that he begins his analysis with the material world, to a description of the first "historical moments" that appears to place women's domain at the center of the early history of the world.

Let us look carefully at those promising early passages in *The German Ideology* to see whether it is possible to distinguish substance from dialectical method.[1] Marx's preoccupation in this work is with materialism, and he is explicit about the link he perceives between a materialist epistemological focus and its consequent political substance. Marx offers a materialist refutation of German idealist philosophy, taking for granted the dialectical aspect of both while assuming that materialism will lead to philosophically justified political radicalism. Can one focus explicitly on materialism *or* idealism and still have a truly dialectical method? If dialectics is the incorporation of *both* idealism and materialism, an emphasis on either aspect would betray the magnificent uncertainty of the method by "rigging" the substantive outcome.

Marx's argument for the philosophical necessity of dialectical materialism begins with the statement, "The premises from which we begin are not arbitrary ones, not dogmas, but real premises from which abstraction can only be made in the imagination."[2] He presents an apparently irrefutable case for beginning at the beginning: "The first premise of all human history is, of course, the existence of living human individuals" (5:31). The basis for "philosophical necessity" is the actual human beings who create their own material history: "Man can be distinguished from animals by consciousness, by religion or anything else you like. They themselves begin to distinguish themselves from animals as soon as they begin to *produce* their means of subsistence, a step that is conditioned by their physical organization. By producing their means of subsistence men are indirectly producing their material life" (5:31). That is, no matter what intellectuals may say, human beings by their life's activity define their own nature in the world. What must happen first is material: the production of goods and the reproduction of life. Their activity must, in the beginning, involve provision of fundamental needs such as food and shelter, and reproduction of the species.

The activities of "everyday people" are thus placed at the very foundation of history by Marx's materialism. Human history is not composed primarily of the great deeds of great men. Rather Marx redefines the basis, or the "first premise" of history as fulfilling the physical needs of everyday life. "We must begin by stating the first premise of all human existence, and, therefore, of all history, the premise, namely that men must be in a position to live in order to be able to 'make history'. But life involves before everything else, eating and drinking, housing, clothing and various other things" (5:42). The first historical act is "production of the means to satisfy these needs." Once these basic human needs are satisfied, new needs arise. Marx refers to the satisfaction of these new needs as another "first historical act." What makes these two acts historical, and specifically human, is that the satisfaction of "mere" animal needs gives rise to *additional* and different needs, whereas animals simply continue to satisfy the same basic needs over and over again. The third circumstance, which "from the very outset enters into historical development," is that "men, who daily re-create their own life, begin to make other men, to propagate their kind: the relation between man and woman, parents and children, the *family*" (5:43).[3]

Marx clarifies the apparent contradiction of three "first" historical acts by noting "these three aspects of social activity are not, of course, to be taken as three different stages, but just as three aspects or, to make it clear to the Germans, three 'moments', which have existed simultaneously since the dawn of history and the first men, and which still assert themselves in history today" (5:43). By including these aspects of life in history itself, Marx accomplishes several things. For his own purposes he establishes a base from which to discuss history as the development of a progressively complex division of labor, with the socially significant division being that between mental and physical labor.

Before he mentions that, however, Marx says something that seems to place sexuality at the very bedrock of productive history. The division of labor, he says, "was originally nothing but the division of labor in the sexual act" (5:44). What arises from that initial division "develops spontaneously or 'naturally' by virtue of natural predisposition, e.g. physical strength, needs, accidents, etc., etc." Does he thereby mean that the sex roles that have survived through history, at least with regard to the division of labor as in child care, are natural? If he does, it is the single human relationship that has defied the influence of social changes throughout history. In fact, if Marx is using an abstract and ahistorical concept of nature here, he is not thinking dialectically and is guilty of imposing an idealist abstraction upon material reality. Perhaps then this passage and the concept of nature generally are worthy of closer scrutiny, in order to determine (1) whether Marx is guilty of assuming an ahistorical concept of nature and imposing it upon women and the "sexual division of labor," and (2) even if he does fall into that substantive conventionalism, whether dialectical method itself permits other possibilities with regard to the concept of nature.

Does Marx violate dialectical method with his use of the concept of nature? His use of nature is a good encapsulation of how dialectical method has an impact on the substantive content of thought. In Mill's discussion of women, *nature* or *natural* carried an implication of immutability. When he turned to woman's nature to demonstrate the "utility" of freeing women, we groaned because it signified static beliefs about "the way women are." *Nature* to Mill stood outside history. Marx's concept of nature is historical and dialectical. Far from carrying the limitations of an imposed concept, it seems potentially liberating. In Marx's use of the term *nature* can be seen a convergence of at least four senses of the word: (1) the natural world external to people (i.e. trees, plants, animals, etc.), (2) the human body, (3) chronologically, as human "prehistory," and (4) also chronologically, as a state in the future that is fully developed so that human beings can live a *species life*. The fourth sense of the term is actually the product of the interaction between consciousness and history, and when Marx wants to focus upon the progress of human existence without focusing on the end point in *fully* developed human existence, he sometimes contrasts *natural* with *voluntary*. *Natural* in that sense means something like "unconscious," and *voluntary* means "conscious." Turning to Marx's texts for specific examples of these different uses, we see that in the essay "Estranged Labour" he states, "The worker can create nothing without *nature*, without the *sensuous, external world*" (3:273). Here the sensuous world is not only external to man: it is also his own body. Man lives in and is *of* nature:

> Physically man lives only on these products of nature, whether they appear in the form of food, heating, clothes, a dwelling, etc. The universality of man appears in practice precisely in the universality which makes all nature his *inorganic* body.... Nature is man's *inorganic body*—nature, that is, insofar as it is not itself human body. Man *lives* on nature—means that nature is his *body* with which he must remain in continuous interchange if he is not to die, that man's physical and spiritual life is linked to nature means simply that nature is linked to itself, for man is a part of nature. (3:276)

The reference to an "inorganic" body is probably an unfortunate choice of terms. It is not a reference to the pollution of nature with inorganic matter in a way that a twentieth-century ecologist might warn about. Marx means that human beings need the raw materials of nature to keep their own physical bodies alive, and that the natural world, while initially perceived as physically external to people, does not remain wholly external. For example, one "internalizes" food sources—crops and animals, and so the natural world and human bodies merge. One uses wool and cotton for clothing, and in being kept warm is kept alive, is physically maintained. One uses wood for building shelters and again, along with coal perhaps, for heating. Hence, inorganic nature is used once more to maintain one's organic, natural body. Thus the finite border between even the objective form of a human subject and the objectivity of the natural world external to it is challenged. What appeared first to be two senses of nature can now be seen as one complex sense: the finite and infinite form of the human body.

We turn now to nature as both prehistory and full human development, or the historically evolved forms of human society. Social activity and consciousness distinguish man from the animals. Nature is both primitive, animal-like, and destined to change in response to conscious human activity. In "Private Property and Communism" Marx notes, "The direct, natural and necessary relation of person to person is the *relation of man to woman.*" In the discussion that follows, it is evident that Marx does not mean to imply that natural is merely primitive, stuck back in "prehistory," unchanging. A natural human essence is also what will emerge through the process of history (the fourth sense); it is man's "own *natural* destination." Marx explicitly states that the "level of development" of the relationship between the sexes is the measure of the development of civilization. It is an indication of the extent to which the second two senses of the term *nature* have merged, how far the origins of human life have evolved toward that "natural destination." The relationship between men and women is a manifestation of "the extent to which the human essence has become nature to man, or to which nature to him has become the human essence of man. From this relationship one can therefore judge man's whole level of development. . . . It therefore reveals the extent to which the *human* essence in him has become a *natural* essence—the extent to which his *human nature* has come to be *natural* to him" (3:296).

Does Marx mean that men, who evolve from a primitive state of nature to fulfill their destiny as fully natural human beings, merely "use" women, who represent nature in a stereotypical, dichotomous sense, as opposed to "reason" or the "higher" faculties? Do women "represent" nature for men? Again, it hardly seems likely. Marx contrasts human with animal. Referring to the relationship between men and women as a measure of the extent to which human existence has become natural does not seem to carry the implication that men *develop* from nature, where women do not.[4] It seems more likely that Marx's terminology can be used for the purpose of arguing that "natural predisposition" (e.g. physical strength), needs, accidents, etc., which develop "spontaneously or 'naturally,'" are themselves destined to develop into a human (natural) form. That is, implicit in Marx's argument about the evolution of human nature is the expectation that gender arrangements are natural in the sense of primitive or animal-like at the beginning of history but are also destined to evolve into a "truly human" form, subject of course to the influence of the economic conditions of any given historical epoch. Even if we take, in its most male-biased light, Marx's subsequent remark that "division of labour only becomes truly such from the moment when a division of material and mental labor appears," with his unexpectedly conventional assumption that significant history is after all the history of the opposition between mental and physical labor, gender arrangements seem subject to the same development as the rest of history, whether or not Marx focuses upon the fact.

Without providing Marx unwarranted assistance, there are plenty of examples in his work of nature as something outside of or prior to history and nature as a sort of essence that is brought to material fruition by history itself. The opposition between undeveloped and developed nature is reflected in Marx's comment that consciousness at the beginning of history is "a purely animal consciousness of nature (natural religion) precisely because nature is as yet hardly altered by history" (5:44). Again, in a description of the division of labor in *German Ideology* he refers to voluntary as an advance over natural, implying that truly human existence is the result of human intervention in natural arrangements: "The division of labor offers us the first example of the fact that as long as man remains in naturally evolved society, that is, as long as a cleavage exists between the particular and the common interest, as long, therefore, as activity is not voluntarily divided, man's own deed becomes an alien power opposed to him, which enslaves him instead of being controlled by him" (5:47).

Now utilizing the vocabulary of subjectivity and objectivity, consider Marx's use of *nature* to mean both the human body and the natural world. The body itself has two dimensions: the subjective (idiosyncratic, inner) experience of the body, and the body as an object in the world, a physical entity that isn't so different from, for example, a tree viewed objectively—externally, tangibly. Marx referred to nature as man's "inorganic body," and we took him to mean that human beings live by internalizing nature as food and appropriating objective nature in the form of clothing and shelter in order to keep physically comfortable. What appears to be a purely objective (physical, external) relationship is also profoundly subjective (internal, experiential). Human labor is required to turn the objects of nature into things that are humanly usable. Hence, human subjectivity (activity) mediates between the objective, tangible, external, passive natural world and the subjective, intangible, internal experience of hunger and its satisfaction, warmth or cold, comfort or discomfort, etc. In a dialectical sense then, even nature in its most overtly physical sense is not static and not objective. The external (objective) world of nature and the natural human body (as object) are in continual interaction, mediated by subjectivity in the form of human activity and experience. Nature is dynamic: it must be understood as both subjective and objective, and constantly changing.

The relationship between (subjective) human activity and the objective material world is also mutable in dialectical thought. For although human beings are the primary subjects, the human subject, or worker, is never in complete control of the objective world, and there are moments, just as in Hegel's discussion of the servant's "shaping and fashioning," when the material world appears to have its own life (subjectivity), to resist and defy the worker's efforts to shape it. If the world were completely pliant and offered no resistance, the self could not develop so profoundly by mixing energy with it. On every level in dialectical thought then, subjectivity and objectivity are capable of losing themselves to one another.

It might be argued that this is not what is meant when reference is made to human or feminine nature. I believe a case can be made that a rather sloppy association exists in Western society between feminine nature and nature in the more physical sense. However, let us grant the point and see how dialectics deals with the more intangible sort of nature.

Consider then dialectical nature in its other sense, as both historical beginnings and the culmination of history. How can they be understood in terms of interpenetrating subjectivity and objectivity? The promising substantive implications for women should be readily apparent. Even if women are more associated with nature than men, in the sense of being more primitive, less rational, less capable of voluntary action, nothing can be associated with primitive history for long and still be natural, because in dialectical terms nature itself is a part of history, constantly changing. If women were to remain "primitive," more like animals, while the world moves on mediated by the activity of men, women would no longer be natural, but anachronistic, standing outside of history, hence outside of nature.

To return to Marx's discussion of the origins of history in the "real existence of real men" who must eat, drink, shelter themselves, and procreate: there are two levels upon which Marx's argument is promising for feminist theory. On the one hand, by "beginning at the beginning," with the material sphere in history and specifically the relationship between the natural world and the human body, Marx disdains the scholarly prejudice, or "extraneous standard" (5:55) that favors a "so-called history" (5:42), which Marx considers more accurately "theological...political... literary rubbish," and includes in his definition of history a sphere that has traditionally belonged to women. Secondly, in defining nature in a dialectical sense, as the interpenetration of body and world, and the understanding that nature is both a beginning and a historical product, Marx eliminates the usual dichotomy between nature and history or culture. He makes it possible to dissolve the dichotomy between nature and reason (or spirit) that has dominated Western culture since the time of the Greeks and caused so many problems for women.

II. STARTING POINTS AND ENDING POINTS

Again, it must be emphasized that Hegelian and Marxian dialectics differ: Hegel was an idealist, and Marx was a material-

ist. Is that primarily a substantive difference, or is it methodological? Materialism is often given as the basis of Marx's radicalism,
while Hegel's idealism is associated with his conservatism, but
Hegel is not simply a conservative, nor has Marx's radicalism
been unequivocally responsible for radical manifestations in the
politics of this century. Besides, Marx was profoundly influenced
by Hegel's dialectic. Is there such a thing as dialectical method
pure and simple, independent, as it were, of both materialism
and idealism? To choose "as a starting point" either the material
world or the world of ideas is to accept from the very beginning
a divided or dichotomized world and to abandon the genuinely
radical potential of dialectical method itself. To "choose" materialism or idealism is to anticipate substance, whereas the radical
potential of dialectics is that it cannot anticipate necessary substantive outcomes. Moments of insight are the result of the
unanticipated and uncontrollable clash of the ideal with the
material. The method assumes conflict between one's idea about
something and its manifestation in reality.

Consider any creative work—writing, building, etc. One
knows in theory, ideally, where one wants to go, what one wishes
to accomplish. The actuality is always at least a little different
from the plan, and one seldom settles for the first draft. Even a
carpenter with an architect's blueprint finds glitches on the job
for which he must compensate as work progresses. Sometimes
the changes take place under the guidance of the architect himself who realizes in the midst of construction that minor alter-
ations are called for. There are also occasions when the architect,
seeing the finished product for the first time, will think that it is
not what she had in mind: "The light in this room isn't exactly
what I expected . . . but it's nice anyway," or "I don't like it, but
we'll (they'll) have to live with it," etc. Sometimes the builder
may make adjustments on the job as it takes actual shape: "This
electrical outlet won't work here, let's move it six inches," or "I
just missed on the fit of this corner, but I can fudge it, or redo it,
use a little wood putty, etc." The fact is that the material world
never precisely fits an abstract blueprint. In writing, art, compos-
ing music, all more flexible mediums than carpentry, the clash is
even more dramatic. One begins with an outline of sorts, sometimes only a vague idea. To actualize it, to get it into a material

form, involves a series of interactions between the idea and its execution. One can focus on the similarities between form and idea: marvel at how amazing it is that any completed work corresponds to the original plan, or one can smugly accept that one's idea "worked." Both perspectives overlook the inevitability of difference from original plans, the difficulty of what goes on between mind and the world.

Dialectical epistemology focuses on the conflict, on the difficulty of reconciling the intangible with the tangible, inner with outer. That problematical border (although even the word *border* is a simplification) is precisely its focus, or should be. The border is assumed to be troublesome, uneven, permeable, but not completely so, for it allows passage in two directions—from inside to outside and back again, but the passage itself leaves nothing intact. Ideas are changed as they pass into reality; reality is changed as ideas perceive it.

If dialectical method focuses on the difficulty of transforming ideas into reality, if it focuses on the undeniable tension between the two realms and admits that the results of the conflict between the two are unpredictable and themselves subject to change, how can dialectical method be either materialist or idealist? The uncertainty at the core of dialectical method is foreclosed when one declares substantive priorities ahead of time. The promise of dialectical method for feminist theory is precisely that it does *not* anticipate outcomes. It can neither predict nor foreclose the possibilities of change, and yet is grounded in familiar terminology and familiar terrain: the material world and ideas.

Consider then the implications of Marx's declararation that he is a materialist because he "begins" in the material world. What does it mean to begin in the world? Does such a starting point anticipate, even try to guarantee an end point? Does it therefore diminish the significance of the conflict between ideal and real that is the very engine of dialectical thought? We begin with Marx's most specific criticism of Hegel's dialectic, the critique of *Philosophy of Right,* to see what beginning in the material world can mean.

Marx indicts Hegel for beginning with ideas rather than actuality and for attributing subjectivity, or activity, to abstractions such as the state. He digs in (at §261), where Hegel is deep within his discussion of the state. Hegel has been arguing for the importance of the state as the "arena of objectivity" for the "actualization" of human existence. How did the state come to be the historically significant arena of objectivity? In a leap from dialectical uncertainty to imposed certainty in the form of ends, Hegel argues that human life, which culminates in the life of the state, is actually dominated and characterized all along by the preordained *idea* of the state. The state is thus both the external objective embodiment and subjective will for all people and all history.

Marx believes Hegel is trying to have it both ways: the state as *result* of family and civil society and the state as the *genesis* of family and civil society. Hegel, Marx argues, cannot proclaim the state to be both "external to" and "immanent within" family and civil society. *Immanent* in Hegel's sense is associated with passive; *external to,* is active. The immanent state is passive, as family and civil society push history toward fruition in the form of the state (which was, however, somehow there, or immanent, all along). The external state is active, forming family and civil society within itself. The substantive import of Marx's argument is that Hegel's idealism, or the attribution of activity, subjectivity, to abstractions such as the state permits Hegel to present mere political opinion as logically grounded.

> Hegel everywhere makes the idea the subject and turns the proper, the actual subject, such as "political conviction" into a predicate.... Paragraph 268 contains a fine disquisition on political *conviction, patriotism,* which has nothing in common with logical exposition, except that Hegel describes this conviction as *"only* the result of the institutions existing in the *state,* in which rationality is *actually* present"; whereas on the contrary, these institutions are just as much an *objectification* of political conviction. (3:11)

Marx claims that Hegel's circular logic can be used to justify whatever politics Hegel desires. "He has turned the subject of the idea into a product, a predicate, of the idea. He does not develop his thinking from the object but expounds the object in accordance with a thinking that is cut and dried—already formed and fixed in the abstract sphere of logic" (3:14). In effect, Marx implies that Hegel's dialectical methodology amounts to rationalism. His complaint is that Hegel begins with idea and imposes it upon the actual. If he had begun with actuality, the idea would have emerged naturally. Hegel's starting point thus forces a division between idea and actuality, where Marx begins with tangible reality, which contains its own idea. From his own viewpoint, Marx begins with an implicit unity between object and idea, while Hegel begins with a dichotomy. Marx's objective starting point for the dialectic is thus a human subject, or rather a multitude of actual human beings: external, active subjects. It is a misconception, he argues, to think that the state has life! The state is but an abstraction, composed of real people. "As if the actual state were not the people. The state is an abstraction. The people alone is what is concrete. And it is remarkable that Hegel, who without hesitation attributes a living quality such as sovereignty to the abstraction, attributes it only with hesitation and reservations to something concrete" (3:28). To Marx, then, where one begins in dialectical method is an important determinant of the substantive outcome of one's theory. Beginning with a focus on ideas guarantees that in dialectical terms one *must* attribute activity to those ideas; beginning with a focus on the material world ensures that theoretical conclusions are legitimate because they are grounded in human activity.

Can Marx claim that his substantive conclusions are more legitimate than Hegel's because he begins in the material world rather than with ideas? Indeed, what distinguishes Marx's materialism from an inductivist's or an empiricist's definition of the state: the "whole" is, quite simply, composed of the parts?

The difference between Marx's dialectical materialism and ordinary empiricism is in fact the activity that Marx *himself* attributes to ideas. Even if he begins with a focus on the material world (the objective world of human subjects), his own adherence to dialectical method soon demands that he admit the activity (subjectivity) of ideas. No matter what the starting point, interchange between ideas and actuality must emerge. In the passage quoted previously, Marx expressed surprise at Hegel's attribution of a "living quality" to an abstraction, such as the state, but not to something concrete, such as people. If Marx believes in interaction between people and the objective, material world, he *must* attribute a form of activity or influence to inert objects in the world. Later we shall see that this is the basis of his theory of alienation. Why is it any less mystical than Hegel's attribution of activity to ideas, or abstractions?

Whether or not we call it mystical, whether or not Marx admits it, ideas have an active, subjective role in his epistemology. The very notion of an interchange of subjectivity and objectivity signifies the "mediation" of ideas between people and the "concrete" world. Marx, because he is a dialectical thinker, must believe that consciousness is not determined merely by material circumstances but that people also bring consciousness to bear on the world. The clash between the solid undeniable force of material reality and the less tangible but equally undeniable force of human consciousness is what makes change inevitable—for both human perception and the material world.

Marx himself does not always adhere to the essential uncertainty of dialectical method. He often insists upon the philosophical certainty of a given outcome rather than allowing the clash between idea and materiality to work itself out to its own uncertain conclusions. One example of this is in his "Critique of Hegel's *Philosophy of Right,*" where Marx discusses "the truth of democracy" as compared to "the truth of monarchy." He states, "Monarchy is not the truth of democracy. Monarchy is necessarily democracy inconsistent with itself; the monarchical element is not an inconsistency in democracy. Monarchy cannot be understood in its own terms; democracy can. In democracy none of the elements attains a significance other than what is proper to it" (3:29). On the one hand, the passage is another statement of Marx's unwillingness to infuse objects with mystical essence: monarchy is rule by a symbol, by an abstraction, while a democracy is composed of real people. The monarch is only a man, but his subjects cannot see that. In a democracy, presumably, such mystification does not take place: there is no projection of life onto an abstraction such as a monarch.

Although he may have a methodological point, Marx does not leave well enough alone. He himself goes on to present democracy as philosophically justified—having its own ideal life. His subsequent claim that "democracy is the solved *riddle* of all constitutions" is a generalization of Hegelian proportions. Marx is not simply declaring a political preference for democracy over monarchy. Nor is he saying that democracy is justified because it is grounded in "real people" rather than Hegel's ideal representative of the abstract concept of the people. He is using his materialist dialectical starting point to launch conclusions with claims for philosophical certainty that rival Hegel's philosophical generalizations. "All other *state forms* are definite, distinct, *particular forms of state*. In democracy the *formal* principle is at the same time the *material* principle. Only democracy, therefore, is the true unity of the general and the particular" (3:30).

To summarize: Marx believes that Hegel begins with abstractions and attributes a living quality to them. Marx, in contrast, begins with the concrete world and attributes active life to it. However, as a dialectical thinker, he cannot view life either as simply human activity, influencing the material world, or as the material world completely determining human behavior. Ideas must intervene or mediate between the world of material objects and human subjects. The ideas, too, must be seen as both active and passive, subjects and objects in a dialectical world.

Our question is whether once that dialectic is engaged it can culminate where Marx wants it to. Does he remain true to his own professed methodology if he announces that beginning in the material world guarantees certain results in the material world? If we can establish that it doesn't much matter whether one begins by focusing on the material or the ideal world, what would be the implications for feminist theory?

The mutual influence of material activity and ideas is in full evidence in Marx's 1844 essay "Estranged Labour." He begins with a proclamation that sounds stunningly empirical, but the reader soon learns that Marx has something else in mind. He proclaims that instead of going back to a "fictitious primordial condition as the political economist does," "We proceed from an *actual* economic fact" (3:271). The fact turns out not to sound like a simple, ordinary, empirical fact at all. It sounds more like a relationship, or an interpretation: "The worker becomes all the poorer the more wealth he produces, the more his production increases in power and size" (3:272). "The worker becomes an ever cheaper commodity the more commodities he creates. The devaluation of the world of men is in direct proportion to the *increasing value* of the world of things. Labour produces not only commodities: it produces itself and the worker as a commodity . . ." (3:272). This paragraph is remarkable not as a statement of concrete fact but rather as an example of an entirely different approach to the relationship between facts and knowledge. It is evident in this essay that Marx's definition of facts is radically different from an empirical conception of facts. Marx's conception of the relationship between objects and subjects is in part compatible with Hegel's perspective, and in part a departure from both Hegel's "idealism" and English empiricism.

Marx's opening gambit about the *"actual* economic fact" is really a statement about the relationship between a human subject—a worker—and the world of objects. Marx calls the uncontaminated relationship between the worker and the object of labor *objectification.* Within the specific confines of the capitalist economic structure objectification is an aspect of alienation. While Marx believes that the end of capitalism will signal the end of alienation, objectification itself is inevitable and not necessarily destructive. It constitutes the very definition of the relationship between human subjects and the material, objective world. "The product of labor is labor which has been embodied in an object, which has become material: it is the *objectification* of labor." Human activity infuses the world, is "captured" or congealed in objects, in whatever people become involved with, put their energy into. "Labor's realisation is its objectification." In the capitalist economy, social forces interfere with the natural relationship between worker and object of labor: "Under these economic conditions this realisation of labor appears as a *loss of realisation* for the workers; objectification as *loss of the object and bondage to it;* appropriation as *estrangement, as alienation"* (3:272).

Objectification to Marx is thus the infusion of human energy into the tangible world, the projection of subjectivity into the world of objects. But then what happens? The notion that a human being should "get something back" from her labor is evident in the distinction Marx draws between objectification and alienation, or "loss of the object" (3:273). There should be some reciprocity between workers and objects of labor: a moment when the object acts as subject to its producer, in the sense of "returning," providing physical life, a sense of aesthetic satisfaction, or whatever else one might expect to get from the object of one's efforts. Even under alienating circumstances, "loss of the object" does not imply that the object has no active impact, but rather that it has an impact on the subject (worker) who made it. Whether positive or negative, there is assumed reciprocity between human being and objective world. Objects of labor "confront" their human makers in a positive or a hostile manner, depending upon economic circumstance.

> The worker puts his life into the object; but now his life no longer belongs to him but to the object. Hence, the greater this activity, the more the worker lacks objects. Whatever the product of his labour is, he is not. Therefore the greater this product, the less is he himself. The *alienation* of the worker in his product means not only that his labor becomes an object, an *external* existence, but that it exists *outside* him, independently, as something alien to him, and that it becomes a power on its own confronting him. It means that the life which he has conferred on the object confronts him as something hostile and alien. (3:272)

When Marx notes that human activity produces "both itself and the worker as commodity" (3:272), it sounds as though he believes it is possible for a human being to "become" an object, but this is only a reflection on the inhumanity of capitalism. The experience of self as object should be a fleeting moment concluding in a return to subjectivity, or something is radically wrong. Capitalism *is* radically wrong, Marx believes, and so it is destined to be changed by the very human beings who are violated, precisely because human beings are inevitably subjects.

Does this conclusion follow from Marx's methodological perspective, or is it a substantive claim? What seems undeniable in purely methodological terms is that a human being has a relationship with the world in which she lives and works, implying that the objects of one's labor will have some active influence on one's experience of oneself. Substantively, however, the quality of that experience cannot be determined with any finality for all people. One can experience loss of control of one's energies and life (alienation), the pleasure of accomplishment, a sense of loss or ambivalence as one's precious work is sold or given away in order to eat and house self and family. While it seems likely that a worker who must sell her life's energy for wages piecemeal and purely quantitatively will not be at peace with herself or with the world, even that is not a foregone conclusion but a probability. The "objective reality" might be as Marx argues, that the laborer is selling not work qualitatively considered but labor power, a quantity of energy. Although dialectical method insists that what one puts into the world returns to one in some sense, dialectical method itself cannot determine with any finality the quality of human experience.

Hegel's dialectical idealism implies that ultimately the material world is itself a "fetter" to spirit. The conditions of capitalism and the ownership of the means of production mean relatively little in Hegel's schema because, in a sense, even the human body is objective, physical, hence particular rather than universal in terms of the world spirit. Alienation for Hegel comes from the experience of the limitations of the human spirit in the concrete, immediate, impermanent world. For Marx, on the other hand, a fully human life, a "free" life *is* possible within this world: transcendence of the spirit is not prerequisite to human freedom. So in a sense, Marx is right in arguing that if Hegel begins with a focus on spirituality, substantively he will end with a focus on spirituality. Hegel's end point is projected into an infinite future, however. The possibility of the absolute idea is not close at hand. Marx claims that communist revolution is possible in this world, and although he does not make specific predictions about life in that future society, he does make universal claims for the experience of unalienated life in this world. Does beginning his dialectic in the material world really lead inexorably to the conclusions he foresees?

III. ACTIVE IDEAS IN MARX'S DIALECTIC

Marx is no empiricist. He is not operating from a mechanistic epistemology, where people unreflectively alter their world and themselves. People *think,* are conscious beings. Ideas, therefore, *do* play an important role in Marx's dialectic and are an active force in Marxian theory. Indeed, the activity granted to ideas is what distinguishes Marx's dialectical materialism from plain old empiricism. The activity of ideas is presented by Marx as a *moment* of human activity. Perhaps it makes sense to view the role of ideas in his terms as a potentially *negative* moment, should illusion, which is most often destructive to human experience, take on an independent existence. When ideas become active, in this sense, it may be said that people have lost control of their own world, which Marx regards as a form of alienation.

From my perspective, it is dialectical method's momentary loss of control of the world that is epistemologically so radical. Dialectics relinquishes control over ideas in a way that empiricism does not. My argument here is that Marx's contention that one must begin and end in the material world is a way of escaping the consequences of that relinquishment. Marx, and Hegel also, hedges his bets against the moments of terrible uncertainty that are the very core of dialectics. Dialectical thought can really be neither idealist nor materialist. It must be both, and to proclaim it one or the other is to manipulate the method toward substantive ends judged desirable.

We turn to Marx's 1844 essay "Private Property and Communism" to see the active role ideas do play in his dialectic and to begin to consider whether he regards the activity of ideas as a negative moment in his dialectic: a moment of "false consciousness," as it were, of mystification that must be overcome.

In "Private Property and Communism" Marx's discussion of the relationship between perception and history permits analysis of the role ideas play in his epistemology. In that essay he argues for the unity of "subjectivity and objectivity, spirituality and materiality, activity and suffering" (3:302). What does such a unity entail? Does it mean that the categories cease to have meaning? That the concrete subsumes the abstract, or vice versa? The essay has two parts: the first is a criticism of existing communist theories for not having transcended the consciousness of capitalism; the second is a discussion of the relationship between history and the human senses.

Marx's initial complaint about the "crude communists" (Proudhon and Fourier in this instance) is that they consider things only in their objective aspect, they accept epistemologically if not politically the world as they find it. This statement parallels his complaint in "Estranged Labour" about the political economists' uncritical acceptance of the necessity of private property. Crude communism actually "universalizes" what it should be doing away with. Because elements of the existing world have not been understood fully, they can persist in the communism envisioned by Proudhon, Fourier, and others. Such a communist society would actually be an exaggeration of the evils of capitalism. To explain this Marx demonstrates how private property doggedly will remain in many forms and particularly in the crude communists' attitude toward women. Without new understanding of the very concept of private property, redistribution of wealth "after the revolution" will only amount to a rearrangement of property, while its devastating effects on human existence will remain. "The category of *worker* is not done away with, but extended to all men. The relationship of private property persists as the relationship of the community to the world of things" (3:295).

This unreflective state of affairs will retain the extension of the "ownership" of women by all men, without questioning the inhumanity of the concept:

> Finally this movement of opposing universal private property to private property finds expression in the brutish form of opposing to *marriage* (certainly a form of exclusive *private property*) the community of women, in which a woman becomes a piece of communal and common property. It may be said that this idea of the *community of women gives away* the secret of this as yet completely crude and thoughtless communism." (3:295)

In order for real political and economic change to transpire, ideas must actively intervene. Passive response to the material world will not bring revolutionary change. How can such an intervention take place, given the materialist base of Marx's epistemology? Return for a moment to Marx's complicated concept of nature. Remember that it signified the convergence of the material and ideal. There are two dimensions to the Marxian concept of nature: physical and historical. The physical involves the convergence of the external physical world with the human body; the historical involves the convergence of the beginnings of history with historical destination. Nature plays an important part in "Private Property and Communism," and Marx is more specific in this essay than anywhere else on the relationship between nature and sexuality. Consider the following:

> The direct, natural and necessary relation of person to per-
> son is the *relation of man to woman*. ... From this relation-
> ship one can judge man's whole level of development. From
> the character of this relationship follows how much *man* as a
> *species being,* as *man* has come to be himself and to compre-
> hend himself; the relation of man to woman is the *most nat-
> ural* relation of human being to human being. It therefore
> reveals the extent to which man's *natural* behavior has
> become human. ... (3:295, 296)

The relationship of "man to woman" is "the most natural," but
that does not mean that it has developed to full capacity. It must
become human, and to be fully human is historical work. Natural
human existence for Marx involves the recognition that people
need one another. The relationship between men and women is
central because the need of both sexes for the reproduction of
the species is an objective concrete manifestation of people's
needs for one another. The less tangible emotional and social
needs follow that physical need and determine its specific content. Nothing natural remains rooted eternally. Material need
begets social organization, which in turn reproduces what is
regarded as natural. The recognition of mutual human need,
derived from the mutual physical need of both sexes for the perpetuation of the species, develops beyond that early necessity
into social relations. Recognition of the mutual needs of men
and women should result in mutual human respect. Respect, the
result of material and social history, is natural on a more highly
developed level than any primitive, physical concept of natural.

While Marx's dialectical method circumvents a static and
limiting concept of nature, his materialism still might create difficulties. Beginning with the material world means only emphasizing the material aspects of nature and perhaps observing the
importance of the intangible aspects of nature. Even the most
physical aspects of nature—human bodies and plants and animals—are not impermeable. They are in constant interaction
with each other. We eat the plants or animals so that we do not
die, and use our living energy to plant more crops and raise more
animals. Such a process is undoubtedly material, as any empiricist could recognize, but it is more importantly also something
beyond material, something conceptual. The famous cherry tree

of *German Ideology*, for another example, is not merely a tree, a bit of nature complete with fragrant blossoms; it is an aspect of economic development, imported for profit. Only human understanding, ideas, consciousness can make that fact available to us.

Overemphasis on materiality, reduction of consciousness to a mediating term, may lead Marx into similar difficulties encountered in the empiricist epistemology exemplified by Mill. For example, on what grounds can Marx criticize the crude communists' inability to think beyond the existing material realities of their time if all consciousness is a product of material circumstances? With regard to the nature of women, if material circumstances are the requisite determinant of political change, how can he account for the lack of political response to women's situation, which has indeed undergone dramatic material change without a full-scale revolution? For example, consider women's material situation in advanced industrial societies today as compared with that during Marx's time. Focusing solely on women's role as reproducers of the species, it becomes evident that dramatic changes have occurred. Women in the mid-nineteenth century had considerably shorter life expectancies, no contraceptives, and had to bear the heartbreak of a much higher infant mortality rate. A woman might expect to live to 50 or 55 and bear children almost continuously for twenty years of maturity. Today a woman expects to live to 70 or 75 and may bear two or three children, planned fairly consciously, with the expectation that all are likely to survive. The physical—that is, material— experience of women has changed dramatically, and with it the social experience of her natural reproductive capacities. Material conditions are ripe for the liberation of women. Why hasn't it happened?

Perhaps Marx would respond that it hasn't happened because women's *economic* circumstances have changed so little in the past century. Indeed, a Marxist feminist would argue that political change is so slow in coming for women because the vast majority of women—whether married to bourgeois or proletarian—have very little economic power of their own. Still, given this example of the inability of material circumstances to produce change on their own, and given Marx's expectation that consciousness changes *after* material circumstances because we begin dialectical analysis with the material world, how can he expect the crude communists to rethink the role of women in communist society before change in the role of women occurs? Given a purely materialist methodology, how can Marx criticize the crude communists' inability to see beyond the existing conditions in which women were much more physiologically constrained?

In part it is not legitimate to expect answers from Marx on these questions. He was not concerned with women's reproductive role; he was admittedly concerned only with the production and reproduction of private property. The issue of actual material differences in women's reproductive lives serves as an example of the limitations of the materialist approach, as does Marx's attitude toward the crude communists. For, given his materialist epistemology, on what basis can he demand that the crude communists see beyond the concept of private property? In the case of the crude communists, Marx's demand for a change in consciousness clearly calls for the transcendence of the prevailing materialist conditions.

Marx does not address these questions but simply declares that the elimination of private property will restore to people their full range of senses. The senses will themselves become "theoreticians," that is, will actively shape the world in which they dwell. Without the predominating need to own, perhaps people will be able to see women as something other than property. "The abolition of private property is therefore the complete emancipation of all human senses and qualities, but it is this emancipation precisely because these senses and attributes have become, subjectively and objectively *human* . . . the senses have therefore become directly in their practice theoreticians" (3:300).

What is truly radical about Marx's methodology is an aspect he is reluctant to acknowledge: the active role ideas play, and their influence on the material world. Marx focuses repeatedly on his materialism, in contrast to Hegelian idealism. "Private Property and Communism" represents a rare moment when Marx openly acknowledges the activity of the senses. More often, when consciousness or imagination is seen to precede action or "material reality," Marx regards the result as mystification. The mutuality between ideas and material reality is there all along, and much more important for a theory of political change than his repeated insistence that the major problem in history is the existence of private property. He proclaims, dramatically, that "the *forming* of the five senses is a labor of the entire history of the world" (3:302). Marx's conceptualization of the human senses as active, although formed by history, is what is truly revolutionary.

His conceptualization of the role of the senses permits circumvention of the empiricist dilemma discussed earlier: senses, in an empiricist universe, are regarded as the essence of subjectivity—intangible and idiosyncratic—and yet in order to receive sensations from the objective world, they must in some degree be active. In Marx's schema, senses do have moments of activity, of subjectivity, at the same time that their formation is a response to the objective world. The human sense organs do not exist outside history. They are not natural in a static sense. They must become human. They may be regarded as initially natural in an undeveloped way, but they are shaped by the material world, which is the product of human history. Ideas, the human senses, in turn, are the active subjective link between human beings as physical objects and the objective material world. People respond to the world, and change it through the mediation of human senses. The senses constitute the flexible medium that permits Marx to break out of the empiricist mold without flirting with idealism.[5]

IV. MARXIAN ECONOMICS AND DIALECTICAL METHOD

Dialectical method, I have argued, must involve idealist moments, moments when ideas are active. The very incompatibility of the idealist and materialist moments is what provides the uncertainty that I take to be the radical potential of dialectical method. Throughout his lifetime Marx's writings became less philosophical and more economic—that is, increasingly more grounded in the material world. If it can be established that ideas play as active a role in the economic writings as in the more philosophical writings, then perhaps we can begin to lift the central methodological dynamic from its imposed starting point and, by implication, from an assumed end point. We shall have extracted the "essence" of dialectical method, or as I prefer to think of it, conceived a minimalist dialectics. We shall be able to see whether in that form dialectics holds any potential for feminism.

In searching for the activity of ideas in the economic writings, we may be surprised to find that the most startlingly active elements are *things:* material objects. The economic writings are peppered with Marx's whimsical sense of humor, presenting commodities as things that lead their makers by the nose around the capitalist marketplace. A table appears, in one instance, "that common, everyday thing, wood." In the next, it "steps forth as a commodity, it is changed into something transcendent. It not only stands with its feet on the ground, but in relation to all commodities, it stands on its head, and evolves out of its wooden brain, grotesque ideas, far more wonderful than 'table-turning' ever was."[6] A coat in the capitalist system possesses both "a sublime reality as a value" and a "buckram body."

Capital is filled with descriptions of objects as active, infused with life by human mystification. Marx takes it upon himself to tear away the veil of appearance, to demystify, to demonstrate that the only really active subjects in capitalism are human beings. This awareness will permit us, he believes, to see that objects are not really active, do not possess their own subjectivity, but only appear to have life. In the capitalist marketplace it feels as though there is a necessity dictated by the objects being exchanged. The objects produced have no meaning as isolated entities: they must find a way to exchange themselves for other objects, for capital, etc. The life or activity thus appears to be coming from the things themselves, rather than from the human beings who manufacture and exchange them. Human beings lose sight of their own activity in all this:

> Since the producers do not come into social contact with each other until they exchange their products, the specific social character of each producer's labor does not show itself except in the act of exchange. In other words, the labor of the individual asserts itself as a part of the labor of society, only by means of the relations which the act of exchange establishes directly between the products, and indirectly, through them, between the producers. To the latter, therefore, the relations connecting the labor of one individual with that of the rest appear, not as direct, social relations

between individuals at work, but as what they really are, material relations between persons and social relations between things. (Tucker 321)

There is a problem revealed by the last sentence of the passage just quoted. Marx says not that things *only appear* to be having "social relations" with each other, but that matters appear to their manufacturers *as they really are:* "material relations between persons and social relations between things." Can things have social relations? Appearance and reality (which in this context seems to mean "the way things ought to be, according to Marx") converge as Marx suggests that activity attributed to objects in this scenario is real. How can things have social relations with each other unless people grant them that reality? How can people grant things active life except by an act of imagination: through ideas? Then what? Do people remain conscious of the fact that they have granted life, or subjectivity, to inert objects?

Marx goes on, actually in a variety of instances throughout *Capital,* to explain that people, because they are the only real subjects in the world, attribute life to objects and then forget what they have done. One example of this is the creation of value. Things are really homely, which is to say that things should be objects that have use value and exist for some humanly defined purpose. People have attributed "value" to things for the simple purpose of exchange. What results, however, is not simply that the objectivity of things is forgotten. Rather, the creation of value signifies, through "social hieroglyphics," the converging of quality and quantity, and the turning of variety into a single common denominator: labor power. The result is utter obfuscation of the simple material reality of objects and the actual work that went into their making. People forget that they have created a code with which to equate unlike objects, and this is what complicates all efforts to "get behind the secret of our own social products" (Tucker 322). After a while the coded view of the world establishes itself, attains "a certain stability," and then the proportions established "appear to result from the nature of the products." For example, one ton of iron appears naturally equal to two ounces of gold, in spite of the physical absurdity of the thought. Marx notes, "we are not aware of this, nevertheless we do it" (Tucker 322).

The question still remains: how do we know which view constitutes reality? Do we really believe that one ton of iron is the same as two ounces of gold? Marx urges people to remember that although the equation of a load of iron with a few ounces of gold seems natural, it is in fact wholly arbitrary, a social creation. It seems an oversimplification merely to say "of course" one ton of iron does not equal two ounces of gold. One is rather tempted to say "of course" to both perspectives. Of course, it is perfectly obvious that we don't mean that the ton of iron is *really* identical, in physical fact, to the two ounces of gold. We know that one is an enormous load of ore and the other hardly anything at all. At the same time, of course, it seems natural that a small quantity of gold should equal an enormous quantity of iron: the gold is after all more valuable than the iron. Marx argues that the real view is the former one, and the moment when he insists upon the superior reality of the physical fact is the moment he abandons dialectics for the simplicity of materialism. He abandons the opportunity to think dialectically and loses perspective on the mutual incompatibility and inseparability of objectivity and subjectivity in dialectical thought.

Viewed dialectically, both perspectives are true, and both are also ridiculous. The belief that one ton of iron is identical, in physical fact, to two ounces of gold may seem the more obviously ridiculous, which is what Marx is trying to demonstrate. If only we stop to think about it, he says, it is obvious that it takes a colossal act of abstraction to imagine that the two are really equivalents. In material fact, one is big and heavy, the other light and small, etc. But the equivalency of the two also, *without thinking too hard,* seems to be natural: we do take for granted and we do act as though a small quantity of gold is the same as a large quantity of something else. We have to remind ourselves that the gold is not in itself more valuable than most other things. Isn't it *also* a "material fact" that gold is valuable since we act as though it is and forget its arbitrary social origins? If we have to perform mental gymnastics to reachieve the perspective that gold is just a rock, aren't those gymnastics every bit as much an act of abstraction as turning gold and iron into equivalents? Indeed, doesn't such a perspective negate the social and economic history that Marx otherwise regards as the basis of material reality?

My question is, given dialectical method, how can Marx insist that one view is real and the other not? If he remains true to dialectics he cannot simply impose the truth of one perspective by stating that it is "more" material. Dialectical reality means precisely that *both* points of view are both true and untrue. The gold is not in physical fact the same thing as the iron. but the gold is in historical fact, in social fact, and by virtue of the way we have come to act, the equivalent of the iron. Although both perspectives are true, neither perspective constitutes the entire truth. Recognition of the two viewpoints is itself historical, a moment in time, a moment of perspective. When Marx demands that we recognize the truth of the statement that one ton of iron does not equal two ounces of gold, he cannot demand that we deny or negate the other perspective and remain true to dialectical method. What arises from the fact of the antagonism of the two perspectives cannot be controlled or foreordained.

It should also be emphasized that Marx himself demands, when he turns our attention to the forgotten moment when we invented social values, that we use our imagination. He demands a moment when ideas are active: a subjective moment. That is, Marx tacitly acknowledges reality to be both material and ideal, but feels compelled to choose one over the other. Because human beings are both subjects and objects, have tangible bodies and intangible minds, both of which are active and passive at different moments, it is impossible to declare an underlying truth without stopping the action, thereby violating a dialectical worldview. Two other examples from the economic writings should serve to demonstrate this.

Consider his discussion of "relative" and "equivalent" value. The terms are really no more than perspectives on an economic equation, for example 1 coat = 20 yards of linen. To begin with, the equation is an example of the social hieroglyphics just discussed. It does not mean that in actual (physical, material) fact it takes twenty yards of linen to sew one coat. (Such a coat would be enormous, or extravagantly tailored, or both. Marx notes that it takes only ten yards of linen to make a coat; contemporary tailors regard even that quantity with amusement.) The statement means in capitalist economics that the labor time involved in the production of one coat is equal to the labor time involved in the production of twenty yards of linen. Only labor power, which is quantified, abstract labor, makes the equation possible.

Marx goes on to demonstrate that the statement actually means two things, depending upon whether the coat or the linen is presented first. "Twenty yards of linen equals one coat" does not mean the same thing as "one coat equals twenty yards of linen." In the first equation, the linen is active (the relative term), setting the standard of value, and the coat is the product, the passive equivalent term. In the second statement, the roles are reversed.

> Here two different kinds of commodities (in our example the linen and the coat) evidently play two different parts. The linen expresses its value in the coat; the coat serves as the material in which that value is expressed. The former plays an active, the latter a passive, part. The value of the linen is represented as relative value, or appears in relative form. The coat officiates as equivalent, or appears in equivalent form. (Tucker 314)

Marx is talking about a "false reality," a reality that exists only within the capitalist system. Within that system it matters very much whether one has a coat and is looking for an equivalent quantity of linen, or the reverse. Yet from a larger perspective the whole equation is palpably absurd in material reality: it takes an active imagination to look at twenty yards of linen and see the equivalent of one coat. The Marxian perspective unmasks the false reality of the capitalist system and tries to establish the absurdity of accepting a world in which one coat equals twenty yards of linen, or one ton of iron equals two ounces of gold.

At the same time that Marx's intention here is to reassert the primacy of material reality, his epistemology is so profoundly dialectical that his credibility in arguing for the material world is somewhat undone. His perspective on subjectivity and objectivity is visible from within his discussion of relative and equivalent value. He accepts the possibility of linen and coats playing "passive" and "active" parts in a "mathematical equation." If we accept his contention that it makes a difference whether the linen or the coat comes first in the equation, that it makes a difference which one plays the equivalent or the relative part, then the equation is not really an equation at all, because it is not reversible, but is more accurately a sentence, with the subject and object playing the usual active and passive parts. If "one coat equals twenty yards of linen" were a mathematical equation (or economic formula), both the coat and the linen would be objects pure and simple. The equation would be reversible because neither the coat nor the linen could have another life, another identity as a subject, with the capacity for activity. *Marx himself* doesn't view coats and linen as mere objects under capitalism. They determine the meaning of one another, depending upon circumstances (that is, depending upon whether one has a coat or the linen at any moment), and they also have something to do with determining the activity of the people who deal with them.

The fact that Marx regards the perspective from within capitalism as a false perspective does nothing to alter the fact that he believes such a perspective to be epistemologically possible. People can lose sense of their primacy over the world of things. Such loss, such experience of reification, or mystification —indeed the very possibility of the "fetishism of commodities"—is possible only if the border between tangible objects and intangible consciousness is understood to be permeable. Coats do not walk themselves to the merchant's exchange: people physically take them there. Marx wants to show us that people don't realize that they are acting as though the coats *themselves* are demanding to be taken and exchanged, and exchanged for the handsomest profit possible. People surrender life to objects, and then forget they have done it: that much constitutes an aspect of Marx's critique of capitalist consciousness. The fact that such an act of forgetting is possible in the first place is Marx's dialectical assumption. Things can appear to have life, to be subjects to such an extent that the meaning of "1 coat = 20 yards of linen" differs from "20 yards of linen = 1 coat" without even mentioning a human being. The interpenetrability of subjects and objects that makes possible the idea that coats and linen can have a relationship with each other is distinctly dialectical. It is not something that would have occurred to John Stuart Mill, who in his wildest imagination could not see the difference between the two formulae to which Marx refers.

This is an example of the active role ideas play in Marx's

dialectical epistemology, even when he is criticizing the life granted to abstractions in capitalism. The border between mind and
material world is not fixed, not stable. Marx seeks the overthrow
of capitalism not in order to render objects lifeless but to end a situation in which material objects are systematically allowed to
usurp the life of their makers, and by implication also of their own-
ers. Marx's vision is not of a world of "dead empirical facts."[7] He
seeks a world where the flow of energy between people, their
ideas, and their material world is not siphoned off for inhuman
purposes. He seeks to reestablish a free exchange of energy
between human subjects and their objective world. If it takes
emphasizing the importance of the material world to do it, Marx
will focus on the material world. He is after mutual interaction
between consciousness and materiality: not a one-sided materialism. In this sense, then, his emphasis on "the material" is a political
response to both Hegelian idealism and capitalism. "Materialism"
itself, however, is only a part of Marx's dialectical epistemology.

   The same perspective is apparent in considering Marx's
"General Formula for Capital," only it is even more schemati-
cized than the discussion of relative and surplus value. The General Formula for Capital is M-C-M'. Translated into English, the
"sentence" means that money is exchanged for a commodity,
which is exchanged for a greater sum of money. Such a state of
affairs reflects the domination of abstraction over concrete experience: the dominance of exchange value over use value, and of
quantity over quality in every aspect of life. It is the reverse of the
description of a more primitive economy where use values dominate: C-M-C. The latter "statement" describes a situation where
commodities are produced for use, and excess use-values are
exchanged for money which is then exchanged for another commodity, needed for its use-value by the original producer. Each C-
M-C circuit thus described is complete because the commodities
are taken out of circulation and used. Corn is exchanged for
money which is exchanged for clothing. The corn is eaten, the
clothing worn, each by its own purchaser. "In the circulation of C-
M-C the money is in the end converted into a commodity, that
serves as a use-value; it is spent once for all" (Tucker 330).

   In the statement M-C-M', on the other hand, the commodity stays in circulation, and money returns to the hands of the

original investor. The commodity is not used as such, but rather exchanged for more money. Neither is the money used as a use-value, a convenient, portable, durable means of exchange. Rather, it exists as capital, as exchange value: it exists only to increase its value, and this it does by ceaseless circulation, using commodities for the purpose of enhancing the value of capital. In the system M-C-M' the purchaser advances money for a commodity whose sole purpose is to be exchanged once again for money. It doesn't matter what the commodity is, of what use it is to be put, so long as it brings in more money than its purchase price. The money goes back into the hands of the original purchaser, whose true identity is now revealed as "investor" rather than farmer, carpenter, person requiring food. Under the logic of this system, the only thing to be done with the money is to advance it once again for still greater anticipated profit. The very logic of the form M-C-M' thus compels endless circulation. It becomes M-C-M'-C-M''-C-M''' and so on *ad infinitum.* The money, or capital, circulates on its own as it were, by the rules of the logic of capitalism. Individual capitalists are objects used by capital, which has its own life. In the situation C-M-C the only reason to exchange goods is particular human need. People dominate in C-M-C; capital dominates in M-C-M'.

Consider the two formulae from another perspective now, and Marx's insight is not so obviously materialist. If we focus upon the middle of each series, there seems to be little difference between the two systems. A capitalist might be seen exchanging a commodity for money and then purchasing another commodity. How can we tell what he's going to do with the goods? How do we distinguish him from somebody purchasing goods for use rather than investment? The difference is certainly not merely material. The material events are nearly identical: the exchange of goods for money, and money for goods. What then distinguishes C-M-C from M-C-M'? Human experience is what distinguishes between the two.... even if the capitalist isn't fully aware of the fact that when he looks at corn he sees not food but a commodity for exchange that might just as well be chairs or shoes.

Once again, Marx's description of reality is dialectical not because he focuses on the material rather than the ideal or spiritual. It is dialectical because it permits us to see that C-M-C and

M-C-M' *can be* so different: they simply cannot be understood in a purely material, concrete, external, objective sense. Focusing on the objective material world does not begin to describe Marx's dialectic. The difference between C-M-C and M-C-M' is human experience; the experience of someone who is investing capital is radically different from that of someone who is purchasing a commodity for use, even if what happens objectively (materially) in both scenarios is that money is put into a person's hands and corn is loaded onto a truck. Although Marx chooses most often to emphasize that human experience is material, in fact it is much more complex than that. Experience is mediated always by consciousness, and consciousness involves ideas. In Marx's dialectic, consciousness or ideas are active, shaping human experience, giving meaning to the material world. The activity of ideas makes it difficult to imagine an end to dialectics at all. Ideas are not determined but rather influenced by the material world. Ideas themselves are unpredictable and do not end anywhere.

What difference then does the starting point make in dialectical epistemology? If it is the *process* of interpenetrating subjectivity and objectivity that constitutes the radical potential of dialectics, what difference should it make whether one begins to look in the material world or in the realm of ideas? If the permeability of the boundaries between subject and object is bound to change dynamically through time, where does one who seeks knowledge stand to begin with?

Hegel and Marx attempted to relieve the tension that accompanied their dialectical approaches to history. Hegel opted for the relative security of ideas, Marx for what appeared to be solid, material ground. In so doing, each in his own way abandoned his commitment to a dialectical epistemology. Marx's argument, appearing in its purest, most schematic form in the economic writings, is that the "starting point" in dialectical thought *must* be the material world. It becomes readily apparent that material reality for Marx is human experience, which opens the doors to all sorts of uncertainties. For human experience is subjective: its tangibility is mediated by consciousness—feelings or ideas—that are intangible, not necessarily material, and not necessarily objective at all.

Starting point in dialectical epistemology, then, may best be viewed as a proclamation of one's subjective priorities in a similar way as end point. A starting point is actually no more dialectical than the inevitable dialectical end in either communism or the absolute idea. The radical promise of dialectical methodology was abandoned by both Hegel and Marx because each believed that his method led inexorably to certain fixed political conclusions, whereas the promise of dialectical method as revealed and then ignored by both is precisely its capacity to avoid such static ends. A necessary starting point is as false as an inevitable end. Remove presupposed dialectical beginnings and ends from their accounts and the disconcerting "determinism" of both Hegel's idealism and Marx's historical materialism vanishes. What is left is an epistemology that dismantles the rigid boundary between objective world and subjective observer: an epistemology that acknowledges the importance of the past in determining the present and the future and yet facilitates reconsideration and reinterpretation of the meaning of the past.

For example, most women *have* been excluded from public and political life since the beginning of time. Human perspective on that past is, however, continually changing, and even "authoritative" interpretations of the past soon become part of the history they interpret. Changes in perspective on the past determine the experience of self in relation to that past and, consequently, the course of future behavior. Knowledge of the past and of one's relation to history is the tool with which the future is forged in both idea and reality.

Feminist theorists might find themselves in conflict with traditional interpretations of history and disagree among themselves about the significance of women's contributions, but there is no need to glorify an alternative female contribution to history, such as private as compared to public, or emotional as compared to rational. Awareness of what has been woman's sphere does not foreclose participation in another capacity in the future. Appreciation of the material does not involve denigration of the ideal. The fact that dichotomies such as subject and object, or passion and reason, have dominated Western thought is neither without significance nor immutable. To deny that the categories have anything to do with women is simply to turn and run: if their significance is to be changed for the future, they must first be understood and accepted as part of the past as well as the present.

Dialectical theory offers promise for feminist theory only if feminist theory utilizes its strength, its force as a radical epistemology, and adds the missing ingredient to both the Hegelian and the Marxian dialectic. Feminist theory must avoid the temptation to end dialectical tension by leaping to *either* idealism or materialism. Catharine MacKinnon's argument that consciousness *is* material for women, with the implication that "consciousness raising" is more than a cliché from the sixties, must be taken seriously.[8] At the same time, consciousness is not enough. The objective reality of history must be acknowledged. The deconstruction of history into a subjectivist haze amounts only to a denial of the importance of the past in the forging of the present. The task of creating a new future falls first to the "senses as theoreticians." When the senses are understood as products of history that can move people beyond a static empirical reality only by understanding their roots in history, then objectivity and subjectivity will have forged a dialectic capable of feminist change. The promise of dialectics for feminist theory is that it makes possible an epistemology that neither accepts nor relinquishes the objective world, neither settles for nor neglects a subjectivist perspective. Change results from a fearless confrontation with and acceptance of the importance of continuity in human life.

CHAPTER 7

CONCLUSION

MINIMALIST DIALECTICS:
BEYOND HEGEL AND MARX

"Minimalist dialectics" calls for no elaborate new technique that must be inculcated into humanity by a knowing elite. It is simply a shift in perspective permitting access to an overlooked dimension of self-knowledge and worldly awareness. Many existing theories make use of themes that may appear similar to minimalist dialectics. The search for a way to integrate subjectivity and objectivity is not new. However, there are some aspects to this methodology that distinguish it from other attempts at epistemological integration.

Minimalist dialectics offers a conception of truth set in motion. It assumes that there *is* truth, involving moments of both objectivity and subjectivity in continual interaction. This conceptualization of truth is thus neither wholly arbitrary nor wholly structured. It involves neither the lack of structure of deconstructionist thought nor the self-appointed task of neo-Marxists: anticipation of where dialectical materialism *must* lead. It avoids the static dichotomies of empiricism, but acknowledges persistent tension between subjectivity and objectivity. In focusing upon the relationship between subjective and objective perspectives, minimalist dialectics is profoundly, self-consciously agnostic about where that interaction may lead. The only faith called for is that mutual understanding, recognition, agreement may arise for moments between people and in response to the material world. These moments are what we call truth. Certainty, however, is the property of no privileged perspective: it is neither objective nor subjective, although it involves both moments conventionally understood. That some human agreement is temporarily possible is certain to the minimalist dialectician, but the stability of that agreement is profoundly uncertain.

The two characteristics of materialist and idealist dialectics that distinguish them from empiricism are *historicism* and the notion of progress through *conflict* between subjectivity and objectivity. Minimalist dialectics also regards truth as a product of conflict and unity between subjectivity and objectivity. Instead of a theory of history, minimalist dialectics operates with *shortened temporal perspective,* which is what permits the method's self-conscious uncertainty. It offers nothing so grand as a theory of history; it does assume that all thought takes place in *time.* That is, nothing is permanent, all things develop, but human perspective is brief and limited compared to a conventional historicist outlook. All perspectives continue to change from the standpoint of this method. That subjectivity and objectivity are moments of perspective is certain, but what change will bring is ultimately unpredictable. History exists only as hindsight, and from a minimalist dialectical perspective the notion of history is not necessarily empirical, but is subject to epistemological abstraction that changes as time goes on. All we have available in the world we inhabit is the short view: time, rather than history.

How can short-run, momentary truth be described? Perspective develops through temporal delays from the moment of an actual material event. Experience itself cannot be discounted, but at the moment of occurrence it must be understood as incomplete. Take as an analogy reading a book. From the moment the text is picked up, it must offer some promise of interest, engagement, involvement for the reader; the reader recognizes something that permits her to continue to read, and which seems "right" or true to her. Continuing to read, of course, she will not see the "rightness" of everything the author has written and will not recognize everything as familiar. Her experience with the text will be a complex combination of recognition, familiarity, surprise, doubt, and disagreement. She will be swept along, lost in the text at times, in Hegelian terms experiencing an objective moment, her subjectivity lost to the work. At other times she might be bored, less involved in the writing, more aware of her subjectivity as distinct from the objective work: "I'd really like a cup of coffee now," "I'm starving; maybe I ought to make myself a sandwich... or would I rather have a doughnut?" Or simply, "This is tedious... I'm bored." In Hegelian terms this would describe a subjective moment: thoroughly conscious of self even while involved in an activity external to the self. Of course there are moments in between, when she is interested but struggling with a difficult passage, perhaps, alternatively lost in the text and self-consciously aware of her struggle to understand.

From such a complex of perspectives, it becomes difficult to provide a single description of her experience with the book. Yet, if a friend should ask our reader whether she enjoyed the book or not, whether she thought it was a "good" book or not, she would most likely be able to provide a fairly succinct answer. The variety of responses while reading describes the interaction between the object (book) and the subject (reader) in *time* in a quite literal, material sense. Assuming for simplicity's sake that our reader begins to read in the morning (she could be a night owl, in which case the time on the clock would change in this description but not much else), the book might easily engage her early in the day: she is well fed, well rested, and in prime condition for ignoring her subjective needs and beginning to read. As time passes she becomes fatigued, hungry, and other obligations (picking up a child at school, an errand she had planned to do) may begin to impinge. She must find the book fascinating at this point for it to sustain and prolong her time of involvement with it. Otherwise her attention might begin to wander, whereas it might not have had she read the same passages several hours earlier.

Yet, in spite of the innumerability of variables, with their sources in both the book and the reader's life, when she has finished the book the experience congeals, permitting succinct summation. The reader can most likely abbreviate her experience by describing the book as "good" or "bad" or "interesting" or "important" or "difficult." What then is the truth of her reading experience? Is it best described by one of the moments along the way, or by the conclusive "That was a good book!" overriding the moments of hunger, boredom, and distracted energy? I would argue that while all the moments contribute to the truth of experience, the astute reader will recognize that any judgment on the book must be deferred until sufficient distance has established itself, enough time has passed so that it makes sense to speak of the experience as a whole. The subjective moments of fatigue or hunger, which seemed so compelling at the time, are now absorbed into the experience identified with the book. The reader can say "how the book was," but that is also not the final truth. Aspects of the reading experience may emerge well after the book has been put on the shelf. A passage that seemed boring or trivial when first read might emerge as important or at least surprisingly vivid or helpful in a later context. Something that seemed crucial or profound at the time of reading may fade into triviality with time, with familiarity, or from the perspective of additional reading and thinking. One can change one's mind about the book. In that case, the truth may be: "The book seemed good at the time, but I now recognize that it was rather limited."

There *is* a truth about the reader's experience with the book. Not just any answer will do when the question "How was that book?" is asked. Yet the truth is momentary: complete for the first time after the book is either read or put down unfinished. The truth must be deferred at least until then. While judgment should be delayed until some sort of initial moment of completion, judgment will not be final then either. The reader anticipates its change through time. Thus she can commit herself to a definite answer about the book and at the same time anticipate the uncertainty of that answer in the future. The whole of her experience, both the certainty and the uncertainty, and the constant change through time can be described as evolving moments of conflicting and reinterpreted subjectivity and objectivity. The long-range historical truth, the excellence or mediocrity of the book, can be decided only by the passage of much more time and the judgment of generations of readers, and even at that it continues to evolve. Plato and Aristotle have been in and out of good grace for millennia. The fact that they continue to be printed says something; the fact that we can count on generations of critics and detractors says something else. The minimalist dialectical approach does not anticipate a historical truth; it self-consciously focuses on the changes that occur in a shorter time frame. It is agnostic about historical truth.

જ⁀

The major difference between this description of the process of acquiring truth and other attempts at integrating subjectivity and objectivity is in the emphasis minimalist dialectics places upon the inevitability of tension and conflict, evolving through time, with no certain outcome. In order to make the differences vivid, let us return to Hegel's "Master and Servant." Feminist theorists, from de Beauvoir to those of the 1980s, have utilized Hegel's description of the master and servant in order to portray a feminist—or simply women's—epistemological standpoint. How does the minimalist dialectical interpretation of Hegel differ from those perspectives?

Most importantly, the usual focus is upon the appropriateness of one perspective—that of the servant, or the oppressed—for feminist consciousness. More traditionally, Hegel's radical potential is identified with his assertion that the essential consciousness belongs to the servant. In contrast, a minimalist dialectical approach focuses upon the process, the development of thought that led to the possibility of seeing the servant's perspective as central. This permits us to move beyond that moment (that is, move beyond even Hegel) to the possibility that the consciousness of the servant is *not* after all definitive. In turn, this leaves room for the more materialist criticism that, in the end, the master still holds power over the servant, that "free in consciousness" is not "free in actuality," that is, the Marxist critique of Hegel. It also permits us to move beyond Hegel to question his own assumptions about the interdependence of master and servant. Perhaps a coterie of masters would be sufficient to provide each master with enough recognition to achieve self-certainty. Perhaps, by extension, men are quite capable of validating each other and need the validation of women less than they need "male bonding" for mutual self-affirmation.

These are not conclusions. They are questions made possible by this epistemological approach, shunning ultimate truths as it embraces short-run moments of truth. Dialectical *process* enabled Hegel to arrive at the understanding that the servant's consciousness is essential. This startling insight was the result of a revolutionary method. As indicated in the chapter on Hegel, as well as the one on Marx, I believe the two dialecticians betrayed their own revolutionary method by settling on the final "essentiality" of any consciousness, or any material state of affairs. That is, there is no end point to a true dialectic, hence no ultimately essential anything, either material or ideal.

Likewise, most contemporary dialectical thinkers, including the feminists who utilize Hegel's "Master and Servant" discussion, focus upon substantive conclusions rather than the neverending dynamic demanded by the method. The Hegelian idealist dialectic brings us to the consciousness of the servant; Marx's materialism brings us to the primacy of production in human existence. In both of these stances there is substantive promise for feminism, but to stop thinking after having arrived at a position that suits one's political predispositions is a violation of dialectical method. In the feminist theory that utilizes Hegelian and Marxian dialectic, focus on conflict or opposition is derived from Hegel, or Marx, depending upon whether the feminist theory leans more toward psychologism or materialism. The dialectical method is lost when that sense of conflict leads to and settles upon the correctness of any one consciousness or the correctness of the stance of Other. The idea of a stable other with oppositional consciousness is what leads to closed-minded political smugness. It can also lead to the romanticization of oppression.

Sandra Harding describes this problem in her wary discussion of the tendency to try to tell "one true story." Instead of focusing on the *evolution* of conflict and oppositional consciousness, and the interpenetration of subjects and objects, the tendency has been to take the easy way out, to look for oppositional consciousness and "who's got one."[1] This simply stalls dialectical method, preventing it from moving beyond a static conception of the world. Dialectical method is radical because of its ability to see the interpenetration of consciousnesses—even of oppressor and oppressed—as systematic and inevitable. It could never truly settle on one static perspective.

The acceptance of a static "appropriate" perspective—oppositional in this case—for women can lead to what Harding describes as "excessive containment within Marxist epistemological assumptions . . . about the political economy . . . that we begin to exist as distinctive social persons only when we get our first paycheck" (194). It also leads to the assumption that women's consciousness is different from men's and better, this time not because of nature but because of a history of oppression that leads to the more promising psychology of the Other.

The acceptance of a static oppositional consciousness for women leads us back to de Beauvoir, who defined woman as Other but regarded that as a problem rather than the basis of any particular excellence. That is, although many feminist theorists have utilized some aspects of dialectic—even drawn directly from Hegel—the far-reaching potential of dialectical method is usually slighted. The dialectic is used to bring us to a point where conflict between subject and object can be understood, but then the method is abandoned, replaced by a conventional perspective grounded in a static oppositional stance. Master and servant, man and woman, oppressor and oppressed exist in a conventional way as roles, essentialities, rather than as dynamic, changeable existences.

Even de Beauvoir, who was certainly influenced by Hegelian thought, freezes the category of Other, regards subjects and objects as embodying essences. She defines men as subjects, women as objects, and uses the Hegelian categories in an un-Hegelian manner. Her application of the passages in Hegel on Master and Servant rests upon the assumption that Hegel did not regard women as fully human. In contrast I have argued that Hegel's substantive beliefs about women do not necessarily undermine the potential power of dialectical method for feminism. De Beauvoir notes:

> Certain passages in the argument employed by Hegel in defining the relation of master to slave apply much better to the relation of man to woman. The advantage of the master, he says, comes from the affirmation of spirit as against life through the fact that he risks his own life; but in fact the conquered slave has known the same risk. Whereas woman is basically an existent who gives life and does not risk *her* life; between her and the male there has been no combat. Hegel's definition would seem to apply especially well to her. He says: "the other consciousness is the dependent consciousness for whom the essential reality is the animal type of life; that is to say, a mode of living bestowed by another entity."[2]

What I have identified as the radical aspect of Hegelian dialectical method is the interchangeability of the consciousness of master and servant, or indeed any two human beings. There can be no essential object or subject because the subjectivity and objectivity of each depends upon the other and are in constant interaction.

There are still some questions left unanswered by this conceptualization of dialectics. I have argued for an epistemology that views a world in motion, where truth is always incomplete, involving the passage of time (but not necessarily enough time to constitute history), and involving conflict between perspectives identified as subjective and objective. This version of dialectical method differs from more conventional Hegelian and Marxian dialectics with regard to the diminished time frame and the unwillingness to settle on the correctness of any one moment of insight as final or essential. One important remaining question, then, is how does this method differ from deconstructionism, which also argues against the finality of any one perspective, any one fix on truth? How can minimalist dialectics embrace a notion of truth if moments of truth are continually changing: not just evolving but going through a process of negation, of becoming what they are not before perhaps reemerging as more complete?

Before embarking upon an analysis of this question, consider two other related questions. I have argued that dialectical truth, in addition to being fuller and more complete, also allows for the possibility of political change in a way that empiricism does not. Doesn't progressive political change of necessity place focus on the perspective of the excluded? For radical political change explicitly involves incorporating the perspective of the unincorporated. Can minimalist dialectics circumvent the contradiction between a privileged "standpoint epistemology" as described by Harding and Hartsock, and the poststructuralism also embraced by Harding? Does the notion of minimalist dialectics as a methodology for change conflict with what I have just argued about there being no privileged epistemological positions in dialectical method? How can the pursuit of even momentary truth be reconciled with a justification for a particular political change? Part of what made Hegel's description of the coming to dominance of the consciousness of the servant so compelling was the idea that the servant, because he was Object, or Other, had access to a consciousness, inaccessible to the master, which entailed familiarity with the material world, as well as with helpless, dependent fear. Doesn't the consciousness of the oppressed then carry particular weight even in Hegel's more conservative dialectic?

Finally, what distinguishes minimalist dialectics from a psychologistic, "encounter-group" consciousness that reduces conflict and opposition to a stagy, contrived "confronting the perspective of the Other" in a safe environment that practically guarantees moments of mutual understanding and self-confirmation? Indeed, what distinguishes dialectical method from the conflict that so effortlessly becomes consensus through talk and rationality in liberal theory?[3] In sum, how do the components truth, conflict, and materiality work together in the never-ending process I have entitled minimalist dialectics?

To begin with, minimalist dialectics is to be distinguished from deconstructionism because it accepts conventional epistemological parameters. Minimalist dialectics regards the perspectives available to human beings in terms of subjectivity and objectivity. The experience described above, for example, of reader and text is approached in quite conventional terms: the book is accepted as having an objective existence external to the reader, divided from her by physical characteristics, the perimeter—skin—of the reader's body and the jacket of the book. (I imagine this excludes the perspective of nuclear physics, which might be able to link the two objects—the woman's body and the book—through some continuum of molecules.) From the minimalist dialectical perspective, both reader and book *do* have a tangible, finite, objective existence. Likewise, both are also regarded as possessing a subjective existence: the woman quite conventionally as a person with feelings, perceptions, idiosyncrasies, an internal life; and the book not so conventionally as possessing the active capacity to engage the reader.

This latter point—the subjectivity of the inert material object—is where dialectical thought departs from conventional empiricism, which regards objects as simply objects. The subjectivity that I attribute to the book should not be associated with the inversion of traditional epistemology common to deconstructionism. Deconstructionist theory does make a point of relocating marginal epistemological categories to center stage, hence of inverting traditional epistemological priorities. This means that deconstructionist theory privileges the position of the reader, undermining the traditional authority of the author over his or her text. Paradoxically, from the dialectical perspective presented here, this can be seen as a rather conventional outlook. What is radical about the dialectical epistemology is its regard for a form of activity, a certain capacity to engage, associated with the text itself, which has subjective as well as objective aspects, and acts as an intermediary between author and reader. However, this radically unconventional attribution of subjectivity to an object is a declaration of neither animism nor epistemological anarchy. The subjectivity of the book is certainly more flexible, but it is also limited by the very objectivity it presupposes. The dialectical assumption is that subjectivity and objectivity are ways of describing aspects that are both in conflict and inseparable. They are momentary aspects of worldly existence. Where there is subjectivity there is objectivity. Acceptance of the conventional categories of subject and object implies that there are certain minimal limits to the meanings that can be attributed to the text. The words *do* have objective existence; the author chose certain words and not others. The reader and author both live in a material historical world. They each have a biography. Everything that contributes toward understanding "the reading" does have both objective and subjective aspects, even though understanding is never frozen into completion.

Thus, not simply anything the reader finds in the text can be considered an appropriate reading, or true. There are objective words on a certain objective number of pages. The truth of the book may not exist as anything final or static, but it must incorporate the intentions of the author, the words he or she chose to include in the book, and the complex subjective experience of the reader. Certain things are not open to debate at all, or at least debate would be rather a waste of time. If the book has 328 pages, each five inches wide and eight inches high, people can agree on that as an objective fact—even if someone prefers to count the pages in Roman numerals and somebody else to measure in metric figures. Objective factors place certain conventional limitations on the book as a flexible, subjective medium. Likewise there are objective aspects to the reader's existence. She lives in a particular country, or locale, at a particular time in history. She has had a particular education, lives with specific circumstances: money, job, size of family, size of house, lighting of the room she reads in, and so forth.

The acceptance of conventional objectivity, even for moments, guarantees that in a minimalist dialectical framework there is a certain stability to history. It is not possible, by some clever act of decentering, to deny events of the past, even if it is possible to interpret them in a new light. Witch hunts actually objectively happened, as did slavery, the holocaust, and countless other examples of atrocious oppression. A disproportionate number of people of color suffer some sort of economic deprivation, and most women throughout history have been confined to a severely limited sphere of life. Minimalist dialectics does not have a theory of history, but it does assume the undeniability of certain events and conventional methods for confirming their existence. The method then proceeds to assume that the simple, empirically confirmable existence of events is only the first step in understanding their relationship to the present and future.

While subjectivity cannot exist without—and indeed presupposes—this objectivity, the objectivity is also an invitation to find the subjectivity of an event. The book demands to be read; printed words mean different things to different readers, and their meaning changes through time. Not only do words have different connotations in different historical times, but consider how dramatically different a book seems to the same reader on its second reading. Of course the difference is dependent upon the experience of the reader, who in fact possesses a human consciousness. However, the book itself as an object demands interaction and is necessary for the growth of the reader's consciousness. The empiricist description of what happens while reading is hopelessly inadequate because it assumes that the book and reader are really, objectively separate from one another. Such a stubbornly limited view does not begin to describe the complexity of the interaction between human being and material world.

Thus does minimalist dialectics' acceptance of the epistemological parameters described by subjectivity and objectivity distinguish the method from deconstructionism. The acknowledgement of conflict between subject and object along with the assumed inseparability of the terms also distinguishes dialectical thought from empiricism. The experience of conflict, loss, and the regaining of the self enriched is the source of progress and growth in dialectical thought.

৯▲

Let us see whether minimalist dialectics can help to resolve a problem of specific importance to feminism by returning to Catharine MacKinnon's discussion of the relationship between rape and heterosexual intercourse. Remember that MacKinnon identified the liberal legal problem with rape with the assumption that an objective event actually happened. Many, even most, rapes, she suggested, occur between "honest men and violated women." In that case, she mused, what can a court possibly find: that a woman was raped, but not by a rapist? MacKinnon argued that the legal system is likely to defer to the male perspective, questioning whether a rape actually occurred, rather than ever acknowledging the equal validity of *two* perspectives.

From a minimalist dialectical outlook, however, it ought to be possible to settle upon an objective perspective, at least for a moment, which would emerge from the clash of two subjectivities without stepping outside the event to acquire an empiricist's distance and detachment. If the method is viable for feminism, it should provide insight that moves beyond the relativism of double subjectivity and avoids the detached finality of traditional objectivity (e.g. if there is "reasonable doubt" that a rape occurred, then the legal system must find for the accused. From MacKinnon's viewpoint, the reasonable doubt is provided by the rapist himself, whose subjectivity is thus privileged.).

What minimalist dialectics adds to MacKinnon's analysis is an assumption that something *did* objectively happen, that understanding it fully may involve acknowledging a powerful conflict of perspectives, which must be allowed to play out completely, without fear that the objective truth will dissolve in a relativistic haze. Let us assume now that the liberal legal system and the man who honestly believes that he did not rape share a perspective, as MacKinnon suggests. Let us also assume that they, at least at the conscious level, believe that rape is wrong and different from "normal" heterosexual intercourse. That is, let us assume that an unrepentant violent rapist will not escape conviction; it is the boundary between rape and intercourse that we are exploring here.

From the woman's perspective there is no doubt: whatever rape may technically be defined as, she *knows* she has been sexually violated. Her subjective experience feels absolute: she is wounded, enraged, would like to strike back, to hurt her assailant. The reality of her sense of violation can be gauged by the intensity of her response. It leaves no room for metaphysical quibbling about what objectively happened. The problem is to create a legal, social, and political environment that acknowledges the objectivity of her position, an objectivity measured in part by subjective experience.

Now let us imagine the position of the accused man: can the intensity of his response match the woman's? I suggest that if there is any possibility in his mind that he may have forced himself on her against her will, he cannot match her outrage, and this lack of subjective affect will manifest itself in his objective behavior. The assumption that emotional reality will manifest itself credibly in objective symptoms or signals is not much of a departure from the assumptions of psychological theory and practice, although it does also presume that a jury comprised of citizens who are not professionally trained psychologists will be able to respond to the signals. That is to say, a rape either occurred or did not occur, and on some level both parties know what happened. It is simply not all that ambiguous to either of them.

The responses of the accused and the accuser are not static states in dialectical epistemology. They will develop from the point of the event, which constitutes an actual (objective) moment. A victim may be shocked, numbed, may experience denial immediately after having been raped. A man may feel uneasy about something "vaguely wrong" and also deny, push the experience and his sense of responsibility for it away. If we can create a conducive social environment, the objective reality of rape will emerge in the form of the victim's subjectively experienced rage and perhaps even allow the rapist's vague unease to develop into awareness of what he has done. That is, the objective event itself has the subjective capacity to evoke the victim's and the perpetrator's responses. The responses develop over time, and possibly in relation to each other. A rape *has* occurred to the extent that someone sustains the extreme outrage. From the victim's perspective, an unwanted kiss or touch, or even verbal sexual harassment may constitute a rape as much as does actual forced intercourse. It is a conventional judgment that determines what sort of sexual imposition constitutes a rape that can send an aggressor to prison. The woman's experience—the undeniable knowledge that she has been violated, even if it takes a while for the anger to emerge—is not privileged to the point of being sufficient to convict a man in court, but neither is its objectivity to be doubted. Currently, it is precisely this sort of "emotionalism" that is not permissible evidence in a court of law. The courtroom, and liberal society in general, seek to separate subjective from objective responses, and to value the dispassionate as more reliable.

In the approach to truth suggested by minimalist dialectics, the passionately subjective response is regarded as part of what objectively happened: it is an aspect of the objective truth. In the case of a rape, not only the woman's sustained anger but the man's subjective response must figure into the judgment. He is likely, in the face of such fury directed at him, to seek to protect himself—either in more vigorous denial or (if a miracle occurs) in recognition and remorse. He will not remain cool and objective. If a judge and jury must determine a course of action, if in fact subjective passion on the part of both accuser and accused are regarded by "the system" as moments of truth in themselves, a judgment is possible to the extent that the jury can participate in, attempt to *lose* their distance and detachment momentarily to, the power of the two parties' subjective passions.

I am hoping of course that, if a rape occurred, the power of the victim's response will be more persuasive than the power of the accused's response. Conversely, if there is doubt that a rape occurred, the power of the accused's experience should prevail. This is not a description of a contest of wills, with the stronger will "winning out." If that were the case, the only likely consequence would be that self-doubt would prevent the oppressed from ever having their day in court. It can work only if truth is regarded as containing objective moments achieved by valuing and participating in the development of subjective moments where distance and detachment are momentarily lost. The hope is that what will emerge from those moments of lost perspective is hard-won understanding, never regarded as final but agreed upon as sufficient to provide justification for action such as convicting a person of a crime and determining appropriate punishment. This is a conception of truth as a process that involves moments of seriously clashing subjective perspectives. Still, the assumption is that when the smoke clears there are moments of completion which, while never absolute, are sufficient to provide a basis for responsible public action.

Of course, should such a perspective ever become adopted by the legal system, the parties would soon know what is expected of them. In this sense, again, the dialectic must be regarded as a never-ending process capable of responding to the possibility of courtroom histrionics to establish one's "passionate" credibility. The judge and jurors, guardians in this case of the dialectical method, know no rest but must be aware of their own participation in the courtroom experience. Their willingness to acknowledge their own (changing) perspectives, and their vulnerability to the partiality of the disputants is what gives them the ability to resist manipulation, and the possibility to make responsible judgements. Static, objectified, codified legal procedures invite a passivity that is incompatible with the vitality of the minimalist dialectical method.

This conceptualization of truth is indeed risky. It calls for a social environment sufficiently nurturing to permit a victim's responses to emerge in their full complexity. Surely a courtroom cannot duplicate a therapist's office, and the constraints of time and expense may inhibit the full development of dialectical tension in, for example, a sexual assault. One risk is that if those objective constraints prohibit the bringing forth of the victim's response, if that emotional bedrock of rage that I am here assuming accompanies a sense of violation, never emerges, the jury will indeed have to find that a rape did not occur. Catharine MacKinnon herself would have to believe in the superiority of conventional objectivity, if she were to argue that such a legal decision is erroneous. The minimalist dialectical approach would have to concede that if the victim did not experience herself as violated, then no rape in fact occurred. Still, the subjectivity of each is protected in a way that conventional empiricism does not do. If the subjectivity of each is protected, it is not privileged. It can be understood only in relation to other subjectivities, in an interactive process where subjectivity and objectivity are acknowledged to be mutually defining.

At the risk of concluding this discussion on a pop-cultural note, I refer to a courtroom scene in a fairly recent movie, *Legal Eagles*. The two stars are lawyers who have the task of defending a young woman who has no alibi, no witnesses on her behalf, and a history of lying to everybody, including her lawyers (played by Robert Redford and Debra Winger), against a murder charge. Still, because this young, seductive liar has also been a victim of more dangerous criminals, the viewer—and her lawyers—are given to a vague, subjective sense that she should be exonerated: she probably is not guilty of murder, although we don't know why because she seems to be guilty of many other things she has lied about.

In his opening remarks to the jury, the usually flamboyant Redford finds that he can rouse neither himself nor the jury to any sympathy for the victim. He is flat. In desperation, he shifts gears and proclaims to the stunned courtroom, "Okay, let's admit it: we all think she's guilty. I think my client is guilty, you think my client is guilty, who could think anything else? So let's convict her and get it over with!" His legal partner, his client, the judge, and the jury are horrified, although the prosecutor seems pleased, if somewhat undone. One juror meekly suggests to Redford, "Isn't she entitled to a fair trial?" Redford retorts, "Oh! Okay, let's give her a fair trial and then convict her! Is that what you want?"

The point I find intriguing about this example is the exposure, the bringing to the surface of the usual subjectivities that the legal system assumes are held in check in a court of law. Only when the prejudgment is brought forth, articulated, admitted, allowed to shock, allowed to be *experienced* publicly, in a court of law, is the trial in a position to proceed. After the scene just described, the trial does proceed. It is not an easy one: objectivity does not win the day, glibly returning and settling over the courtroom. The moment of confrontation between subjectivity and objectivity permits the trial to continue. This is a description of a dialectical moment.

ã⊛

We are now in a position to begin to see the relationship between this description of dialectical truth and the potential of minimalist dialectics to support or justify political change that is not possible in an empiricist framework. The limitations of empiricism's capacities to link the pursuit of truth with the pursuit of political change are obvious enough. Empiricism has no theory of history. It is a "rationalist" method in that its categories—subjectivity and objectivity—exist outside time. Truth is equated with objectivity, which is viewed in static terms as something "out there." The subject may accumulate more objective data (bearing in mind the limitations and logical questions raised earlier), but the data itself is impermeable and does not change by virtue of interaction with the subject. Empirical evidence, then, is by definition unchanging, and empirical truth must be grounded in existing objective reality. The pursuit of truth and the pursuit of political change are thus antithetical projects, given an empiricist epistemological outlook. Truth is to be found in the existing world, which has no innate capacity to change because it is objective, inert, unchanging without human intervention. Should human subjects intervene in the objective world, they contaminate it as data, and in the act of changing it sacrifice their privileged, detached Archimedean stance and render themselves incapable of seeing truth. One acts, *or* one reasons: to the empiricist, the two activities are distinct, and indeed incompatible.

This hands-off stance that prevents the empiricist from becoming involved enough with the world to change it can be viewed as an invitation to political irresponsibility and "knownothingism": "Don't blame me because these poor people are homeless and starving; I'm just collecting data. The policy planners will change things." Even worse, "The data will determine what changes are possible." There is also a more benign way of viewing the separation of knowledge from political action. It is, as Hannah Arendt would argue, a safeguard against totalitarian systems that assume a link to exist between a particular political stance and truth. In *Origins of Totalitarianism* Arendt associates such claims of a monopoly of truth with totalitarian theory and sees little difference between the assumption of historical destiny in right-wing fascism (Hitler, Mussolini) and communism (Marxism, Leninism, and Stalinism).[4] I agree that the assumed necessity of certain historical ends connected with a methodology is indeed dangerous, and that both Hegel's and Marx's assumption of inevitable historical outcomes court the danger of totalitarianism. However, I have also argued that in assuming historical ends Hegel and Marx ceased to think dialectically. They abandoned the method. Minimalist dialectics avoids the danger of postulated historical ends because of its self-conscious agnosticism about ends and its unwillingness to indulge in sweeping theories of history. Still, minimalist dialectics is grounded in actual, material time.

How then can minimalist dialectics embrace the pursuit of both truth and political change, avoiding the conservatism of empiricism and the totalitarianism of dialectical theories of history? The conflict between subjective and objective moments is a conflict between moments in time. Each moment in which a truth establishes itself generates its own negation. The present is in conflict with its own future. In the case of the reader, she knows that her perspective on the book is always incomplete (even if there are moments that are more complete than others). She knows she is not in a position to declare once and for all the truth about either her book or her position on it. Yet she is a human subject, who is not merely passive but who has a hand in shaping the circumstances in which she finds herself. She contributes actively to the shaping of her experience with the book, finds an environment in which she can give it full, honest attention, or allows herself to be distracted by physical needs, previous intellectual allegiances, etc. She also knows that the true judgment about the excellence of the book is something that she contributes to by her reading, but which is not fully determinable by her or anybody else.

What does it mean to say that the present is in conflict with the future in dialectical thought, and that the shortened time frame in which minimalist dialectics operates precludes the possibility of assumptions of political correctness or totalitarianism? The statement that the present is in conflict with the future means only that whatever exists will of necessity beget its own negation, beget a perspective that is not available in the present. A moment of unity of self and other (subject and object) is destined to fall asunder: the sun sets, a car horn honks, and the magic moment of blissful unity is destroyed. Awareness of the inevitability of change makes it impossible to settle on the ultimate truth of any one moment. Still, subjectivity and objectivity circumscribe the possible perspectives on change: not just any change is possible, but, and this is the distinctive property of minimalist, as compared to more sweeping historical dialectics, there is no presumption of the outcome of the long historical view. The order that Hegel presupposes will emerge after chaos at the "slaughterbench of history" is too distant to figure into a minimalist dialectical approach. There is no possibility in minimalist dialectics, then, for a leap of faith such as "Reason rules the world," which could be used to justify short-term political horrors. Hitler or Stalin could not be "comprehended" as a moment of historical negation, destined to beget its own ultimate negation. There is no sacrificing of generations to a political future because minimalist dialectics does not see time in terms of historical epochs but rather as moments in a single human existence. Nor is there the possibility of a privileged intellectual position. The present will not hold still long enough for its truth to congeal. A political problem must be worked through by means of interaction between actors—for example the politically privileged and the politically oppressed—with the understanding on the part of all parties that every perspective will be undone and redone. Neither oppressor nor oppressed, man or woman, black or white, possesses the correct consciousness. The only correct consciousness is one that is capable of continually striving to comprehend its own relationship to the consciousness of the other, and this comprehension comes only by means of moments of negation.

What prevents this methodology from being reduced to psychologism, to an ahistorical, antimaterial interchange of consciousnesses? In order to regain access to the materialist aspect of dialectics, let us return to the reader and the book. There is a hint of the inevitable materialism when we recall the assumption of conventional objectivity of both the person and the book, that they are objects in time and space. Imagine now, instead of an interaction between a lifeless object (even if the lifeless object is an intermediary for a real human author), an interaction between two human beings.

Considering interaction between human beings permits us to see more about the relationship between truth and politics and to find more vividly the material aspect of minimalist dialectics. It is the materialism that prohibits its reduction to a psychologistic interaction, contained between two individuals but not related to a larger social and political environment. Even in something as apparently "innocent" as two people reading a book, a material dimension in a social and political sense will begin to make itself apparent. In the instance of the solitary reader and book, the material dimension was limited to the physical objectivity of each. When two people read a book and try to communicate with each other about it, how is the pursuit of the truth about the book related to the complexities of interaction between the two human subjects?

To begin with, there is each reader's parallel relationship with the text, with the full range of complexities described previously. There is now also a double pursuit of truth as well. Two people read a book and differ on its quality and meaning. Can both people be right? Is there a truth contained somewhere in the book that determines its meaning? A dialectical view of the situation assumes that in addition to the interaction between the subjective and objective aspects between reader and book, each reader will participate in an exchange of subjectivity and objectivity with the other. In a sense, each reader tests her own experience of the book against and through the other reader. A superficial discussion between the two readers leading to a quick consensus about the quality or meaning of the book yields little to each person. In the case of disagreement, however, each one stands to grow to the extent that she is able to confront the areas of disagreement.

The psychological context of the encounter I describe here is not a safe one. I am not referring to a benign conversation between acknowledged equals who are unthreatened by each

other (as if two such individuals actually exist!). Nor am I referring to liberal consensus theory: "There's room for both of our
opinions; no harm in differing." I am talking about focusing
upon and acknowledging the conflict, the resistances each reader
puts up when confronted with the opinion of the other, even if
the dispute is relatively mild. The other is temporarily regarded
as "enemy." The thought, "If she's right, I've completely misread
this book and I am an idiot. I will no longer trust my own judgment," might be an exaggeration, but it captures the urgency of
the conflict. One always has some stake in protecting one's own
judgment. There is a problem between self and other; there are
boundaries that can be crossed only with difficulty and some psychological risk. I would contend that the celebrated capacity of
women to find the sources of unity with other human beings will
be strengthened if the unity is the result of discord risked and
fully played out. Untested harmony awaits the first disagreement
to fall.

Part of the reason this description of an encounter between
two readers need not be considered merely "psychologistic" in a
contrived and self-contained way is that it focuses upon the
problem of the boundary between people, anticipates that interpenetration, unity, and growth can take place only by acknowledging and going through the conflict, and that the conflict cannot be safely contained. It is dangerous because of the
uncertainty of the outcome (minimalist dialectical uncertainty
about the future). Genuine conflict does not come with a guaranteed outcome. As in Hegel's master and servant scenario, I am
not talking about any slight anxiety but rather something perceived as a threat to one's very existence. Two "acknowledged
equals" might find, once engaged in disagreement, that there is
some unconscious question about their equality. One really feels
"smarter" than the other. Perhaps an unacknowledged sibling-
type rivalry has always existed between the two friends.

Why should a disagreement over a book be perceived in
such dramatic and conflictual terms? In part because I believe
such drama *does* take place between any two human beings over
many more innocent issues than we would prefer to imagine.
Indeed, the drama lurking beneath the innocent surface of most
human interactions is what makes a psychological approach so

compelling in our society, and psychotherapy prevalent enough to be comparable to a modern religion. I seek here to demonstrate why the minimalist dialectical approach does *not* become reduced to psychologism and is, rather, solidly grounded in social and political materiality.

This social and political grounding becomes apparent if we factor into our literary dispute any actual hierarchical relationship. Suppose the two readers are teacher and student, professional critic and lay reader, perhaps even man and woman. Hegel's master and servant immediately reappears, as does Marx's material world. The material reality of status difference complicates the encounter enormously. The status difference is material and not only psychological because it is manifested materially in the lives of the people involved. The teacher is paid money for his literary interpretations; the student is judged and graded for hers. The teacher moves within a sphere of different people than the student, is usually older, economically more comfortable (or at least established), and involved in a more "adult" culture. These differences are objective, tangible, external. They are not fully separable from subjective manifestations. The teacher may feel bolder about making a judgment about the book, but his interpretation may be circumscribed by the critical conventions to which he paid homage in order to achieve his professorial rank. The student may value her opinions more lightly, but she may, either wittingly or unwittingly, take risks, make much more daring and innovative judgments than her teacher. Her teacher may recognize a certain unshackled innovativeness, a sort of brilliance no longer available to him, and feel the need to defend himself from it. A life and death struggle of Hegelian proportions ensues. If there is no agreement whatsoever, then the struggle is futile and nothing is accomplished. In a sense, both consciousnesses die. If the professor bullies the student into submission or the teacher flees in terror from his critic, not much is accomplished either.

Another possibility exists: if the professor can allow himself to be threatened to the depths of his being, can endure that profound doubt about his expertise, identity, life's work as he loses himself to the student's perspective, then he has a chance of achieving, ironically enough, the consciousness of the servant and the freedom Hegel anticipates will result. The student already has, objectively, structurally, the advantage of the servant's stance, but if she can, more conventionally, "lose herself" to the professor's interpretation, she will grow as well. There is no privileged position in such an encounter; there is no essential consciousness. There is a dialectical interpenetration of consciousnesses: an acknowledged conflict, and with risk, a confrontation that results in an exchange of consciousnesses, without relinquishing the meaning of subjectivity and objectivity, the conventional stances.

ૐ

Specifically, then, what does minimalist dialectics offer as an epistemology for feminist theory? It assumes that it doesn't matter whether one begins from a material or a psychological perspective, that is, from objectivity or subjectivity, because both will be incorporated into knowledge about anything in the world. As one endeavors to understand another, one must be willing to risk losing the security of ego boundaries. As one allows oneself to be overtaken by the psychological subjectivity of the other, one also learns something about the other person's relationship with the material, objective world. A man seeking to understand something about the reality of a woman's existence will seek to understand not only the psychological particularity of a given woman (a friend, perhaps). He will in some way have to seek out details about the objective reality of her life. For example, he might never have experienced the additional thought that goes into leaving the house at night for a simple errand, or to attend a movie: "Where will I park? Is that area well lit and busy at that hour of night?" He might have to understand something about her economic situation, which is statistically likely to be more precarious than his own. He might have to try to understand something about her struggle with conventions about a woman's role: "I know I'm a lousy housekeeper, but I just can't do everything." Some things might be nearly inaccessible to him—for example, a woman's concern about coordinating a desire for children with the demands of a career in a professional world that doesn't structurally recognize such a desire.

If the dialectic is to work, he will have to strive to feel these aspects of her existence as his own. They must be perceived as negating his own everyday reality. He must experience the woman's consciousness as the essential one, his own grasp of the world regarded *at the moment* as wholly inadequate: negated, dissolved by his insight into her experience. Perhaps this cannot be achieved at will. It may take a catalyst of some kind. There are, for example, descriptions by the men themselves, of college football players weighing in, standing naked before scouts from the pros and "feeling like a piece of meat." To perceive that experience as, in this society, more feminine than masculine might begin to undermine the "manly" atmosphere of the locker room, to say nothing of forging a new line of communication between the "most masculine" men in popular imagination and their female "negations." The naked, vulnerable depersonalization of an armed forces physical exam, when understood to resemble a feminine at least as much as a masculine experience, might begin to erode complacent attitudes about the essential masculinity of life in the military. Surely there are more common examples reaching a broader spectrum of men that might act as similar catalysts: literally undermining the culturally traditional interpretation of everyday experiences.

Yet what must be understood is that the woman's consciousness is not by definition more essential than the man's. The *interchange* of consciousness is what creates the possibility of social and political change. A man and a woman are not engaged in a contest about whose experience is more essential or more oppressed. A woman, too, must risk her sureness about her own feminist consciousness by striving to lose herself in the consciousness of the man. Does the expectation of a conventionally successful career feel like a source of power or like a trap? How does he feel walking alone to his car late at night? Invulnerable? Oblivious? Or more likely to be killed than raped? What is it like for him never to expect his body to experience the dramatic moments of pregnancy and childbirth? Is there perhaps a desperation to being thirty years old and anticipating a progressive, linear weakening of his physical prowess, rather than possessing a woman's capacity for one or two flamboyant displays of fertility, resulting in the most intimate possible physical bond with another being? Perhaps some aspects of male existence just feel good, and the feminist must face her own envy or curiosity about them. Likewise, the feminist may have to face and allow herself to be overcome by the consciousness of an "ordinary housewife," or even a Phyllis Schlafly. Still, there is no anticipated correct consciousness, and there is no guarantee of political outcomes with this method. There is risk, and the belief that only through risk is there the possibility of more than the safest, most controlled change.

In Hannah Arendt's terms, each is called upon to take the stance of the conscious pariah, to voluntarily seek to understand the experience of the outsider from the *inside,* from the places in one's own experience where active identification with the outsider is appropriate.[5] This does not sanctify the consciousness of the outsider, or the oppressed, in a static way. It assumes that there are strengths to be drawn *not* from exclusion or oppression per se, but from subjectively seeking out and accepting the stance of object. Again, what distinguishes dialectical method from the more conventional view is that it isn't possible to dwell in any particular political or psychological stance for long. The meaning, the experience of the outsider's stance is continually changing, and changing in relation to its opposite or negation. Even the most abjectly oppressed people in the world must have a vestige of subjectivity left if there is to be any hope of escaping the misery of their situation. That spark of subjectivity, activity, selfhood is the only possible basis for progress toward a more fully human existence.

What about the thorny political problem of how one can expect the world to begin to behave dialectically, in the minimalist sense described in these pages? Why should someone who possesses actual power and privilege bother to risk the unsettling consequences of losing himself to another? Minimalist dialectics is a somewhat combative method, or at least conflict oriented. However, it is not coercive. It is difficult to imagine how one would force another to risk himself if he were wrapped up in elaborate self-protective systems. How can minimalist dialectics be implemented?

I don't have a ready answer to the question. It raises again the spectre of the difficult relationship between truth and politics. Two possible lines of thought occur to me. One is to think of the liberation available to the professor described above (in relation to the bright student of literature), when we imagine him placing himself in the unlikely position of servant by allowing his professorial defenses to be undermined by her unlicensed insight. If he emerges from the ordeal, and makes a habit of allowing himself to be undone as a way of learning, he earns more than our admiration. He stands a decent chance of avoiding the depression, alcoholism, and mid-life crisis that most likely await him as the price of his pompous defensiveness. A few courageous souls may find the risk worthwhile.

On the other hand, perhaps there *is* room for if not coercion at least more aggressive confrontation from feminists. Militant blacks forced white liberals to face themselves and their political pretenses in the 1960s. A more confrontational radical feminism might force liberal or not-so-liberal antifeminist souls to do some hard thinking. What would make such a radicalism uniquely compelling would not be merely the forcing of confrontation, the highlighting of differences and boundaries. Radical feminists must have the courage to abandon a stance of defensive moral self-righteousness and risk their own political certainties. Not only would they thereby set a unique historical example, but the moments of resolution to conflict and the ensuing significant change that dialectical method offers as possibility but not promise might indeed come to pass.

NOTES

CHAPTER 1

1. Hannah Arendt, *The Human Condition* (Chicago: University of Chicago Press, 1958), 137.

2. Arendt, *Human Condition,* 274.

3. Arendt, *Human Condition,* 260, and see 280.

4. Arendt, *Human Condition,* 276.

5. See Susan Hekman's discussion of this development in "Subjects and Objects: Gender and Epistemology in the Social Sciences," paper delivered at the 1987 American Political Science Association meetings in Chicago.

6. Part 1: "Feminism, Marxism, Method and the State: An Agenda for Theory," *Signs* 7, no. 3 (Spring 1982); Part 2: "Feminism, Marxism, Method and the State: Toward Feminist Jurisprudence," *Signs* 8, no. 4 (Summer 1983). Part 1 appears in the anthology *Feminist Theory, A Critique of Ideology,* ed. N. O. Keohane, M. Z. Rosaldo, and B. C. Gelpi (University of Chicago Press, 1982), and citations to it here are from the anthology. Part and page references will be given within parentheses in the text.

7. See my "Saving Objectivity for Feminism: MacKinnon, Marx and Other Possibilities," *The Review of Politics,* Fall 1987.

8. See also Catharine MacKinnon, *Feminism Unmodified, Discourses on Life and Law* (Cambridge: Harvard University Press, 1987).

9. Carol Gilligan, *In a Different Voice* (Cambridge: Harvard University Press, 1982), 1. Page references will be given within parentheses in the text.

10. An example of the moral dilemma presented for considera-

tion to participants in the study is: Should a man (named Heinz) steal a drug which he cannot afford to buy in order to save the life of his wife who is sick and desperately needs the drug?

11. Nancy Chodorow, *The Reproduction of Mothering* (Berkeley: University of California Press, 1978).

12. Dorothy Dinnerstein, *The Mermaid and the Minotaur* (New York: Colophon, 1977).

13. Sara Ruddick, "Maternal Thinking," *Feminist Studies* 6, no. 2 (Summer 1980): 347.

14. See 349.

15. And one good source would be Anne Fausto-Sterling's *Myths of Gender* (New York: Basic Books, 1985). Fausto-Sterling presents criticism of theories of difference based on biological determinism. Hers is primarily a methodological critique of male scientific findings on the subjects of hormones, genes, brain structure.

16. Luce Irigaray, *Speculum of the Other Woman,* trans. Gillian C. Gill (Ithaca, N.Y.: Cornell University Press, 1985), 246–47. Other page references will be given within parentheses in the text.

17. See Linda Alcoff, "Cultural Feminism versus Post-Structuralism: The Identity Crisis in Feminist Theory," *Signs* 13 (Spring 1988), 417, and Julia Kristeva, "Woman Can Never Be Defined," in *New French Feminisms,* ed. Elaine Marks and Isabelle de Courtitron (New York: Schoken Books, 1981), 137.

CHAPTER 2

1. Totowa, N.J.: Rowman and Allenheld, 1983. Page references will be given within parentheses in the text.

2. Ithaca, N.Y.: Cornell University Press, 1986. Page references will be given within parentheses in the text.

3. New Haven, Conn.: Yale University Press, 1985. Page references will be given within parentheses in the text.

4. Mary O'Brien, *The Politics of Reproduction* (Boston: Routledge and Kegan Paul, 1981); "Feminist Theory and Dialectical Logic," in *Feminist Theory: A Critique of Ideology,* ed. N. O. Keohane, M. Z. Rosaldo and B. C. Gelpi (Chicago: University of Chicago Press, 1982).

5. O'Brien, "Feminist Theory," 102.

6. O'Brien, "Feminist Theory," 108.

7. O'Brien, *Politics of Reproduction,* 29, 34.

8. O'Brien, *Politics of Reproduction,* 8.

9. O'Brien, *Politics of Reproduction,* 24.

10. Nancy Hartsock, *Money, Sex and Power* (New York: Longman, 1983). Page references will be given within parentheses in the text. See also Hartsock's "The Feminist Standpoint," in *Discovering Reality,* ed. Sandra Harding and Merrill B. Hintikka (Dordrecht, Holland: D. Reidel, 1983).

11. Other feminists who have written about Marxism and dialectics are Zillah Eisenstein, *The Radical Future of Liberal Feminism* (New York: Longman, 1981); Jane Flax, "Do Feminists Need Marxism?" in *Building Feminist Theory* (New York: Longman, 1981); Heidi Hartmann, "The Unhappy Marriage of Marxism and Feminism: Towards a More Progressive Union," in *Women and Revolution,* ed. Lydia Sargent (Boston: South End Press, 1981). The focus in all these works is more on the political substance of Marxism or socialism than on dialectical methodology per se.

12. In Harding and Hintikka, *Discovering Reality.* Page references will be given within parentheses in the text.

13. For a superb survey and critical analysis of modern dialectical thought see Scott Warren, *The Emergence of Dialectical Theory* (Chicago: University of Chicago Press, 1984).

14. See Jonathan Culler, *On Deconstruction: Theory and Criticism after Structuralism* (Ithaca, N.Y.: Cornell University Press, 1982).

15. I read somewhere of an old Indian woman in Mexico who said to a younger woman, "We spend our whole life learning to feel at home in our body and then it is time to leave it."

CHAPTER 3

1. John Stuart Mill, *The Subjection of Women,* intro. Wendell Robert Carr (Cambridge: MIT Press, 1970). Page references are given in the text within parentheses.

2. Sir Leslie Stephen, *The English Utilitarians,* 3 vols. (London: Duckworth, 1900).

3. Stephen, *English Utilitarians,* 3:76.

4. J. B. Schneewind, *Mill: A Collection of Critical Essays* (London: Macmillan, 1968), 4.

5. Schneewind, *Mill: A Collection,* 2.

6. Gertrude Himmelfarb, *On Liberty and Liberalism* (New York: Knopf, 1974), xii, 328.

7. Roger Scruton, *From Descartes to Wittgenstein* (New York: Harper Colophon, 1981), 232.

8. Schneewind, *Mill: A Collection,* 2.

9. See Mill's *Autobiography* for his own account of the influence of his father, and any number of psychoanalytic accounts, but especially Bruce Mazlish, *James and John Stuart Mill* (New York: Basic Books, 1975), and the chapter on Mill and Taylor in Phyllis Rose, *Parallel Lives, Five Victorian Marriages* (New York: Alfred A. Knopf, 1984). Both accounts suggest that Mill was overpowered first by his father and then by the woman he chose to love, so that he was always in some sense dependent upon them as the intellectual authorities in his life. He had a stake in reconciling their influences upon him, rather than choosing one over the other. One could say that Mill had a life-long problem with being an adult. A cautionary note should accompany the suggestion that James Mill represented rationalism to Mill. For there is also evidence that Mill was attracted to German rationalism precisely because it represented a way to escape the complete influence of his father's and Jeremy Bentham's empiricism.

10. "Now the prevailing theory of the eighteenth century was that proclaimed by Locke, 'that all knowledge consists of generalizations from experience'; or what is the opinion both of Locke and Mill comes to the same thing, that 'sensations on the mind's consciousness of its own acts are not only the exclusive sources but the sole material of our knowledge.' According to this theory there is no knowledge *a priori* —'no truths,' as Mill puts it, 'cognizable by the mind's inward light and grounded on intuitive evidence.' Coleridge, however, along with the German philosophers since Reid, takes the opposite view. He admits that no knowledge is possible without experience but he holds that in some cases 'the visible appearances of nature excite in us by an inherent law of ideas of the invisible things on which they depended.' And thus he believes that it is possible by direct intuition to perceive things and recognize truths not cognizable by our senses." (Schneewind, *Mill: A Collection,* 48)

11. John Stuart Mill, *Dissertations and Discussions,* 5 vols. (London: Longman's Green, Reader and Ryan, 1867), "Coleridge," 1:415.

12. Whether or not James Mill was an empiricist is the subject of a complicated debate, which would only be a distraction in this context.

13. Mill, "Coleridge," 409.

14. Alan S. Ryan, *J. S. Mill* (London: Routledge and Kegan Paul, 1974), 86.

15. See Sandra Harding, *The Science Question in Feminism* (Ithaca, N.Y.: Cornell University Press, 1986).

16. Willard Van Orman Quine, "Two Dogmas of Empiricism," in his *From a Logical Point of View* (Cambridge: Harvard University Press, 1961), 20.

17. Evelyn Fox Keller and Christine Grontkowski, "The Mind's Eye," in *Discovering Reality,* ed. Sandra Harding and Merrill Hintikka (Dordrecht, Holland: D. Reidel, 1983).

18. This is not peculiar to Plato: the Greek verb εἴδω, *see,* has a perfect tense οἶδα, which means both "to have known" and "to see."

CHAPTER 4

1. John Stuart Mill, *A System of Logic,* 2 vols. (London: John W. Parker, 1851), 1:9. Subsequent volume and page references are given in the text within parentheses.

2. See his *Autobiography,* ed. Jack Stillinger (Boston: Houghton-Mifflin, 1969): "I grew up ... with great inaptness in the common affairs of every day life. I was far longer than children generally are before I could put on my clothes. I know not how many years passed before I could tie a knot.... I never could, nor can I now, do anything requiring the smallest manual dexterity, but I never put even a common share of the exercise of understanding into practical things.... I was, besides, utterly inobservant: I was, as my father continually told me, like a person who had not the organs of sense: my eyes and ears seemed of no use to me, so little did I see or hear what was before me, and so little, even of what I did see or hear, did I observe and remember..." (23, 24, n. 12).

3. This experimentation in the imagination seems to have had a reality in Mill's young life. See his *Autobiography:* "During this part of my childhood, one of my greatest amusements was experimental sci-

ence; in the theoretical, however, not the practical sense of the word; not trying experiments, a kind of discipline which I have often regretted not having had—not even seeing, but merely reading about them" (12).

CHAPTER 5

1. In *An Enquiry Concerning Human Understanding* Hume remarked: "I shall venture to affirm as a general proposition which admits of no exception, that the knowledge of this relation [causation] is not, in any instance, attained by reasonings a priori, but arises entirely from experience, when we find that any particular objects are constantly joined with each other" (in *Philosophical Works of Hume*, ed. T. H. Green and T. H. Grose, 4 vols. [London: Longman's Green, 1875], IV:24), and in his *Treatise of Human Nature:* "All those objects of which we call the one *cause* and the other *effect*, considered in themselves are as distinct and separate from each other as any two things in nature; nor can we ever, by the most accurate survey of them, infer the existence of one from the other. It is only from the experience and the observation of their constant union that we are able to form this inference; and even after all, the inference is nothing but the effects of custom on the imagination" (in *Hume's Moral and Political Philosophy*, ed. Henry D. Aiken [New York: Hafner Publishing Co., 1948], 16).

2. See Scott Warren, *The Emergence of Dialectical Theory* (Chicago: University of Chicago Press, 1984), esp. 30–33, and Robert Tucker, *Philosophy and Myth in Karl Marx* (Cambridge: Cambridge University Press, 1972), esp. 34–38.

3. Warren notes of Kant, "Although he appears to overcome the duality of subject and object, he introduces a new duality of phenomenon and noumenon, which effectively expresses the fundamental problem of existence itself outside the realm of human knowledge as the mysterious *Ding an sich*. This new dualism reveals how the empiricist and rationalist strains in Kant's thought are still too clearly separated. The view that knowledge is possible only of phenomena given in sense experience is still too strongly influenced by empiricism" (Warren, *Emergence of Dialectical Theory*, 33).

4. See for example, many of the essays in Sandra Harding and Merrill B. Hintikka, *Discovering Reality*, (Dordrecht, Holland: D. Reidel, 1983).

5. G. W. F. Hegel, *Philosophy of Right*, trans. T. M. Knox (New York: Oxford University Press, 1967). Subsequent section references will be given in the text within parenthesis.

6. Indeed, the parallels between dialectical thought, sex, and birth have been noted by at least one feminist theorist. Mary O'Brien, *The Politics of Reproduction* (Boston: Routledge and Kegan Paul, 1981).

7. In the sections that follow, I present in some detail Hegel's discussions of "Master and Servant" from the *Phenomenology of Spirit,* and of marriage and the family from the *Philosophy of Right.* I include so much material from these well-known passages in Hegel because readers who are not specialists in Hegelian philosophy might be unfamiliar with them or not have read them recently. There is, of course, extensive scholarly literature on Hegel's political philosophy and dialectical method, as well as feminist commentary on Hegel. I do not mean to slight Hegelian scholarship by not making more explicit use of the wealth of interpretive work already done. Rather, I offer an interpretation of this material specifically for the purpose of considering its possibilities for feminist theory. For references to feminist commentary on Hegel, see the discussion and notes on feminist dialecticians in chapter 2. For additional material on "Master and Servant" and *The Philosophy of Right,* see, for example, the following sources: Avineri, S., *Hegel's Theory of the Modern State,* London: Cambridge University Press, 1972; Bernstein, J. M., "From Self-Consciousness to Community: Act and recognition in the Master-Slave Relationship," in Pelczynski, Z. A., ed. *Hegel's Political Philosophy: Problems and Perspectives,* London: Cambridge University Press, 1971, pp. 14–39; Gadamer, H-G., *Hegel's Dialectic,* New Haven: Yale University Press, 1976; Kojeve, A., *Introduction to the Philosophy of Hegel,* New York: Basic Books, 1969; Navickas, J. L., *Consciousness and Reality: Hegel's Philosophy of Subjectivity,* The Hague: Martinus Nijhoff, 1976; Reidel, M., *Between Tradition and Revolution,* London: Cambridge University Press, 1984; Verene, D.P., ed. *Hegel's Social and Political Thought,* Atlantic Highlands, N.J.: Humanities Press, 1990; Westphal, M., *History and Truth in Hegel's Phenomenology,* Atlantic Highlands, N.J.: Humanities Press, 1979.

8. Carl J. Friedrich, *The Philosophy of Hegel* (New York: Modern Library, 1954), 399. Subsequent page references will be given in the text within parentheses.

9. In academic life, "Ethnic Studies" or "Women's Studies" are not regarded as "legitimate" scholarly fields. Rather, whatever white men have studied defines the central areas of inquiry and does not require the specification "white" or "male." "Men's History," "Men and Politics," "Men's Economics," "Men's Literature" would appear absurd to the male scholars who dominate these fields.

10. The following passage in "Master and Servant" illustrates the point:

In the first instance, the master is taken to be the essential reality for the state of the servant; hence, for it, the truth is the independent consciousness existing for itself, although this truth is not yet taken as inherent in the servant's position itself. Still, it does in fact contain within itself this truth of pure negativity and self-existence, because it has experienced this reality within it. For this self-consciousness was not in peril and fear for this element or that, nor for this or that moment of time, it was afraid for its entire being; it felt the fear of death, it was in mortal terror of its sovereign master. It has been through that experience melted to its inmost soul, has trembled throughout its every fiber, the stable foundations of its whole being have quaked within it. This complete perturbation of its entire substance, this absolute dissolution of all its stability into fluent continuity, is, however, the simple, ultimate nature of self-consciousness, absolute negativity, pure self-referent existence, which consequently is involved in this type of consciousness. (407)

11. G. W. F. Hegel, *The Philosophy of History,* trans. J. Sibree (New York: Dover Publications, 1956).

12. Consider also other statements about woman's incapacity for learning, her placidness, the "vague unity of feeling" that characterizes women as compared to "stress of thought and . . . technical exertion" that characterizes men (§166). Hegel's misogyny is also exemplified in passages such as:

The difference in the physical characteristics of the two sexes has a rational basis and consequently acquires an intellectual and ethical significance. This significance is determined by the difference into which the ethical substantiality, as the concept, internally sunders itself in order that its vitality may become a concrete unity consequent upon this difference. (§165)

An addition supplied by Hegel's student Gans:

Women are capable of education, but they are not made for activities which demand a universal faculty such as the more advanced sciences, philosophy, and certain forms of artistic production. Women may have happy ideas, taste, and elegance, but they cannot attain to the ideal. The difference between men and women is like that between animals and plants. Men correspond to animals, while women correspond to plants because their development is more placid and the principle that underlies it is the rather vague unity of feeling. When women hold the helm of government, the state is at once in jeopardy, because women regulate their actions not by the demands of universality but by arbitrary inclinations and opinions. Women are educated—who knows how?—as it were by breathing in ideas, by living rather than by acquiring knowledge. The status of manhood, on the other hand, is attained only by the stress of thought and much technical exertion. (§107 addition to §166)

13. "Marriage is but the ethical Idea in its immediacy and so has its objective actuality only in the inwardness of subjective feeling and disposition. In this fact is rooted the fundamental contingency of marriage in the world of existence. There can be no merely legal or positive bond which can hold the parties together once their dispositions and actions have become hostile and contrary" (§176).

14. See Katherine MacKinnon's essay, "Difference and Domination" in *Feminism Unmodified*, (Cambridge: Harvard University Press, 1987).

CHAPTER 6

1. This is a specialized reading of Marx, an extraction of aspects of his dialectical method to see what they might contribute to the formulation of an epistemology for feminism. Scholarly literature on Marx's theory abounds. The sources I most often rely upon, although not specifically for the purposes of this chapter, are: Robert Tucker, *Philosophy and Myth in Karl Marx*, New York: Cambridge University Press, 1961; Bertell Ollman, *Alienation*, New York: Cambridge University Press, 1971; George Lichtheim, *Marxism*, London: Routledge and Kegan Paul, 1967; Schlomo Avineri, *The Social and Political Thought of Karl Marx*, Cambridge: The University Press, 1969; Ernst Mandell, *The Formation of the Economic Thought of Karl Marx*, New York: Modern Reader, 1971; Steven Lukes, *Marxism and Morality*, New York: Oxford University Press, 1985; David McLellan, *Karl Marx, His Life and Thought*, New York: Harper Colophon Books, Harper and Row, 1977; Roger S. Gottlieb, *An Anthology of Western Marxism*, New York: Oxford University Press, 1989.

For works specifically on Marxism and feminism, see notes 10 and 11, chapter 2.

2. Karl Marx and Frederick Engels, *Collected Works* (New York: International Publishers, 1976), 5:31. Subsequent references to volume and page will be given in the text within parentheses.

3. Mary O'Brien takes objection to Marx for saying that *men* propagate their own kind, and for placing this "circumstance" third, when it would appear to be first. Perhaps she is being too hasty: Marx mentions women specifically before the end of the sentence, and he also establishes that he does not claim to know whether the chicken or the egg came first in the passages that follow. In addition, use of the generic in German—*mensch* or even *man* does not have the explicitly male connotation it does in English. It is more accurately translated as "human beings," or "people." If Marx sought explicitly to exclude women, he would have had to break with German linguistic tradition and use the word *mann,* which means man in the sense of male and is also the word for husband. Such usage is most unlikely.

4. See, for example, Mary O'Brien, *The Politics of Reproduction,* Boston: Routledge and Kegan Paul, 1981, especially pages 116 ff., and "Feminist Theory and Dialectical Logic" in *Feminist Theory: A Critique of Ideology,* ed. Nannerl O. Keohane, Michelle Z. Rosaldo, and Barbara C. Gelpi, Chicago: University of Chicago Press, 1981. O'Brien argues that women have been defined as the gender with one, biologically defined nature, which is unchanging and unresponsive to history. Men, on the other hand, have claimed *two* natures for themselves. They are natural in a biological sense similar to women, but, in addition, have claimed to be the only species capable of making its own "second" nature, characterized by rationality and developing in response to the history that it alone, of all the species, is capable of creating.

5. In fact this may be compatible with Freud's insistence that the ego is a *bodily* ego: a part of the mind, capable of consciousness and unconsciousness, but dependent upon its physical body, and sense perception. "The ego is first and foremost a bodily ego; it is not merely a surface entity, but is itself the projection of a surface." Sigmund Freud, *The Ego and the Id,* trans. Joan Rivere, ed. James Strachey (New York: W. W. Norton, 1962), 16.

6. Robert C. Tucker, *The Marx-Engels Reader,* 2d ed. (New York: W. W. Norton, 1978), 320. References to *Capital,* vol. 1, are taken from this work.

7. Marx, *German Ideology, Collected Works,* 5:37, ". . . history ceases to be a collection of dead facts, as it is with empiricists."

8. Catharine MacKinnon in "Feminism, Marxism, Method and the State: An Agenda for Theory," *Signs* 7, no. 3 (Spring 1982), provides a powerful statement of the limitations of materialist outlook: "What is objectively known corresponds to the world and can be verified by pointing to it (as science does) because the world itself is controlled from the same point of view" (24). "For this reason the reality of women's oppression is, finally, neither demonstrable nor refutable empirically. Until this is confronted on the level of method, criticism of what exists can be undercut by pointing to the reality to be criticized" (28).

CHAPTER 7

1. Sandra Harding, *The Science Question in Feminism* (Ithaca, N.Y.: Cornell University Press, 1986), 194, 195.

2. Simone de Beauvoir, *The Second Sex,* trans. and ed. H. M. Parshley (New York: Random House, Vintage Books, 1974), 73.

3. Including specifically John Stuart Mill himself in, for example, *On Liberty:* "Truth, in the great practical concerns of life, is so much a question of the reconciling and combining of opposites that very few have minds sufficiently capacious and impartial to make the adjustment with an approach to correctness, and it has to be made by the rough process of a struggle between combatants fighting under hostile banners" (ed. Currin V. Shields [New York: Bobbs Merrill, Library of Liberal Arts, 1956], 58).

4. (New York: Harcourt, Brace, 1951).

5. Arendt, in *The Jew as Pariah* (ed. Ron H. Feldman [New York: Grove Press, 1978]), describes "The Conscious Pariah" in her essay on Bernard Lazare. "Living in the France of the Dreyfus Affair, Lazare could appreciate at first hand the pariah quality of Jewish existence. But he knew where the solution lay: in contrast to his unemancipated brethren who accept their pariah status automatically and unconsciously, the emancipated Jew must awake to an awareness of his position and, conscious of it, become a rebel against it—the champion of an oppressed people. His fight for freedom is part and parcel of that which all the downtrodden of Europe must needs wage to achieve national and social liberation" (76).

INDEX